What readers are saying about
Everyday Scripting with Ruby

What a wondrous collection of recipes, guidelines, warnings, comprehensive examples, metaphors, exercises, and questions! It's a terrific value to software testing practitioners who want to get the most from their test automation effort.

▶ **Grigori Melnik**
 Lecturer, University of Calgary

A fantastic type-along-with-me introduction to a powerful scripting language that starts in the shallows and then moves into the depths turning the reader into an accomplished Ruby scripter, almost without them noticing it!

▶ **Erik Petersen**
 Emprove

Finally a hands-on book that is filled with gems of wisdom for the testing community. By following the book's easy-to-read chapters, real-life code samples, and superb coverage of complex topics like test-driven design and inheritance, a tester will not only take her testing career to the next level but also contribute immensely to the software development at her organization.

▶ **Gunjan Doshi**
 VP of Product Development and Process Excellence,
 Community Connect, Inc

Marick explains the Ruby language using a series of short, practical examples. Watir users and other testers who want to learn Ruby will find it very accessible.

▶ **Bret Pettichord**
 Lead Developer, Watir

When you've read this book, you will be able to automate software tests, which will give you an edge on most of your QA workmates. You will be able to program in Ruby, which is a joy in itself. You will have created several very useful utilities and will know how to adapt them to meet your particular needs. All of the above will have been achieved briskly and pleasantly. You will become a more effective tester and, most likely, will have a fine time in the process.

▶ **George Hawthorne**
    Consultant, Oblomov Consulting

The book is an excellent read, is very informative, and covers a lot of ground in a relatively slim book. I think this is always a good idea. I have a lot of 800+ page tech books that I've read about the first half or two thirds of, because they are padded toward the end with very esoteric information. This book held my interest throughout—I have a full-time job and a ten-month-old son and still managed to get through these examples in around a week! Brian's personality comes through (e.g., the Kennel containing Barkers) in a good way that helps rather than hinders in understanding the material.

▶ **Paddy Healey**
    Enterprise Systems Engineer, Aventail Corporation

The chapters, examples, and exercises on regular expressions are worth the cost of the book alone! Everything else is more than just gravy—it's every kind of dessert you didn't know you could have. Whether you are just beginning to script or have been scripting for several years, this book will be an invaluable resource. The examples and exercises, Ruby facts, step-by-step approach, and explanations will help you kick up your automation efforts to a whole new level!

▶ **Paul Carvalho**
    Consultant, Software Testing and Quality Services

Everyday Scripting with Ruby

For Teams, Testers, and You

Everyday Scripting with Ruby

For Teams, Testers, and You

Brian Marick

The Pragmatic Bookshelf

Raleigh, North Carolina   Dallas, Texas

Many of the designations used by manufacturers and sellers to distinguish their products are claimed as trademarks. Where those designations appear in this book, and The Pragmatic Programmers, LLC was aware of a trademark claim, the designations have been printed in initial capital letters or in all capitals. The Pragmatic Starter Kit, The Pragmatic Programmer, Pragmatic Programming, Pragmatic Bookshelf and the linking *g* device are trademarks of The Pragmatic Programmers, LLC.

Every precaution was taken in the preparation of this book. However, the publisher assumes no responsibility for errors or omissions, or for damages that may result from the use of information (including program listings) contained herein.

Our Pragmatic courses, workshops, and other products can help you and your team create better software and have more fun. For more information, as well as the latest Pragmatic titles, please visit us at

> http://www.pragmaticprogrammer.com

Printed in the United States of America.

ISBN-10: 0-9776166-1-4

ISBN-13: 978-0-9776166-1-9

Printed on acid-free paper with 85% recycled, 30% post-consumer content.

First printing, December 2006

Version: 2006-12-22

To Dawn, my Best Beloved, best friend, and role model
And to shoemakers' children everywhere

Contents

1 Introduction   **1**

1.1   How the Book Works   3

1.2   An Outline of the Book   4

1.3   Service After the Sale   5

1.4   Supplements   6

1.5   Acknowledgments   6

2 Getting Started   **7**

2.1   Download the Practice Files   7

2.2   In the Beginning Was the Command Line   8

2.3   Do You Need to Install Ruby?   10

2.4   Installing Ruby   10

2.5   Your Two Basic Tools   11

2.6   Prompts, Command Lines, Prompts, and irb   12

2.7   It's Time to Make Mistakes   14

I   The Basics   **17**

3 A First Script: Comparing File Inventories   **19**

3.1   A Script in Action   19

3.2   The Ruby Universe   20

3.3   Objects Send and Receive Messages   20

3.4   Variables Name Objects   22

3.5   Comparing Arrays   23

3.6   Printing to the Screen   24

3.7   Making a Script   25

3.8   Where Do We Stand?   27

3.9   Exercises   27

4   Ruby Facts: Arrays   **29**

5   Three Improvements and a Bug Fix   **33**
  5.1   Command-line Arguments   33
  5.2   Ignoring Case   35
  5.3   Methods   39
  5.4   Dissecting Strings   41
  5.5   Fixing a Bug   43
  5.6   Where Do We Stand?   45
  5.7   Prelude to the Exercises   46
  5.8   Exercises   48

6   Ruby Facts: If, Equality Testing, and Unless   **51**
  6.1   if . . . elsif . . . else   51
  6.2   When Are Objects Equal?   53
  6.3   A Shorthand Version of if   53
  6.4   unless   54
  6.5   The Question Mark Operator   54

II   Growing a Script   **57**

7   The Churn Project: Writing Scripts without Fuss   **59**
  7.1   The Project   59
  7.2   Building a Solution   61
  7.3   Where Do We Stand?   83
  7.4   Exercises   83

8   Ruby Facts: Booleans   **87**
  8.1   Other Boolean Operators   87
  8.2   Precedence   87
  8.3   Every Object Is a Truth Value   89
  8.4   Boolean Expressions Can Select Objects   89

9   Our Friend, the Regular Expression   **91**
  9.1   Regular Expressions Match Strings   92
  9.2   Dissecting Strings with Regular Expressions   94
  9.3   Reordering an Array   95
  9.4   Where Do We Stand?   97
  9.5   Exercises   97

10 Ruby Facts: Regular Expressions   **99**
    10.1 Special Characters 99
    10.2 Grouping and Alternatives 101
    10.3 Taking Strings Apart 101
    10.4 Variables Behind the Scenes 102
    10.5 Regular Expression Options 102
    10.6 Wait, There's More. 103
    10.7 Exercises 103

11 Classes Bundle Data and Methods   **105**
    11.1 Classes Define Methods 107
    11.2 Objects Contain Data 108
    11.3 Where Do We Stand? 112
    11.4 Exercises 112

12 Ruby Facts: Classes (with a Side Order of Symbols)   **119**
    12.1 Defining Accessors 119
    12.2 Self 122
    12.3 Class Methods 126
    12.4 Class Variables and Globals 129
    12.5 Exercises 129

III Working in a World Full of People   **131**

13 Scraping Web Pages with Regular Expressions   **133**
    13.1 Treating Web Pages Like Files 134
    13.2 Restricting Attention to Part of the Page 136
    13.3 Plucking Out the Title and Authors 138
    13.4 Hashes Store Named Data 140
    13.5 Taking the Trip 141
    13.6 Exercise Yourself 143

14 Other Ways of Working with Web Applications   **147**
    14.1 Handling XHTML 147
    14.2 Driving the Browser 149
    14.3 Direct Access to Underlying Protocols 150

15 Working with Comma-Separated Values   **153**
   15.1 The CSV Library 154
   15.2 Using Blocks for Automatic Cleanup 154
   15.3 More CSV Operations 155
   15.4 Applying It All to affinity-trip.rb 155
   15.5 Discovering and Understanding Classes in the Standard
       Library 156
   15.6 Replacing Code with Data 158

16 Ruby Facts: Hashes   **161**

17 Ruby Facts: Argument Lists   **165**
   17.1 Optional Arguments 165
   17.2 Rest Arguments 166
   17.3 Keyword Arguments 167

18 Downloading Helper Scripts and Applications   **171**
   18.1 Finding Packages 171
   18.2 Using setup.rb 172
   18.3 Using RubyGems 173
   18.4 Understanding What You've Downloaded 175

19 A Polished Script   **177**
   19.1 The Load Path 178
   19.2 Avoiding Filename Clashes 178
   19.3 Avoiding Class Name Clashes Using Modules 179
   19.4 A Script to Do the Work for You 181
   19.5 Working Without Stepping on Yourself 184
   19.6 The rakefile 185
   19.7 Location-independent Tests 188
   19.8 Exercises 190

20 Ruby Facts: Modules   **193**
   20.1 Nested Modules 194
   20.2 Including Modules 195
   20.3 Classes Are Modules 197

21 When Scripts Run into Problems   **199**

   21.1 Use Exceptions to Report Problems 200

   21.2 An Error-handling Strategy 200

   21.3 Your Exception-handling Options 202

   21.4 Methods That Use Blocks 206

   21.5 Exercises 208

IV The Accomplished Scripter   **211**

22 Frameworks: Scripting by Filling in Blanks   **213**

   22.1 Using the watchdog Script 214

   22.2 Inheritance 217

   22.3 Gathering User Choices 223

23 Discovery Is Safer Than Creation   **231**

   23.1 The Story of Barker 232

   23.2 What Happens Where? 235

   23.3 Modules Instead of Superclasses 240

24 Final Thoughts   **243**

V The Back of the Book   **245**

A Glossary   **247**

B Solutions to Exercises   **259**

   B.1 Solutions for Chapter 3 259

   B.2 Solutions for Chapter 5 261

   B.3 Solutions for Chapter 7 264

   B.4 Solutions for Chapter 9 268

   B.5 Solutions for Chapter 10 272

   B.6 Solutions for Chapter 11 273

   B.7 Solutions for Chapter 12 284

   B.8 Solutions for Chapter 21 289

C Bibliography   **291**

   Index   **293**

## Chapter 1

Introduction

The shoemaker's children are running around barefoot.

People on the outside of software development projects see them spew out a multitude of tools that shift work from people to computers. But the view inside a project is—all too often—different. There, we see days filled with repetitive manual chores. At one desk, a tester is entering test data into a database by hand. At another, a programmer is sifting through the output from a version control system, trying to find the file she wants. At a third, a business analyst is copying data from a report into a spreadsheet.

Why are these people doing work that computers could do perfectly well? It's a matter of *knowledge* and *skill*. The tester thinks programming is too hard, so he never learned. The programmer knows programming, but none of her languages makes automating this kind of job easy, and she doesn't have time to do it the hard way. The analyst once wrote a script to do a similar chore, but it broke when she tried to adapt it to this report. Getting it working would take more time than copying the data by hand, even if she has to copy it six times over the next month.

 **Joe Asks...**

Scripting? Programming? What's the difference?

There isn't one. I'm using "scripting" for this book because it sounds less imposing and more suited to everyday chores.

This book is for all those people.

- *For the person who thinks programming is too hard* (our tester): it's not as hard as all that. Programming has a bad reputation because computers used to be too slow. To make programs run fast enough, programmers had to use programming languages that made them tell the computer all kinds of fiddly details. Computers are now fast enough that we can use languages that make *them* figure out the fiddly little details. As a result, programming is now much easier.

- *For the person who gets bogged down when writing or changing larger scripts* (our analyst): you don't yet have the skills to master complexity. This book teaches them. It's a tutorial in the modern style of programming, one that emphasizes writing tests first (test-driven programming), borrowing other people's work in bits and pieces, growing programs gradually, and constantly keeping them clean.

  Many scripts will be one-shot: write it, use it, throw it away. But for scripts you plan to keep around, these skills will let you do it. (In truth, many professional programmers I meet haven't yet learned these particular skills, so they will find this book a useful introduction.)

- *For the person who knows the wrong languages well* (our programmer): languages like Java, C#, C++, and C are perfectly fine languages—in their niche. But their niche is not writing smaller programs quickly, especially not smaller programs that manipulate text and files rather than numbers and internal data structures. You need to add another language to your repertoire.

In this book, you'll learn a language—Ruby—that is well suited to each of these three audiences. It's easy to learn and quick to write. While it has the features needed for simple scripts that transform or search text, it also has all the features needed to cope with complexity. If you're a tester, you'll be pleased to know that testing is considered one of Ruby's niches (largely due to Watir, http://wtr.rubyforge.org/, a tool for driving web browsers). If you're a programmer, you may already know that Ruby has recently become explosively popular because of its "killer app," Rails (a framework for building web applications, http://www.rubyonrails.org/). Despite that, it's more than a decade old, so it's not just some passing fad or unstable prototype. And everyone will be pleased with the Ruby community, which is notably friendly.

1.1 How the Book Works

This is a *hands-on* book. Scripting is like riding a bicycle: you don't learn it by reading about it; you learn it by doing it. And you get better by doing more of it. The purpose of a book, or of a coach, is to direct your practice so that you get better faster.

Therefore, the book is organized around four separate projects that are similar to those you might do in real life. I build the first two projects slowly, showing and explaining all my work. You'll learn best if you type along with me, building the project as we go. In the third and fourth projects, I move faster and explain only the finished result.

The *practice files* that come with the book contain a series of snapshots *practice files* for each of the first two projects. The snippets of Ruby code in the book identify the file they come from. You can look at the file to see the snippet in context, to diagnose problems by comparing what you've typed to what I have, or to start your own typing in the middle of a project instead of at the beginning.

Some of you won't create the projects along with me. I do still urge you to work through the exercises and compare your solutions to the solutions I give.

The Projects

The first project is an uninstaller checker. If you uninstall your company's product, does the uninstaller remove everything it should? Does it remove something it shouldn't? This script will tell you. More generally, it lets you take snapshots of any part of your hard disk and compare them.

The second project reaches out to a version control system, retrieves change information, and summarizes it for you. It's a typical example of manipulating text.

The third project visits to a website, "scrapes" data out of it, and puts that data into a comma-separated value file for use by a spreadsheet.

The final project is a "watchdog" script. It can watch long-running programs or tests and then send you an instant message or email when they finish.

A Special Note to Testers

You were the original audience for this book. It used to be called *Scripting for Testers*, but people kept saying it would be useful to a broader audience. Even programmers I expected to be uninterested said things like "with only a few changes, this book would be for me." So I made the changes, but testers still have a special place in my heart.

As a tester, I bet you came to this book hoping to learn how to automate test execution: how to push inputs at a program (probably through the user interface), collect the results, and compare what the program produced to what it should have produced. Even when this book was exclusively for testers, I didn't create any projects like that. I had two reasons:

- *Automating test execution is not the most efficient way for you to learn.* I aim to teach you the practices, habits, and Ruby features you'll need in real life. You don't need those things to write one automated test or even ten, maybe not even a hundred, so it would feel artificial, false, and unconvincing for me to teach them in the context of a small automated test suite. They're better taught with small projects of a different sort.

- *Automating test execution may not be the most effective thing for you to do.* Is test execution the *only* task you do by hand? Probably not. People overly focused on test automation often miss opportunities for simple scripts that yield outsized improvements.

1.2 An Outline of the Book

This is a book about both the features of Ruby and the craft of scripting. Each part of the book teaches some of both. Ruby features are introduced as they're needed for that part's project. Each part also introduces new skills that build on earlier ones.

Part I, on page 19, teaches you the basics of Ruby and the basics of scripting. If you've never programmed, work through it carefully. If you already know a language, you can read it more casually, but do still read it. Ruby is based on ideas you might not know and has features you may not have seen before; if you skip them, you won't be prepared for the rest of the book.

At the end of Part I, all three kinds of reader will be ready to learn how to script better. Part II, on page 59, adds more Ruby facts, but it's mainly about teaching you how to write scripts in a steady, controlled way. All programmers know the feeling of hitting that wall where they can't make any change without breaking something. I want to show you how to push that wall further away.

Part III, on page 133, concentrates on accomplishing more with less effort. It shows how to save work by finding, understanding, and including libraries written by others. It shows you how to set up your scripts so that your co-workers can download, install, and use them easily. While demonstrating still more features of Ruby, this part also elaborates on an important topic from Part II, "regular expressions," a powerful way of searching text.

Part IV, on page 213, covers the advanced topic of inheritance. Inheritance can sometimes save even more work than libraries because someone else designs a framework for part of your script. You need only plug in pieces that the framework orchestrates. Part IV shows you both how to use complicated frameworks others create and how to make simpler ones for yourself. You may want to get experience writing scripts of your own before learning about frameworks.

The book ends with a glossary, solutions to exercises, and an index. What else? Throughout the book, you'll find chapters called "Ruby Facts." When I introduce a Ruby feature in the process of creating a script, I'll describe only the bits used in the script we're writing. But you'll want to know more about such features when you write your own scripts, so I use the fact chapters to tell you more. Skip them if you like.

Despite those chapters, this book is not a complete reference on Ruby. Eventually you'll want to buy one. I heartily recommend Dave Thomas and friends' *Programming Ruby* [TH01]. It's also from the Pragmatic Bookshelf—indeed, Dave is one of the owners of the press. But I'm not recommending their book because they're my publisher. They're my publisher because I kept recommending their book.

1.3 Service After the Sale

Everyday Scripting with Ruby has its very own Pragmatic Programmers' web page at http://www.pragmaticprogrammer.com/titles/bmsft/. There, you will find updates, errata, source for all the examples and more.

1.4 Supplements

As time and demand permit, I'll be publishing supplements to this book; each will be devoted to a particular topic. Please check the book's home page for details.

1.5 Acknowledgments

This book would not exist were it not for the prodding of Bret Pettichord.

Thank you, those who commented on drafts: Mark Axel, Tracy Beeson, Michael Bolton, Paul Carvalho, Tom Corbett, Bob Corrick, Lisa Crispin, Paul Czyzewski, Shailesh Dongre, Gunjan Doshi, Danny Faught, Zeljko Filipin, Pierre Garique, George Hawthorne, Paddy Healey, Jonathan Kohl, Bhavna Kumar, Walter Kruse, Jody Lemons, Iouri Makedonov, Chris McMahon, Christopher Meisenzahl, Grigori Melnik, Sunil Menda, Jack Moore, Erik Petersen, Bret Pettichord, Alan Richardson, Paul Rogers, Tony Semana, Kevin Sheehy, Jeff Smathers, Mike Stok, Paul Szymkowiak, Jonathan Towler, and Glenn Vanderburg.

Special thanks to Paul Carvalho for teaching me something I didn't know about Windows and for working through Part IV before Part III, and to Paul Czyzewski for how thoroughly he reviewed the pages I gave him time to review.

My editor, Daniel Steinberg, provided just the right mix of encouragement, support, and pressure.

I'll be eternally grateful to my publishers, Andy Hunt and Dave Thomas, for not seeming to mind as their children were born, grew up, left home, got married, and had children of their own—all during the writing of this book.

And I'd like to thank my family. You wouldn't *believe* what they've let me get away with.

Chapter 2

Getting Started

This chapter gets you ready for the rest of the book.

- Everyone will need to download the practice files.
- If you're not familiar with the *command line* ("the DOS prompt," "the shell"), you'll need to learn a bit about it.
- Ruby might be preinstalled on your system. If it isn't, you'll need to install it.
- Anytime you type, you make typographical errors. Typing scripts is no different. You need to learn to recognize the signs you've made a mistake.

2.1 Download the Practice Files

This book comes with a number of Ruby scripts you can practice on. You can download them as a zip archive from the book's web page at http://www.pragmaticprogrammer.com/titles/bmsft/. Download it anywhere you please.

Your browser might "unzip" the file for you when you download it. If not, double-clicking or right-clicking it will probably work. Failing that, on Mac OS X and other Unix variants you can type unzip bmsft-code.zip to the command-line interpreter.[1] On Windows, download an application like WinZip (http://winzip.com/), and set it to work.

Unzipping the file creates a folder named code. I recommend renaming that to something more specific, like scripting-book, but I'll use code to refer to it throughout the book.

---

1. The command-line interpreter will be explained shortly.

Within code, there is a subfolder for each of the scripts in the book. Do your work within those subfolders. There's also a subfolder with solutions to the exercises and several subfolders with more Ruby examples.

2.2 In the Beginning Was the Command Line

command-line interpreter

When you use Ruby or any other scripting language, you're likely to use your computer's *command-line interpreter*. The command-line[2] interpreter is a program that lets you command the compiler by typing in text, rather than by pointing and clicking with a mouse. If you've never used the command-line interpreter, here's an introduction.

Windows

In Windows, you get to the command-line interpreter from the Start menu. Click the Run menu item, type cmd, and then press Enter. You'll see something like this:

```
Microsoft Windows XP [Version 5.1.2600]
(C) Copyright 1985-2001 Microsoft Corp.
C:>
```

The C:\> you see is called the *prompt*. It's called that because it's supposed to prompt you to type some commands for the computer to execute. Not everyone who reads this book will have the same prompt, so I've arbitrarily chosen to show the prompt as prompt> from now on, except when I'm talking about something specific to Windows. When you see an instruction to type something like this:

```
prompt> irb
```

I want you to type i r b Enter. Don't type the prompt. Let's suppose you installed the practice files in C:\unzip-place. Type this:

```
C:\> cd c:\unzip-place\code
```

(cd stands for "change directory"—"directory" is a synonym for "folder".)

current working folder

When you change to a folder, it becomes your *current working folder*. If a command doesn't name a specific folder, the command-line interpreter assumes you mean the current working folder. For example, you can view the contents of the current working folder like this:

```
C:\unzip-place\code\> dir
```

---

2. The title of this section refers to an essay by author Neal Stephenson. You can find it at http://www.cryptonomicon.com/beginning.html.

If you're working on the file-inventory project, you can now go there like this:

C:\unzip-place\code\> cd inventory

Note that you don't have to preface inventory with C:\unzip-place\code because that's your current working folder.

You can move back up to the enclosing folder like this:

C:\unzip-place\code\inventory\> cd ..

That's all you need to know to run the examples in this book (though you'll want to learn more).

Mac OS X, Linux, BSD, and Other Unix Variants

The Mac command prompt is an application named Terminal. It lives in the Utilities subfolder of the Applications folder. On other Unix variants,[3] the command prompt might be named Konsole, Terminal, gnome-terminal, or xterm. You should be able to find it in one of your window manager's menus.

Regardless of how you start it, the command prompt looks something like this:

Last login: Sat Dec 16 11:45:37 on ttyp1
Welcome to Darwin!
computer-name:~ user$

The computer-name:~ user$ you see is called the *prompt*. Your prompt is probably different, so from now on, I'll show the prompt as prompt>. When you see an instruction to type something like this:

prompt> irb

I want you to type [i][r][b][Return]. Don't type the prompt.

Let's suppose you installed the practice files in the unzip-place folder in your home folder. Type this:

prompt> cd ~/unzip-place/code

cd stands for "change directory"—"directory" is a synonym for "folder." The twiddle (~) means your home folder.

---

3. Mac OS X, the other systems in the title of this section, and still others I didn't name all have a common ancestry: the Unix operating system developed at Bell Labs in the 1970s. To a scripter, Mac OS X is just Unix with an exceptionally pretty face added. Oh, and it has some nice applications too.

current working folder

When you change to a folder, it becomes your *current working folder*. If a command doesn't name a specific folder, the command-line interpreter assumes you mean the current working folder. For example, you can view the contents of the current working folder like this:

prompt> ls

If you're working on the file-inventory project, you can now go there like this:

prompt> cd inventory

Note that you don't have to preface inventory with ~/unzip-place/code because that's your current working folder.

You can move back up to the enclosing folder like this:

prompt> cd ..

That's all you need to know to run the examples in this book (though you'll want to learn more).

2.3   Do You Need to Install Ruby?

Ruby runs on Windows 2000, Windows XP, or later; Mac OS X; and any version of Unix you're likely to find. You may already have Ruby installed on your machine. To find out, type this at the command prompt:

prompt> ruby -v

If you see a complaint like "command not found," you'll have to install Ruby.

If Ruby is installed, the response will look something like this:

ruby 1.8.1 (2003-12-25) [powerpc-darwin]

The version of Ruby shown there, 1.8.1, is older than the one I used when writing this book. I used 1.8.2. All the examples here might work perfectly, but I wouldn't count on it. Install the latest version.

2.4   Installing Ruby

Windows

There is a one-click Ruby installer. You can find it here: http://www.ruby-lang.org/en/downloads/. After you download it, double-click it in Windows Explorer to run it, and then follow the directions.

After installing Ruby, close any command-line windows, open a new one, and then follow the directions in Section 2.3, *Do You Need to Install Ruby?*, on the facing page, to check that it was installed correctly.[4]

Mac OS X

Tiger (version 10.4) and later versions of Mac OS X come with recent enough versions of Ruby. If you're using an older release of OS X, see http://www.ruby-lang.org/en/downloads/ or the book's website for instructions.

Other Unix Variants

You may be able to find precompiled versions of Ruby (RPMs, etc.) in the usual places and retrieve them via the usual tools (apt-get, pkg-get, ports, etc.). Otherwise, see the book's website for instructions.

2.5   Your Two Basic Tools

There are two basic tools: an editor and an interpreter.

Your Editor

You can use any editor that works with text files to create Ruby scripts. On Windows, I recommend you use SciTE, which is installed with Ruby. It's more than just a text editor: it understands Ruby well enough to color-code parts of a script to make it easier to read, and it lets you run scripts without having to switch to the command line. (In the Start menu's Programs entry, you'll find a Ruby entry, and SciTE is under that.)

On a Mac, I recommend TextMate (http://macromates.com/). It costs money, but you can try a free download.

On the Mac and other Unix-like systems, you can use pico. It's free. Start it by typing its name at the command prompt. It shows its available editing commands at the bottom of the screen. In that help, Control + X is denoted by ^X.

If you use the Gnome window system on Linux, gedit is worth trying.

---

4. You have to close and open a new command line because the old one may not "notice" that Ruby has been installed.

irb

The second useful tool is irb. It lets you try your ideas without having to write a whole script. You can type a little snippet of Ruby and quickly check what it does. You'll see many examples later in the book. For now, check that irb is ready for use. At the command prompt, type the following. (Remember not to include the prompt.)

```
prompt> irb
```

You'll see something like this:

```
irb(main):001:0>
```

Most of the pieces of the prompt are unimportant. You'll learn about the parts that are later in this chapter.

Now type a Ruby expression, and press Enter (on Windows) or Return (on Unix-like systems):

```
irb(main):001:0> 1+1
=> 2
irb(main):002:0>
```

irb displays the result and then prompts you to type something more.

result

2 is the *result* of *evaluating* the expression 1+1. In the rest of the book you'll be evaluating more exciting expressions, but that's enough for now. Exit from irb like this:

```
irb(main):003:0> exit
prompt>
```

2.6 Prompts, Command Lines, Prompts, and irb

There are two kinds of prompts in this book, command-line prompts and irb prompts. If you type a command meant for the command-line interpreter to irb (or vice versa), you'll get confusing results. If what you see on your screen is nothing like what the book tells you to expect, check that you're typing at the right prompt.

If you're typing the command line and should be typing to irb, start irb:

```
prompt> irb
```

If you're typing to irb and should be typing at the command line, exit irb:

```
irb(main):001:0> exit
```

Two Things People Often Forget at First

- Do your project work in the folder containing that project's practice files. For example, if you're working on the inventory project, type this on the Mac and Unix-like systems before you start irb:

```
prompt> cd ~/unzip-place/code/inventory
```

On Windows, type this:

```
C:\> cd \unzip-place\code\inventory
```

- You exit from irb by typing exit at its prompt. On Windows, you'll sometimes then get the query "Terminate batch job (Y/N)?"—type y.

Working with Prompts

You'll often make typing mistakes at a prompt. On some systems, the Up Arrow key will reinsert the previous line at the current prompt. You can then use the Back Arrow and Forward Arrow keys to move around in the line.

It's often convenient to edit complicated text in an editor and then copy and paste it to irb. It's easier to switch back to the editor, correct the mistake, and repaste it than it is to fool around with the arrow keys.

On the Mac and other Unix-like systems, the cut, copy, and paste keystrokes work as you'd expect. For example, on the Mac, ⌘ V pastes into the Terminal window. In that window, you can select a range of text, copy it with ⌘ C, and then paste it into an editor window.

On Windows, you'll paste to the command line with a right click rather than the normal Ctrl+V. Alternately, you can use an Edit menu that you get by right-clicking the title bar.

To copy from the Windows command line, select text with the mouse, and then press Enter. If that doesn't work, make sure you have "quick edit" turned on. Open the Properties dialog (via the control menu you get with Alt+Space or by right-clicking in the title bar), go to the Options tab, and check Quick Edit Mode.

2.7 It's Time to Make Mistakes

In a lot of this book, I'll be telling you to type commands to irb and see what the result is. No matter how carefully you type, you'll make mistakes. irb gives you clues about what went wrong, but those clues can be hard for a Ruby beginner to understand. So let's get some confusion out of the way now by deliberately making a few mistakes.

Suppose you wanted to know the value of 100 - 43. Start irb again (if it's not still running), and type that calculation. You should see this:

```
irb(main):001:0> 100 - 43
=> 57
```

Swell. But on my keyboard and probably yours, the ⎡-⎤ key is right next to the ⎡=⎤ key. Because I'm a klutz, I often hit them both at once. What would irb do if I pressed ⎡Enter⎤ after doing that? Try it...

```
irb(main):002:0> 100 -= 43
```
❶
```
SyntaxError: compile error
(irb):3: syntax error
100 -= 43
```
❷
```
       ^
     from (irb):3
```

Hmm. All the detail there is hard to explain. Fortunately, you don't need to understand it. Whenever you see a syntax error like you did on line ❶, just know that the previous line has something wrong with it, most likely a typo. The caret at line ❷ may point at or near the error, but that's not guaranteed.

Here's another way to make a typing mistake: parentheses usually come in matching pairs, but it's easy to leave one off. For example:

```
irb(main):003:0> (1 + 3) * 2 + 1)
SyntaxError: compile error
(irb):12: syntax error
     from (irb):12
```

Notice that irb didn't try to guess where the opening parenthesis should have been. You can also leave off a closing parenthesis, but that turns out to be harmless. irb gives you a slightly different prompt and lets you continue typing. In the following, I wanted to type (1 + 3) * (2 * 4), but I hit ⎡Enter⎤ instead of the last parenthesis. At the next prompt, I typed the forgotten parenthesis and hit ⎡Enter⎤ again:

```
irb(main):004:0> (1 + 3) * (2 * 4
irb(main):005:1> )
=> 32
```

> **Syntax Errors in Script Files**
>
> At this point, you're making mistakes while typing to irb. You'll make the same sort of mistakes when creating script files. When you run the broken scripts, the error messages may be different; that's covered in the sidebar on page 36.

The prompt gives a subtle clue that there's more to type by changing its last bit from :0> to :1>. That's called a *continuation prompt*. The more obvious clue is that irb doesn't show any result until you add the right parenthesis.

continuation prompt

Ruby's *strings* give you another way not to finish something you started. A string is a sequence of characters enclosed by quotes, like this:

strings

```
irb(main):001:0> "a string"
=> "a string"
```

If you leave off the closing quote, Ruby's prompt changes. Instead of ending with an >, it ends with " to say that you're to continue typing in a string. Like this:

```
irb(main):010:0> "an unfinished string
irb(main):011:0"
```

When you now add text with a closing quote, you'll get this:

```
irb(main):012:0> "an unfinished string
irb(main):013:0" ... is now finished"
=> "an unfinished string\n... is now finished"
```

Notice that the result string has something odd in the middle. The \n shows that an end-of-line character is treated like all the others when it's typed into the unclosed string: it's included in the result. (The end-of-line character is either Enter or Return, depending on whether you use Windows, Mac OS X, etc.) That's nice when you want such a character in the string. When it's because of a mistake, you'll need to retype the string correctly.

Ruby actually lets you use two different characters to start and end strings. Strings surrounded with double quotes are created a little differently than ones you surround with a single quote. (You'll learn about the difference in Section 7.2, *Formatting Strings*, on page 70.) If you're anything like me, you'll sometimes start a string one way and end it the other. irb will dutifully do what you don't want: include what you thought was the ending character in the string and then give you a prompt to end the string. You have two options. One is to end the string with the appropriate character and then type the correct string at the next noncontinuation prompt:

```
irb(main):014:0* 'a string "
irb(main):015:0' '
=> "a string \"\n"
irb(main):016:0> 'a string'
=> "a string"
irb(main):017:0>
```

Notice that the irb still prints the string surrounded by double quotes. A string is a string is a string, no matter how you created it, and irb always prints strings the same way. Because you've created a string that contains a double quote, irb needs to show the difference between the double quote *in* the string and the double quotes that it prints to tell you that the result *is* a string. It does that by prefacing the internal quote with a backslash. (In strings, a backslash always means the next character is special somehow.)

Many times you get a continuation prompt because you mistyped something on a previous line. In that case, there's no point in trying to tidily close off the string or parenthesized expression or whatever it was that you started. You just want some quick way to get back to the regular prompt and start over. On Mac OS X and Linux, the way to do that is to type Ctrl+C.

On Windows, Ctrl+C might also work. If it doesn't, either nothing will happen or you'll be asked "Terminate batch job (Y/N)?" If nothing happens, try pressing Enter after the Ctrl+C.

Here's an example where I started a string and didn't finish it right. Each try at fixing things made them worse. Ctrl+C to the rescue:

```
irb(main):017:0> ("irb + "irb"
irb(main):018:1" "
irb(main):019:1> "
irb(main):020:1" '
irb(main):021:1"   ^C^C
irb(main):022:0>
```

Often I get a little, um, enthusiastic and type Ctrl+C several times, with vigor, just to make sure irb gets the point. That's not needed, but it's satisfying.

Part I

The Basics

## Chapter 3

A First Script:
Comparing File Inventories

In this chapter, you'll create a simple but useful script. Along the way, you'll learn some basic Ruby terminology and techniques. In Chapter 5, *Three Improvements and a Bug Fix*, beginning on page 33, you'll add more abilities to the same script.

3.1 A Script in Action

At a command prompt, go to (using cd) the inventory subfolder of your code folder. (If you've forgotten how, see the sidebar on page 13.) There's a Ruby script, inventory.rb, there. Run it like this:

```
prompt> ruby inventory.rb
```

You'll see this:

```
exercise-differences.rb
inventory.rb
old-inventory.txt
recycler
recycler/inst-39.tmp
snapshots
snapshots/differences-version-1.rb
snapshots/differences-version-2.rb
snapshots/differences-version-3.rb
snapshots/differences-version-4.rb
snapshots/differences-version-5.rb
snapshots/differences-version-6.rb
snapshots/differences-version-7.rb
snapshots/differences-version-8.rb
temp
temp/inst-39
```

run a Ruby script

You've just *run a Ruby script*, one that makes an inventory of everything in the current folder (including everything in all the subfolders).[1] In the course of this chapter, you'll create another script that compares two inventories, telling you what files have been added to or removed from the first. If you're a tester, these scripts can be useful to you in at least two ways:

- Suppose you're given a new "test build" every Friday. The test build is supposed to come with a list of all the changes since last week's build. People being fallible, sometimes that list is wrong. A list of what files have been added or deleted can help you decide what needs testing.
- You could take an inventory of the entire filesystem (C:\, for example), install a product, uninstall it, and compare the old snapshot to a new one. You might find that the uninstall leaves litter behind.

3.2 The Ruby Universe

When you run the inventory.rb script, you create a little Ruby universe. That universe, in essence, contains only three kinds of things: *nouns*, *verbs*, and *names*. The nouns are usually called *objects*. They are the "things" in the Ruby universe. Objects just sit there until they're told to do something. That's where the verbs come in. All the verbs in the Ruby universe are imperative: verbs like "sit!" and "stay!" and "roll over!" In Ruby, these verbs are called *messages*, and telling an object to do something is called *sending a message*.

objects

messages

sending a message

name

You don't have direct access to the objects inside the Ruby universe. To get at one of them, you have to use a *name* that refers to it. It's similar in our universe: I am an object. My children refer to me as "Dad," my wife refers to me as "hubster" or even more embarrassing names, and a clerk at the Philadelphia airport referred to me as "31" and "hey, you." All of them used names to talk about the object that is me.

3.3 Objects Send and Receive Messages

The previous section is pretty abstract, so let's see Ruby names, objects, and messages in action. Create an inventory file by typing the following at the command prompt:

```
prompt> ruby inventory.rb > new-inventory.txt
```

---

1. The idea for this project came from tester Chris McMahon.

The > new-inventory.txt tells the command-line interpreter to put the script's output into the file named new-inventory.txt. That's not a part of Ruby—it works with any command. (I chose the name new-inventory.txt to suggest this is an inventory taken after installing and uninstalling a product. You may have noticed that old-inventory.txt already exists; that's supposed to be the one taken before installation.)

Start irb, and type the following. Note that File begins with a capital letter. Ruby is a *case-sensitive* language, meaning that the names File and file are completely different. If you use file, you'll get an error message.

case-sensitive

```
irb(main):001:0> File.open('new-inventory.txt')
=> #<File:new-inventory.txt>
```

I'm going to step through what just happened in great detail: don't worry, it'll soon become second nature.

File names a particular object in the Ruby universe. It's the object that knows how to open files and prepare them for use. The open message commands it to do so. Since File needs to know which file to open, open takes an *argument*, which is the string *'new-inventory.txt'*.

argument

Upon receipt of the message, File does the work to open a file. That involves creating another object that *is* the open file (as far as Ruby is concerned). File then *returns* that newly created object to whatever object sent the message (usually called the *sender*). In this case, the sender happens to be irb. (Since irb is a Ruby script, it lives as an object in the Ruby universe.) When irb gets the return value, it prints to the screen in a form intended to be useful to people writing scripts. Here, #<File:new-inventory.txt> says the object was created by File to give access to the filesystem's file new-inventory.txt. Other objects print out in different ways; in fact, each object can choose how it wants to be printed.

returns

sender

But there are more things to do with that open file than print a description of it. We can ask it for all the lines in the file, like this:

```
irb(main):002:0> File.open('new-inventory.txt').readlines
=> ["exercise-differences.rb\n", "inventory.rb\n", "new-inventory.txt\n", ↩
"old-inventory.txt\n", "recycler\n", "recycler/inst-39.tmp\n", "snapshots ↩
\n", "snapshots/differences-version-1.rb\n", "snapshots/differences-versi ↩
on-2.rb\n", "snapshots/differences-version-3.rb\n", "snapshots/difference ↩
s-version-4.rb\n", "snapshots/differences-version-5.rb\n", "snapshots/dif ↩
ferences-version-6.rb\n", "snapshots/differences-version-7.rb\n", "snapsh ↩
ots/differences-version-8.rb\n", "temp\n", "temp/inst-39\n"]
```

As before, we've told irb to send File the open message. File responds with an open file object. But irb doesn't print the result because we've told it to send that result another message, readlines. readlines converts

string

array

every line in the file into a *string*. "String" is the name Ruby gives to a sequence of alphabetic characters. readlines then returns all those strings in an *array*. You can think of an array as a bunch of objects arranged in a row. In this case, they're in the same order they appeared in the file. irb prints strings surrounded by double quotes, and it prints arrays as a comma-separated list enclosed in square brackets. You'll be seeing a lot more about strings and arrays throughout the book.

If you look at the file new-inventory.txt, you'll see that it indeed does contain the same lines in the same order. The only differences are the quotes irb puts around strings to tell you they're strings and the peculiar \n at the end of the Ruby strings. That's the way irb indicates the separator between the lines.[2]

You may also have noticed that in typing the string 'new-inventory.txt', I used single quotes, but irb used double quotes to print the strings out. If you like, use double quotes when typing strings. It makes no difference in this part of the book.

3.4 Variables Name Objects

Having gotten an array with the file's contents, let's give it a name, new_inventory. (Notice that the name uses an underscore, not a dash.) That's done like this:

```
irb(main):003:0> new_inventory = File.open('new-inventory.txt').readlines
=> ["exercise-differences.rb\n", "inventory.rb\n", "new-inventory.txt\n", ↩
"old-inventory.txt\n", "recycler\n", "recycler/inst-39.tmp\n", "snapshots ↩
\n", "snapshots/differences-version-1.rb\n", "snapshots/differences-versi ↩
on-2.rb\n", "snapshots/differences-version-3.rb\n", "snapshots/difference ↩
s-version-4.rb\n", "snapshots/differences-version-5.rb\n", "snapshots/dif ↩
ferences-version-6.rb\n", "snapshots/differences-version-7.rb\n", "snapsh ↩
ots/differences-version-8.rb\n", "temp\n", "temp/inst-39\n"]
```

variable

In keeping with historical terminology, Ruby calls new_inventory a *variable*. (That made more sense when computers were all about doing mathematics.)

---

2. On Windows, the separator is a carriage return followed by a line feed; on Linux/Unix, it's just a line feed; on the Mac, it's just a carriage return. There's no more meaning to those differences than there is to the fact that Germans drive on the other side of the road than the English do. It's completely arbitrary; accidents would be avoided if everyone did it the same way, but it's too late to change now. Ruby tries hard to let you not care which choice the builders of your operating system made: \n means "whatever's correct on this machine."

The inventory project holds a file named old-inventory.txt. It contains an inventory supposedly taken before the one in new-inventory.txt. Read it in like this:

```
irb(main):004:0> old_inventory = File.open('old-inventory.txt').readlines
=> ["exercise-differences.rb\n", "inventory.rb\n", "old-inventory.txt\n", ←
"financial-records.xls\n", "snapshots\n", "snapshots/differences-version- ←
1.rb\n", "snapshots/differences-version-2.rb\n", "snapshots/differences-v ←
ersion-3.rb\n", "snapshots/differences-version-4.rb\n", "snapshots/differ ←
ences-version-5.rb\n", "snapshots/differences-version-6.rb\n", "snapshots ←
/differences-version-7.rb\n", "snapshots/differences-version-8.rb\n", "te ←
mp\n", "temp/junk\n"]
```

Now we can compare arrays.

3.5 Comparing Arrays

The way to find the difference between two arrays is to "subtract" one from the other, like this:

```
irb(main):005:0> new_inventory - old_inventory
=> ["new-inventory.txt\n", "recycler\n", "recycler/inst-39.tmp\n", "temp/ ←
inst-39\n"]
```

These strings are in the newer inventory but not in the older. To find what files have been deleted since the old inventory was taken, subtract in the other direction:[3]

```
irb(main):006:0> old_inventory - new_inventory
=> ["financial-records.xls\n", "temp/junk\n"]
```

If you check the contents of the files, you'll see that the results are correct.

Notice that the subtraction doesn't change either array. Subtracting old_inventory from new_inventory doesn't affect new_inventory's array. It doesn't remove strings from it; instead, it produces a completely new array with those strings found only in new_inventory's array.

Names Follow Certain Rules

A Ruby name may contain letters, numbers, and the underscore character (not a hyphen). Names can't begin with a number, nor may they include spaces. Case matters: my_ship is not the same name as my_Ship.

---

3. If everything in Ruby is objects, messages, and names, where's the message send here? You can read the line as "send the array named old_inventory the message named '-' with the argument being the array named by new_inventory." But Ruby would be less popular if it prevented you from writing subtraction (be it of numbers or arrays) in the way you learned as a child.

When a name begins with a capital letter, you're telling Ruby that you expect it always to refer to the same object. Ruby will complain if you try to use the same name for a different object:

```
irb(main):007:0> MyShip = "a cutter"
=> "a cutter"
irb(main):008:0> MyShip = "a bark"
(irb):4: warning: already initialized constant MyShip
=> "a bark"
```

(Ruby complains but still obeys.)

When a multiword name begins with a lowercase letter, it's conventional to separate the words with underscores, like my_fine_name. When one begins with a capital letter, the convention is to capitalize each word: MyFineName. I don't know the rationale behind the difference.

As a special case, message names can end with a question mark or an exclamation point. When one ends in a question mark, it's a signal that the message asks a true/false question of its receiver. An exclamation point is a signal to the reader that the message does something special and perhaps unexpected.

3.6 Printing to the Screen

We have nearly all the information needed to report on changes between inventories. All we need to do is make a script that prints it. The main tool here is a message named puts (short for "put string"). Here's how to generate part of a report:

```
❶    irb(main):009:0> puts "The following files have been added:"
❷    The following files have been added:
❸    => nil
```

Let's look at the lines in order.

❶ Although it doesn't look like it, puts is just another message. A message to *what?* Unlike before, there's no dot separating the object receiving the message and the message name. In Ruby, you don't need to name the message *receiver* if it's clear (to Ruby) from context. In this case, you can think of the object that receives the message as irb itself. When you run a Ruby script from the command line, it would be the script itself.

receiver

Another reason puts looks odd is that there are no parentheses around its single argument. You can leave parentheses off if Ruby knows where you would have put them.

❷   The string is printed to the screen. This printing has nothing to do with the way irb prints results. puts does its work before irb has any results to print.

    Although puts is printing a string, it doesn't put quotes around it like irb does. irb's output is formatted for you, a scripter. puts formats its output for end-user consumption. If you want the irb-style output, use the *inspect* message:

inspect

```
irb(main):010:0> puts "I'd like some quotes, please".inspect
"I'd like some quotes, please"
=> nil
```

❸   This line is puts's return value. Every Ruby message must return *something*, and nil is a common choice when there's actually nothing interesting to say. (The word "nil" means "nothing.")

    irb is written to print the return value from the last message it sends. If you run a script from the command line, that doesn't happen. The result of each script line vanishes—only what puts prints goes to the screen.

puts also works with arrays:

```
irb(main):011:0> puts old_inventory
exercise-differences.rb
inventory.rb
old-inventory.txt
financial-records.xls
snapshots
snapshots/differences-version-1.rb
snapshots/differences-version-2.rb
snapshots/differences-version-3.rb
snapshots/differences-version-4.rb
snapshots/differences-version-5.rb
snapshots/differences-version-6.rb
snapshots/differences-version-7.rb
snapshots/differences-version-8.rb
temp
temp/junk
=> nil
```

Notice how array elements are conveniently printed one per line. (That has nothing to do with the fact that the strings end with an end-of-line character, \n; puts would do the same for strings without them.)

3.7   Making a Script

We have all the steps needed to create an inventory-comparison script. Name it differences.rb, and add the lines that follow this paragraph.

(If you don't want to type the lines, you can copy them from the file named in the gray box. I bet you'll understand them better if you type them.) Section 2.5, *Your Editor*, on page 11, lists editors you might use. Whichever one you pick, be sure to save the file in the inventory folder.

code/inventory/snapshots/differences-version-1.rb

```
old_inventory = File.open('old-inventory.txt').readlines
new_inventory = File.open('new-inventory.txt').readlines

puts "The following files have been added:"
puts new_inventory - old_inventory

puts ""
puts "The following files have been deleted:"
puts old_inventory - new_inventory
```

Make sure you've exited from irb, and then run that script[4] like this:

```
prompt> ruby differences.rb
The following files have been added:
new-inventory.txt
recycler
recycler/inst-39.tmp
temp/inst-39

The following files have been deleted:
financial-records.xls
temp/junk
```

Some editors make it easier to run scripts. If you press F5 while editing a script in SciTE, it will run it and display the output in one half of a split screen. If you press ⌘R in TextMate, it will run the script and display the output in a new window.

This script has some definite weaknesses. For example, it insists you put your inventories in files named new-inventory.txt and old-inventory.txt. But it's a good start. Let's take stock.

---

4. If you didn't create a script but instead want to run the version in the snapshots folder, you need to copy it from there into differences.rb in the inventory folder. On Windows, do this:

C:>copy snapshots\differences-version-1.rb differences.rb

On Unix-like systems, do this:

prompt>cp snapshots/differences-version-1.rb differences.rb

3.8 Where Do We Stand?

We have a useful script. If you don't already compare inventories, or if you've always done it manually, there's something new in your bag of tricks.

You've learned a little bit about the simplicity underlying Ruby: everything is done by sending messages to objects. More important, you've seen the first of a variety of useful *data types*, the array. The combination of underlying simplicity and lots of built-in tools is what makes good scripting languages so powerful.

data types

3.9 Exercises

When working on the exercises, continue to use the inventory subfolder of your code folder.

1. The message length asks an array how long it is:

   ```
   irb(main):001:0> [1,2,3].length
   => 3
   ```

   Suppose you added this to your script:

   ```
   x = (new_inventory - old_inventory).length
   ```

   What would be the value of x for the inventories new-inventory.txt and old-inventory.txt? What information does x give you? What would be a better name than x?

2. What happens if you change the line in the previous exercise to this:

   ```
   x = new_inventory - old_inventory.length
   ```

   Why?

3. Change the script so that it prints three additional pieces of information: the number of files added in old-inventory.txt, the number removed, and (the trickiest one) how many files were unchanged.

4. Notice that both old-inventory.txt and new-inventory.txt are in alphabetical order, so the arrays named by them are too. Does the script depend on that? Would it work if the inventories were scrambled?

Chapter 4

Ruby Facts: Arrays

Because arrays are such a useful general-purpose container, Ruby lets you do many, many things with them. The following is just a sample.

Each row of the table below has three parts: an expression you could type to irb, the result irb would produce, and a commentary on the right.

Expression	Commentary
a = ['zero', 'un', 'dos', 'tre'] ↪ ["zero", "un", "dos", "tre"]	A **literal array** is created by putting square brackets around a comma-separated list of *elements*. I've named this particular four-element array a so that I can refer to it in the following examples.
a.length ↪ 4	You can ask for the **length** of an array...
a.size ↪ 4	...in two different ways. (This shows one of the reasons I like Ruby so much. In some languages, the way to ask for the length of an array is a size message. In others, the way to ask for the size of an array is the length message. The authors of those languages typically insist that you remember which one they chose. Ruby's author wanted to be friendly, so he lets you use either.)
[].size ↪ 0	The length (or size) of an empty array is 0.
a[0] ↪ "zero"	You refer to the first element of an array with *index* 0. The second element is selected with index 1, and so on. That's called **zero-based indexing**. (There have been vicious battles over whether indexing should be zero-based or one-based. I think the general consensus is that zero-based indexing works better in practice, once you get used to it.)

a[3] ↪ 'tre'	This is one way to select the last element of this four-element array.
a[-1] ↪ "tre"	This is another way.
a[-2] ↪ "dos"	**Negative indices** march backward through the array.
a[200] ↪ nil	Indices that are **out of bounds** return the value nil. You'll see a use for that in the next chapter.
a[0,3] ↪ ["zero", "un", "dos"]	You can select more than one element. Here, we've selected a **slice** of three elements, starting with a's 0th element.
a[1..3] ↪ ["un", "dos", "tre"]	This selects a slice containing elements 1 *through* 3 (an **inclusive range**).
a[1...3] ↪ ["un", "dos"]	This selects elements 1 *up to but not including* 3 (an **exclusive range**). *More* dots select *fewer* elements. (That doesn't make sense to me either.)
a[3] = 'z' ↪ "z"	You can **change an element** of an array.
a ↪ ["zero", "un", "dos", "z"]	See?
a[1..2] = ['x', 'y'] ↪ ["x", "y"]	You can change a range of elements.
a ↪ ["zero", "x", "y", "z"]	
a.delete_at(0) ↪ "zero"	**Deleting an element** at an index returns that element...
a ↪ ["x", "y", "z"]	...and also changes the array. Notice that delete_at's argument is surrounded by parentheses, not square brackets. (It's a message name, and message arguments are always in parentheses.)
a.delete("y") ↪ "y"	You can also delete an element because of its value, not where it's found in the array.
a ↪ ["x", "z"]	
a.slice!(0..1) ↪ ["x", "z"]	You can remove a slice from an array. The slice is returned...

a ↪ []	. . . and the array is changed. (The exclamation point is often used to signal methods that change the receiver when—as with arrays—most messages leave their receiver unchanged.)
a.empty? ↪ true	You can ask whether an array has any elements.
a.push(7) ↪ [7]	You can **push elements onto the end** of the array. . .
a ↪ [7]	(Notice that an array can hold numbers as well as strings.)
a << 8 ↪ [7, 8]	This is an alternate notation for push that some people like.
a = [0, "un", nil] ↪ [0, "un", nil]	You can put **different kinds of objects** in an array, all at the same time.
a << [10.1, "ten.two"] ↪ [0, "un", nil, [10.1, "ten.two"]]	You can even put arrays inside arrays.
a.length ↪ 4	An array within an array is just like any other element, so adding an array adds only one to the length.
a[-1] ↪ [10.1, "ten.two"]	And arrays within arrays are indexed in the usual way.
a[-1][0] ↪ 10.1	If you want an element of an array within an array, you need to index twice.
a.pop ↪ [10.1, "ten.two"]	You can **pop elements off the end** of the array. . .
a ↪ [0, "un", nil]	. . . and that changes the array.
a.shift ↪ 0	You can **shift things off the front** of the array. . .
a ↪ ["un", nil]	. . . and that again changes the array.
a.unshift(0) ↪ [0, "un", nil]	You can **put something on the front of the array** with unshift or. . .
a[0,0] = ['new element'] ↪ ["new element"]	. . . replace a zero-length slice before the 0th element. That returns the new element and. . .

a ↪ ["new element", 0, "un", nil]	. . . changes the array.
a[1..2] = [19600219] ↪ [19600219]	The slices you replace can be of any size, and the arrays you replace them with can be larger or smaller.
a ↪ ["new element", 19600219, nil]	Here, we've replaced two elements with one.

I encourage you to play around with these methods. If you want a concise list of *everything* an array can do, try this:

```
irb(main):006:0> any_old_array = []
=> []
irb(main):007:0> puts any_old_array.methods
```

You'll get quite a list. There'll be no documentation, but sometimes it's fun just to experiment.

ri

If you do want documentation for sort, say, you can use *ri* (think of it as short for "Ruby information"): type this to the command line:

```
prompt> ri Array.sort
```

On some systems, you'll need to type ⬚q to exit from ri. See the sidebar on page 111 for more.

Chapter 5

Three Improvements and a Bug Fix

The script in Chapter 3, *A First Script: Comparing File Inventories*, beginning on page 19, has three problems:

- The inventories always have to be in files named old-inventory.txt and new-inventory.txt. We should be able to specify them on the command line:

  prompt> ruby differences.rb old-file new-file

  old-file and new-file are called differences.rb's *command-line arguments*.

  command-line arguments

- On Windows, case is irrelevant in filenames. At least one user (Chris McMahon) doesn't want to be told that a file named bibtex has been deleted and a file named Bibtex has been added.
- When inventorying an entire filesystem (like C:\), Chris doesn't want to know about files in the temp directory or in the recycling bin.

In this chapter, we'll fix these problems. Along the way, you'll learn about Ruby control structures, how to define your own messages, and a bit more about arrays and strings.

5.1 Command-line Arguments

Command-line arguments are available as strings in the array named ARGV. For example, consider this command line:

prompt> ruby differences.rb old-inventory.txt new-inventory.txt

Within differences.rb, ARGV[0] will name (that is, provide a way to refer to) the string *"old-inventory.txt"*, and ARGV[1] will name *"new-inventory.txt"*. Instead of "hard-coding" the two files' names into the script, we can require the user to give them on the command line. The code to do that would look like this:

```
old_inventory = File.open(ARGV[0]).readlines
new_inventory = File.open(ARGV[1]).readlines
```

Replace your script's two File.open lines with these two, and give it a try:

```
prompt> ruby differences.rb old-inventory.txt new-inventory.txt
```

You should get the same results as before.

I'm always forgetting to give required arguments to scripts. Let's see what this script does in that case:

```
prompt> ruby differences.rb
differences.rb:1:in 'initialize': cannot convert nil into String (TypeError)
        from differences.rb:1:in 'open'
        from differences.rb:1
```

Not a friendly error message. I encourage you to try to figure out what happened before reading on.

If you give no arguments to a script, ARGV still names an array, but it's empty. You can see that using irb. irb is just a Ruby script, and you start it without any arguments, so...

```
prompt> irb
irb(main):001:0> ARGV
=> []
irb(main):002:0>
```

Since there's nothing in the array, every array index is out of bounds and will return nil:[1]

```
irb(main):003:0> ARGV[0]
=> nil
irb(main):004:0> ARGV[1]
=> nil
```

Because ARGV[0] is nil, the script has a problem when it hits this line:

```
old_inventory = File.open(ARGV[0]).readlines
```

open expects a string that names a file. The error message is the result of giving it nil instead. open tries its best to interpret nil as a string but

---

1. See Chapter 4, *Ruby Facts: Arrays*.

fails. I'd prefer that our script produce a more graceful error message when the user doesn't give both required arguments. That can be done by putting the following code at the beginning of the script (before ARGV is used):

```
code/inventory/snapshots/differences-version-2.rb
unless ARGV.length == 2
  puts "Usage: differences.rb old-inventory new-inventory"
  exit
end
```

Ruby's **unless** construct begins with **unless** and ends with **end**. The *body* *body* is the text between the two. Unless the expression following the **unless** is true, the body is executed. Otherwise, it's skipped. In this case, the body is executed unless the number of elements in the array is equal to 2 (meaning that both arguments were given).[2]

The body of an **unless** is just like any other Ruby code; it executes one line at a time. In this case, it prints a message. Then it uses the exit message to stop the script; otherwise, Ruby would continue to try (and fail) to open a file. You don't have to indent the body, but it makes the code easier to read. I usually indent two spaces.

Chapter 6, *Ruby Facts: If, Equality Testing, and Unless*, beginning on page 51, will tell you more about Ruby's **unless** construct, as well as the more common **if**.

5.2 Ignoring Case

Case is irrelevant to Windows filenames, but it's not irrelevant when strings are compared. So a switch from manifest.txt to Manifest.txt will look like an addition and a deletion. An easy way to avoid that is to make all the strings lowercase before comparing them.

When sent the downcase message, a string responds with another string that is its lowercase version. (The original string is not changed.) Like this:

```
irb(main):005:0> "STRING".downcase
=> "string"
irb(main):006:0> "string".downcase
=> "string"
```

2. Ruby uses == to mean "is equal to" because a single equal sign is already used to make variables name objects.

An Annoying Mistake to Make

You used your first **end** on the previous page. As you write more complicated scripts, you'll find that you sometimes leave off the **end**. That can lead to an annoying error message:

```
prompt> ruby differences.rb
differences.rb:20: syntax error
```

(Try it, and see for yourself.)

The error message is jargon for "the structure of the script is wrong—some word was in the wrong place, missing, or something."

The reason the message is annoying is that line 20 is the very end of the file. Ruby is saying "something went wrong between the beginning and end of the file." Gee, thanks. That narrows it down.

It would be nice if Ruby would give the exact line number where the **end** should be, but it can't. The **end** could appear on any line up to the end of the file. You'll have to search for where it belongs.

There are other ways to cause a syntax error, but usually they're caught before the end of the file. For example, consider this line, which is missing the closing parenthesis:

```
old_inventory = File.open(ARGV[0].readlines
```

Here's the resulting error message:

```
prompt> ruby differences.rb
differences.rb:13: syntax error
new_inventory = File.open(ARGV[1]).readlines
                    ^
```

That's a little closer to the actual problem, but the line shown is still the one *after* the one with the problem. Ruby couldn't complain on that line because everything there is valid, provided the parenthesis is closed on some later line. It's only at the next line that Ruby can tell that the script is irretrievably broken, so that's the line it shows.

The general rule for syntax errors is that the source of the problem isn't necessarily on the line where it's noticed. Look backward.

All we need to do is downcase each string in both old_inventory and new_inventory. That's easily done with one of Ruby's most powerful features, *iterators*. An iterator lets you work with each element of an array in turn. Here's a simple example:

iterators

```
irb(main):007:0> [1, 2, 3].each do | element |
irb(main):008:1*   puts element
irb(main):009:1> end
1
2
3
=> [1, 2, 3]
```

The each message tells the array to do something to each of its elements. You tell the array what to do by giving it a *block* delimited by **do. . . end**. The block contains Ruby code of your choosing, and the array hands it each element, one after the other. The block will want to do something to the element, so it needs to give the element a name. That's the variable, element, within the vertical bars.

block

The block is executed three times. The first time, element is 1, the second it's 2, and the third it's 3. Finally, each returns the original array.

each is the most basic iterator. There are a host of others, such as collect. It's like each, but it doesn't return the original array. Instead, it gathers the value of each execution of the block into a new array, which it returns. Like this:

```
irb(main):010:0> [1, 2, 3].collect do | element |
irb(main):011:1*   element * 1000 + element
irb(main):012:1> end
=> [1001, 2002, 3003]
```

collect doesn't care what's in the array. The elements can be strings, like the strings in old_inventory, and those strings can be sent the downcase message:

```
irb(main):013:0> ['ab', 'AB', 'aB'].collect do | string |
irb(main):014:1*   string.downcase
irb(main):015:1> end
=> ["ab", "ab", "ab"]
```

We can do the same sort of iteration to strings read from the inventory:

```
old_inventory = File.open(ARGV[0]).readlines.collect do | line |
  line.downcase
end
```

Here, open returns an open file that receives the readlines message. readlines returns an array, which immediately receives the collect method.

collect gathers up the downcased strings and returns them in an array, which finally is named with the variable old_inventory.

I didn't see a point in naming the intermediate values because we're never going to use them again. You might think that using some intermediate names might make it easier to understand the code:

```
file_lines = File.open(ARGV[1]).readlines
new_inventory = file_lines.collect do | line |
  line.downcase
end
```

I might agree with that, but perhaps there's a better solution. Consider what's happening here. Our code first asks the open file for an array. Then it downcases each element. Wouldn't it be better to skip the intermediate array and just ask the open file to downcase everything and return the results? That would look like this:

```
new_inventory = File.open(ARGV[1]).collect do | line |
  line.downcase
end
```

polymorphic

It works. That's because collect and each are examples of *polymorphic* messages. That means different kinds of objects accept them, and each kind does something appropriate with the block. Open files apply the block to each of their lines, and arrays apply it to each of their elements. Polymorphic iterators reduce the size of the vocabulary you need to know: whenever an object can be seen as composed of pieces, you can be pretty sure it responds to each and friends. Because of that, you'll spend less time flipping through manuals.[3]

Here's what we now have in the script:

```
code/inventory/snapshots/differences-version-4.rb
```

```
old_inventory = File.open(ARGV[0]).collect do | line |
  line.downcase
end
new_inventory = File.open(ARGV[1]).collect do | line |
  line.downcase
end
```

That can still be improved. Here's how I made the second three lines: I copied the first three, pasted them, changed ARGV[0] to ARGV[1], and changed old_inventory to new_inventory... (except I almost forgot to make

---

3. each wasn't our first example of a polymorphic message. We earlier used the polymorphic message -, which works for both arrays and numbers. I just didn't make a big deal about it then.

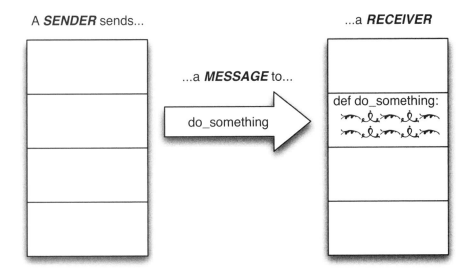

A **SENDER** sends...

...a **MESSAGE** to...

do_something

...a **RECEIVER**

def do_something:

It can be hard to remember the difference between messages and methods. A message is a request sent from some sender object. When the receiver object receives the message, it looks to see whether it has a method with the same name. If so, the Ruby code within the method is run, and the results are returned to the sender. The message is the request; the method fulfills it.

Figure 5.1: MESSAGES AND METHODS

the second change). In the future, whenever I change the first lines, I'll have to remember to change the second three as well. There's a good chance I'll forget. *Duplicate code is a major cause of unmaintainable scripts.* If you do not keep firm control of duplication, you'll spend too much time fixing bugs in your scripts. And other people won't use your scripts because they're buggy or too fragile to build upon.

Let's fix the duplication.

5.3 Methods

Ruby *methods* let you create new verbs (messages) in the Ruby language. It's a bit confusing that two closely related ideas—messages and methods—have such similar names. See Figure 5.1, for a picture showing how they work together.

methods

> ### Delimiting Blocks
>
> Blocks can start with a **do** and end with **end**, or they can start with { and end with }. The following two snippets of code mean the same thing:
>
> ```
> array.each do | element |
>   puts element
> end
>
> array.each { | element |
>   puts element
> }
> ```
>
> My sense is that Rubyists prefer the first except for short blocks, especially those that can fit on one line:
>
> ```
> array.each { | element | puts element }
> ```
>
> In this book, I'll use the first form almost exclusively.

Here is our first example of a method and its message.

`code/inventory/snapshots/differences-version-5.rb`

```
❶   def inventory_from(filename)
      File.open(filename).collect do | line |
        line.downcase
      end
    end

❷   old_inventory = inventory_from(ARGV[0])
❸   new_inventory = inventory_from(ARGV[1])
```

The new message is defined at ❶. It looks something like a block—it's a chunk of ordinary Ruby code that works on named objects handed to it. There are minor syntactic differences—it starts with **def** instead of **do**, and arguments are enclosed in parentheses like (filename) instead of vertical bars like | line |—but the most important difference is that methods have names and blocks don't. You won't go far wrong if you think of a method as a named block.

Once a method is defined, there's a new message in the Ruby universe. Lines ❷ and ❸ show it being sent. Each of those lines replaces three.

Clumping lines of code into methods may seem silly in such a small script, but you'll soon be modifying inventory_from. I think you'll appreciate not having to make the changes twice.

5.4 Dissecting Strings

Recall that Chris doesn't want to see temporary files or files in the Recycle bin. A simple solution is to reject the entire contents of any folder named temp or recycler.

Let's start by figuring out how to reject a single filename. Here's a list of examples that should be filtered out. (All the examples are lowercase because the script already uses downcase on each line in the inventory.)

- c:/temp/file[4]
- c:/temp
- d:/temp
- temp
- /temp
- /wretched/temp/file
- /recycler
- /temp/recycler
- h:/recycler

Here are some we *don't* want to filter out:

- c:/temp2
- c:/tmp/file
- /recycle
- /trash
- /program files/temp-file

My first thought was that we want to reject a file from the inventory if it includes the string */temp* or */recycler*. But it turns out that that won't work—consider *temp*, which wouldn't match, and *c:/temp2*, which would. It seems we want to reject a file if its name contains "temp," possibly after a slash but after no other character and possibly followed by a slash but by no other character. And the same rules apply to "recycler."

Yuck. That could be expressed in Ruby, but it seems way too complicated. What I've found as I've aged is that if my solution looks too

---

4. You may have noticed that Ruby's folder separator character is the forward slash (/). If you're working on Unix or Mac OS X, that's unsurprising—it's what the operating system uses too. On Windows, it looks odd, since Windows uses the backward slash (\). Ruby takes care of the translation, just as Windows web servers do for URLs like http://www.example.com/folder1/folder2/file1.html.

complicated, it's probably because I'm not looking at the problem from the right angle. The right angle here is that the line in question isn't just a string—we can also think of it as a *series* of strings separated by slashes. Instead of simultaneously looking for "temp" and worrying about slashes, why don't we treat them as separate issues?

So: worrying about slashes. It turns out that Ruby has a way to split a string wherever there's a separator. It's the split method. Here are some examples:

```
irb(main):016:0> "c:/temp/file".split('/')
=> ["c:", "temp", "file"]
irb(main):017:0> "c:/temp".split('/')
=> ["c:", "temp"]
irb(main):018:0> 'temp'.split('/')
=> ["temp"]
irb(main):019:0> '/temp'.split('/')
=> ["", "temp"]
```

Once the original line is split up, it's easy to look for *temp* because of another handy message, include?:

```
irb(main):020:0> ["c:", "temp"].include?('temp')
=> true
irb(main):021:0> ["c:", "temp"].include?('recycler')
=> false
```

Armed with include?, we can write a method to detect the kind of boring files Chris doesn't want to hear about:

`code/inventory/snapshots/differences-version-6.rb`
```
def boring?(line)
  line.split('/').include?('temp') or
    line.split('/').include?('recycler')
end
```

Now that we can identify one boring line, we want to reject (exclude, ignore, delete) every boring line in an inventory array. Fortunately, Ruby's arrays respond to the reject method. Like each and collect, it takes a block. Like collect, it returns a new array that depends on what the block returns. Unlike collect, though, reject filters out all the elements for which the block is true. In other words, assuming the inventory is in inventory, the following code would produce an array with boring lines stripped out:

```
inventory.reject do | line |
  boring?(line)
end
```

That code can be plugged into the script's inventory_from method, which would look like this:

```
code/inventory/snapshots/differences-version-6.rb
```

```
   def inventory_from(filename)
❶    inventory = File.open(filename)
❷    downcased = inventory.collect do | line |
       line.downcase
     end
❸    downcased.reject do | line |
       boring?(line)
     end
   end
```

For clarity, I rearranged it into three parts:

❶   First, it reads the file into an array named inventory.

❷   Next, it downcases all the lines, naming the new array downcased.

❸   Finally, it rejects the lines that name boring files, returning the result.

Here's how the new method works:

```
prompt> ruby differences.rb old-inventory.txt new-inventory.txt
The following files have been added:
new-inventory.txt
recycler

The following files have been deleted:
financial-records.xls
```

Wait a minute—what's recycler doing there in the list of added files?

5.5 Fixing a Bug

If you look at new-inventory.txt, you'll see that it has four files that ought to be filtered out:

```
recycler
recycler/inst-39.tmp
temp
temp/inst-39
```

But only three of them seem to be. Can you figure out the bug from the information you have now? (I couldn't.)

Since I couldn't see the bug, I did something quick 'n' dirty to learn more: I put a puts at ❶ in the following. Each time boring? is invoked, the puts will tell me what string it's working with.

Note that + concatenates two strings to produce a new string. I use inspect for debugging because it gives a more exact representation of objects. (See inspect's description on page 25.)

`code/inventory/snapshots/differences-version-7.rb`

```
def boring?(line)
❶   puts "boring? " + line.inspect
    line.split('/').include?('temp') or
      line.split('/').include?('recycler')
end
```

Running that tweaked script, I see this:

```
prompt> ruby differences.rb old-inventory.txt new-inventory.txt
boring? "exercise-differences.rb\n"
boring? "inventory.rb\n"
boring? "old-inventory.txt\n"
...
boring? "recycler\n"
boring? "recycler/inst-39.tmp\n"
...
The following files have been added:
...
```

Aha! I forgot about the trailing \n.[5] It's easy to check whether that makes a difference:[6]

```
irb(main):022:0> "recycler\n".split('/')
=> ["recycler\n"]
```

split leaves the \n on. Will that affect the inclusion check? Let's see:

```
irb(main):023:0> ["recycler\n"].include?('recycler')
=> false
```

It does. That makes sense, since a string with a trailing \n really is a different one than one without. Now, thousands of scripts have had to deal with trailing \n characters; in fact, one helps build this book. So it's not surprising there's a message just for getting rid of them: chomp. It works like this:

```
irb(main):024:0> "recycler\n".chomp
=> "recycler"
```

---

5. This is the same \n we encountered on page 21 when executing a bit of this script in irb. If you've forgotten what \n is all about, see that page.

6. The string *"recycler\n"* has to be typed with double quotes for the \n to mean "put a line separator here\." If you type it within single quotes, it means "a backslash followed by an 'n'." See the sidebar on page 72 for more on the differences between single and double quotes.

We could chomp the line in either boring? or inventory_from. I arbitrarily chose to do it at ❶ in inventory_from:

`code/inventory/snapshots/differences-version-8.rb`

```
def inventory_from(filename)
  inventory = File.open(filename)
  downcased = inventory.collect do | line |
❶   line.chomp.downcase
  end
  downcased.reject do | line |
    boring?(line)
  end
end
```

Does it work? Yup:

```
prompt> ruby differences.rb old-inventory.txt new-inventory.txt
The following files have been added:
new-inventory.txt

The following files have been deleted:
financial-records.xls
```

As a tester, I know better than to say "I fixed the last bug," so I'll just say that I see no further reason to change this script right now.

5.6 Where Do We Stand?

Scripting is about stringing messages and objects together in some coherent way. Methods let you define new messages to use. Without that ability, it'd be as if you couldn't tell someone "go to the store"; instead, you'd have to provide every little detail of the journey. ("Go out the front door to the sidewalk. Turn left. Proceed until you reach the cross-street. Look both ways. If no car is coming, cross the street. . . .")

By the time you'd finished giving the instructions, you'd have forgotten what you wanted. To accomplish any substantial task without getting hopelessly confused, you have to use a specialized vocabulary. Methods let you define that vocabulary's verbs.

Blocks are essentially unnamed methods. The methods can remain unnamed because you're using them only once. You give a block to collect to tell it what to do and then forget about it.

Every time we needed some behavior—transforming each element of an array, rejecting elements of an array, splitting a string, downcasing a string—it turned out to be built in to Ruby. That's important: it's all too

> ### Joe Asks. . .
>
> #### Why Didn't temp Also Incorrectly Appear in the Output?
>
> The folder temp appeared identically in both the old and new inventories. Although it wasn't correctly chomped, that didn't matter because there was no change to show anyway.
>
> Files like temp/junk *were* correctly filtered out because they were split into ["temp", "junk\n"]. The line separator only "polluted" the last part of the name.

common for beginning scripters to learn a small set of messages and not to get into the habit of looking beyond them. Get into the habit of looking—not just at the Ruby documentation but also on the internet. (See Chapter 18, *Downloading Helper Scripts and Applications*, beginning on page 171, for more.)

5.7 Prelude to the Exercises

From this point on, you'll be working with larger and larger chunks of Ruby code. It's likely, though, that you'll still want to try out methods in irb. But method definitions are awkward to type. Once you hit [Enter], you can't correct an error without retyping the whole method. One alternative is to edit the method in a file and then paste it into irb (as described in Section 2.6, *Working with Prompts*, on page 13).

An alternative I often prefer is to make the whole Ruby script *loadable*. That means the script executes normally when run from the command line but can also be loaded into irb so that all its methods are available.

```
prompt> irb
irb(main):001:0> load 'exercise-differences.rb'
=> true
irb(main):002:0> boring?('/temp/foo')
=> true
```

A loadable script has to detect whether it's being run from the command line or being loaded. Figure 5.2, on the facing page, shows how that's

`code/inventory/exercise-differences.rb`

❶
```ruby
def check_usage
  unless ARGV.length == 2
    puts "Usage: differences.rb old-inventory new-inventory"
    exit
  end
end

def boring?(line)
  line.split('/').include?('temp') or
    line.split('/').include?('recycler')
end

def inventory_from(filename)
  inventory = File.open(filename)
  downcased = inventory.collect do | line |
    line.chomp.downcase
  end
  downcased.reject do | line |
    boring?(line)
  end
end
```

❷
```ruby
def compare_inventory_files(old_file, new_file)
  old_inventory = inventory_from(old_file)
  new_inventory = inventory_from(new_file)

  puts "The following files have been added:"
  puts new_inventory - old_inventory

  puts ""
  puts "The following files have been deleted:"
  puts old_inventory - new_inventory
end
```

❸
```ruby
if $0 == __FILE__
  check_usage
  compare_inventory_files(ARGV[0], ARGV[1])
end
```

inventory/exercise-differences.rb

Figure 5.2: A SCRIPT THAT WORKS INSIDE IRB

done. (That script, exercise-differences.rb, is in the inventory folder, so you can use it for this chapter's exercises.)

The work of deciding how the file is being used is done at ❸. The names on that line are rather cryptic.[7] Variable $0 holds the name of the running script as it appeared on the command line. __FILE__ is the name of the file it appears in. (Note there are two underscores before and two after.) When differences.rb is run as a script, those are the same thing. For irb, they're not. The name of the running script is *irb*, and the value of __FILE__ is something else. (You can type __FILE__ to irb to see what it is.) So the **if** statement can be read as "if I am the script running at the command line, check_usage and compare_inventory_files. Otherwise, I'm being loaded, so do nothing."

The methods at ❶ and ❷ simply wrap two chunks of code that originally weren't in methods. The first chunk was at the beginning of the file and checked that arguments had been given. The second did the work of comparing two inventory files. They could have simply been copied into the **if** statement at ❸, but I thought the script would be easier to read if each chunk had a name. And compare_inventory_files, at least, might be something usefully used within irb:

```
irb(main):003:0> compare_inventory_files('old-inventory.txt',
   'new-inventory.txt')
The following files have been added:
new-inventory.txt

The following files have been deleted:
financial-records.xls
=> nil
```

5.8 Exercises

1. differences-version-8.rb (in snapshots) is a version that wasn't changed to be loadable. What happens if you load it anyway? Can you explain the behavior?

2. Start the next set of exercises by copying exercise-differences.rb into differences.rb.

---

7. The names go back a long way and were chosen to be memorable to people who also go back a long way, especially people familiar with the C programming language.

Now change differences.rb so that chomping off the \n is done inside boring?. Check your work by running the script. Hint: Move the use of chomp from inventory_from to boring?. There, instead of splitting a line, split a chompedline.

3. boring? asks the question "does the line contain *'temp'* **or** does it contain *'recycler'*?" The actual code that asks the question is a little complicated; what it's doing doesn't just jump out at you. In such cases, it's often a good idea to move the code into a method with a helpful name. So, first change boring? to look like this:

```
def boring?(line)
  contains?(line, 'temp') or contains?(line, 'recycler')
end
```

(The name here is a little awkward: contains?(x, y) should be read as "x contains y." That kind of awkwardness is not uncommon because the verb of the sentence has to come first. It's something you'll get used to.)

Next, implement contains?. Its body should look like part of what you deleted from the original boring?. The difference is that the string to look for (either *'temp'* or *'recycler'*) is handed to contains? instead of being used explicitly. That is, the second argument to contains? names the string to check for.

4. Another useful iterator is any?. It returns true if any of the array elements make the attached block return true. To ask whether any deposit is big enough to report to the authorities, you could type this:

```
irb(main):004:0> deposits = [1, 0, 10000]
irb(main):005:0> deposits.any? do | deposit |
irb(main):006:1*    deposit > 9999
irb(main):007:1> end
=> true
```

You can read that as "you are given a list of three deposits. Is anydeposit greater than *9999*?"

Write a new version of boring? that takes two arguments. The first is the inventory entry (a string). The second is an array of boring component names (like *"temp"* and *"recycler"*). It would be used like this:

```
boring?("temp", ["temp", "recycler"])
boring?("/foo/bar", ["food", "bart", "quux"])
```

The first should return true, and the second false. Here's a skeleton for the method to get you started:

```
def boring?(line, boring_words)
end
```

The body of that method should say, in Ruby, what this English sentence says: "a line is boring if it contains any boring word (as defined by the array boring_words)."

Check your new boring? by loading the new version of differences.rb and trying the two previous examples.

Hints:

- If you're going to ask a question about any of the words in an array, that would look like this:

```
boring_words.any? do | a_boring_word |
    ... ask the question about that word ...
end
```

- The question "does the line contain a boring word?" can be written like this:

```
contains?(line, a_boring_word)
```

5. The new version of boring? works, but the script now breaks. Run it to see. Then fix it.

Chapter 6

Ruby Facts: If, Equality Testing, and Unless

Here are the most common ways to tell Ruby that you want something
to happen only under certain circumstances.

6.1   if ... elsif ... else

Here is Ruby's if statement in all its glory, wrapped in a method:

`code/if-facts/describe.rb`

```
def describe(inhabitant)
  if inhabitant == "sophie"
    puts 'gender: female'
    puts 'height: 145'
  elsif inhabitant == "paul"
    puts 'gender: male'
    puts 'height: 145'
  elsif inhabitant == "dawn"
    puts 'gender: female'
    puts 'height: 170'
  elsif inhabitant == "brian"
    puts 'gender: male'
    puts 'height: 180'
  else
    puts 'species: Trachemys scripta elegans'
    puts 'height: 6'
  end
end
```

If given 'paul', the method would work like this:

```
irb(main):001:0> load 'describe.rb'
=> true
```

```
irb(main):002:0> describe 'paul'
gender: male
height: 145
=> nil
```

test expressions
The expressions on the if and elsif lines are called *test expressions*. Ruby
executes each of them in turn until it finds one that's true. Then it
body
executes the immediately following *body* (in this case, the lines that
use puts). If none of the test expressions is true, the body of the else is
executed.

Just like everything else in Ruby, if returns a value. The value of a body
is the value of its last statement (just as with method bodies), and the
value of the entire if construct is the value of the selected body. So in
the case of describe 'paul', the value of the if is the value of puts 'height:
145' (which happens to be nil).

You can leave out either or both of elsif and else. The if and end are
required. If there's no else and none of the test expressions is true, the
if "falls off the end," in which case its value is nil.

Scripters often use if to pick which of several values is returned from a
method. The following method returns a description of an inhabitant of
my house:

code/if-facts/description.rb

```
def description_of(inhabitant)
  if inhabitant == "sophie"
    ['gender: female', 'height: 145']
  elsif inhabitant == "paul"
    ['gender: male', 'height: 145']
  elsif inhabitant == "dawn"
    ['gender: female', 'height: 170']
  elsif inhabitant == "brian"
    ['gender: male', 'height: 180']
  else
    ['species: Trachemys scripta elegans', 'height: 6']
  end
end
```

I had the method return an array because puts prints each element of
an array on a separate line:

```
irb(main):004:0> load 'description.rb'
=> true
irb(main):005:0> puts description_of('dawn')
gender: female
height: 170
=> nil
```

Warning: elsif Is a Typo Magnet

If you're like me, about half the time you use **elsif**, you'll type it as either **else if** or **elseif**.

6.2 When Are Objects Equal?

In the previous section, I checked whether inhabitant was a particular first name. == is *boolean-valued*. That is, it returns either true or false: *boolean-valued*

``` a = 0 a == 0 ↪ true ```	Notice that equality is tested with == because = has already been used up by variable assignment. That's another of those accidents of the history of programming. It means you'll certainly sometimes type = when you meant to test equality.
``` a == 1 ↪ false ```	
``` "string" == "string" ↪ true ```	You can use == on anything. Each kind of object can have its own version of what equality means.
``` "string" == "String" ↪ false ```	For example, string equality takes case into account.
``` 0 == '0' ↪ false ```	0 is a number; '0' is a string. For the most part, different types of objects can never be equal.
``` 1.0 == 1 ↪ true ```	The numeric types are an exception. Numbers that can have decimal points (*floating-point* numbers) and numbers that can't (*integers*) are, strictly, different kinds of things, but they can still be equal. To be absolutely sure what equality means for a data type, you need to look at documentation.

6.3 A Shorthand Version of if

Consider this English sentence: "I'll carry an umbrella if it's raining." That could be written in Ruby like this:

```
if raining?(here)
  carry('umbrella')
end
```

Three lines for such a simple idea seem a bit much. For that reason, Ruby has a one-line form that has the same format as the English:

```
carry('umbrella') if raining?(here)
```

This form doesn't allow an else or elsif, and it doesn't use end. Everything has to fit on one line.

6.4 unless

The word "unless" is in the English language for a reason. Contrast "unless the judge is unfair, you'll win" with "if the judge is not unfair, you'll win." Negations—especially negations of already negative ideas—can be confusing. The same is true of Ruby code:

```
unless unfair(judge)
  winner = you
end

if not unfair(judge)
  winner = you
end
```

You can also use unless with the one-line form:

```
array.pop unless array.empty?
```

6.5 The Question Mark Operator

You'll often find yourself selecting between two alternative values for a variable. That can be done like this:

```
if input < 0
  output = 0
else
  output = input
end
```

But it seems wrong to take up five lines for such a simple idea. You can reduce it to two by picking one of the values and then possibly overriding it:

```
output = input
output = 0 if input < 0
```

But it's a little confusing for the code to do something and then immediately say, "Wait! I didn't mean that!" So there's a compact version of **if** for just this purpose:

```
output = (input < 0) ? 0 : input
```

You can read that as "**if** input is less than zero, **then** return 0, **else** return whatever object input names."

This **?:** construct is called either the *question mark operator* or, more often, the *ternary operator*. ("Ternary" because it uses three expressions, unlike operators such as +, which have two and are called *binary operators*.)

question mark operator

ternary operator

binary operators

Part II

Growing a Script

## Chapter 7

The Churn Project: Writing Scripts without Fuss

Scripting can be straightforward or horrible. When it's horrible, it feels like the script is actively fighting you and that every try at making something better makes something else worse. The way to make it straightforward is to proceed in tiny, tested steps. In this chapter, I'll show you how to do that.

"Straightforward" doesn't mean "error-free." Expect to make mistakes all the time; the trick is to recover from them smoothly and quickly. This chapter will demonstrate that by showing how I handle two blunders of the sort that often lead to a quagmire.

One warning: in this chapter, I'm going to explain my thinking as I write a script. It takes a lot longer to explain thoughts than to have them. Don't let all the words in this chapter fool you into thinking that scripting requires agonizing over every decision. Instead, strive to make decisions crisply. If you can't decide which of two possibilities is better, it probably doesn't matter which you pick. If you're wrong, just recover and move on.

7.1 The Project

If you ask a programmer what she's working on, she might say "auditing" or "the persistence layer." Systems are usually divided into named subsystems with boundaries that are more or less clear. The source code for different subsystems is usually stored in different folders.

```
prompt> svn log --revision 'HEAD:{2005-07-30}' svn://rubyforge.org/var/ ↩
svn/churn-demo/inventory
------------------------------------------------------------------------
r2 | marick | 2005-08-07 14:26:21 -0500 (Mon, 07 Aug 2005) | 1 line

added code to handle merger
------------------------------------------------------------------------
r1 | marick | 2005-08-07 14:21:47 -0500 (Mon, 07 Aug 2005) | 1 line

first touches
No commit for revision 0.
------------------------------------------------------------------------
```

Figure 7.1: CHANGES TO A SUBSYSTEM

```
prompt> ruby churn.rb
Changes since 2005-08-05:
        audit ********* (45)
  fulfillment **** (19)
  persistence *** (17)
          ui *** (15)
        util * (3)
    inventory * (2)
```

Figure 7.2: OUTPUT FROM THIS CHAPTER'S PROGRAM

When deciding where to concentrate effort, a tester might want to know which subsystems have changed the most. That information is available from the project's version control system. My favorite is called Subversion. Figure 7.1 shows one way of asking Subversion about a fake project I've set up. If you have Subversion on your system and are on the Internet, you can type the same line to get similar information. Subversion, like the best things in life, is free. You can find it at http://subversion.tigris.org. You don't need it to work on this project, though.

Subversion's output shows that the "inventory" subsystem has changed twice since July 30. That's a pretty ugly way to get the information, though, and it shows you only one subsystem at a time. In this chapter, we'll write a script that asks the same question of all the subsystems in a project, producing output like that of Figure 7.2.

The output isn't fancy, but there's nothing wrong with simple and functional. Notice the script somehow knows what subsystems there are (the six listed) and from when it should start counting changes (the date one working month before the script is run). It might be nice to allow those defaults to be overridden, but we won't bother for this script. (We will for later ones.)

7.2 Building a Solution

A technique that often works well is one I call *scripting by assumption*.[1] The trick is to start writing the script by *assuming* that Ruby provides all the methods you need. Here's some starting code I wrote for churn, all the while assuming that everything hard would be done for me:

scripting by assumption

```
code/churn/snapshots/churn.v1.rb
```

```
❶ if $0 == __FILE__
❷   subsystem_names = ['audit', 'fulfillment', 'persistence',
                          'ui', 'util', 'inventory']
❸   start_date = month_before(Time.now)

❹   puts header(start_date)
    subsystem_names.each do | name |
❺     puts subsystem_line(name, change_count_for(name))
    end
  end
```

I'll explain these lines over the next several pages. Unless you *like* flipping pages back and forth, you may find it more convenient to look at the source online. The callout symbols (like ❹) are included in the file. They're shown as *end-of-line comments* like this:

end-of-line comments

```
puts header(start_date)   #(4)
```

When it sees the comment character **#**, Ruby ignores everything from there until the end of the line.

Our script must produce two things: a header string containing not much more than the starting date of the changes, and a series of strings, one for each subsystem, that contains a name, a change count, and asterisks for a simple visual representation of the change count. The asterisks make the output look something like a histogram tipped on its side.

---

1. That's not a name I made up, but I can't find who said it first. Abelson and Sussman write of "programming by wishful thinking" in *Structure and Interpretation of Computer Programs* [ASS84]. It's the same idea, but I like "assumption" a bit better.

At ❹, I assume Ruby comes with a method, header, that produces a correctly formatted header string. When writing that line, I came to a fork in the road. I could have the script tell header what date to print, or I could have it figure it out (by calculating the date one month before the moment the script runs). The choice comes down to this:

```
puts header(start_date)
```

or this:

```
puts header
```

I chose the first because the second implies that the header string is always the same. It's not: it varies, so it seems sensible to make the cause of variation explicit. When I wrote that line, I didn't know what start_date really was. I assumed it'd become obvious later.

At ❺, I assume a method, subsystem_line, that returns a string ready to print. The contents of that string will vary depending on the subsystem's name and count of changes. Should the count of changes be given to subsystem_line directly or indirectly?

- "Directly" means that the script will get a subsystem's change count from Subversion and hand it to subsystem_line. In that case, subsystem_line's definition would start like this:

  ```
  def subsystem_line(name, change_count)
  ```

- "Indirectly" means subsystem_line will itself ask Subversion for the change count. To do so, it would need to know the starting date, so its definition would start like this:

  ```
  def subsystem_line(name, start_date)
  ```

separation of concerns

I chose the direct approach because it makes it more obvious what's in the string that subsystem_line will create. It also follows a guideline called *separation of concerns*. In the indirect case, subsystem_line has two concerns: how to format a string and how to communicate with Subversion. In the direct case, subsystem_name is only about formatting, and some other method is about Subversion.

Since subsystem_line has to be called for each subsystem, it makes sense to stash all the subsystem names in an array and iterate over them with each. The array is created and named at ❷. Since a project's list of subsystems will rarely change, it makes sense to "hard-code" it.

I'm assuming everyone always wants to know the number of changes in the last working month, so start_date is defined that way at ❸. I could have defined it as an argumentless method last_month, but what I've got seems to read more clearly: "the starting date is the month before right now." (When the Time object is sent the message now, it returns an object that represents the current instant of time.) And, as you'll learn in Section 7.2, *Test-driving month_before*, passing in a date also makes test-driven scripting easier.

I created a variable start_date to name the day from which to start looking for changes, but when I needed a change count to give to subsystem_line, I passed it along directly:

```
puts subsystem_line(name, change_count_for(name))
```

I could have written this:

```
change_count = change_count_for(name)
puts subsystem_line(name, change_count)
```

Why didn't I? There are two reasons for adding a variable to a script. The first is that you're using an object more than once and you're either unable or unwilling to create it twice. That doesn't apply here. The other is that the variable helps someone understand the script. My main reason for creating start_date was that I could put it next to subsystem_names at the beginning of the script. All the data the script works with depends on the data those two variables name, so it makes sense to draw attention to that by putting them first and together. I can't see any way that creating a variable change_count would help a reader.

There's one more bit of code to mention: ❶. Because of it, the script can both be run from the command line and also be loaded into irb. (The trick was explained in Section 5.7, *Prelude to the Exercises*, on page 46.)

Test-driving month_before

It's increasingly common for programmers to build their code *test-first*: if the code doesn't do something you want, first write a test that fails because of that, and then write the minimal amount of code that passes the test. If more is needed, write the next test and then the next bit of code. Continue until the code does what you want. Along the way, clean up code whenever it starts to get messy, making sure that the cleaned-up code always passes all the tests. (The technical term for such cleanup is *refactoring*.)

test-first

refactoring

With practice, writing code with tests is faster than writing code alone (because of the time you don't have to spend hunting for bugs), and it's usually a lot more pleasant.

```
code/template-for-tests.rb
```

❶ require 'test/unit'
❷ require 'X'

❸ class X < Test::Unit::TestCase

❹   def test_X
❺   assert_equal('expected', 'actual')
    end

end

template-for-tests.rb

Figure 7.3: A TEST TEMPLATE

Test::Unit

Ruby comes with a package called *Test::Unit* that lets you set up tests without having to write much support code. You can find a test template in Figure 7.3. Parts you'll need to fill in are marked with an *X*.

❶ The test file is run like any other script. require loads all the Ruby code that makes up Test::Unit into that running script. It's almost the same as using load in irb.

❷ Usually, there's one test file for each script file. This line loads the script under test. In this case, 'X' will be replaced with *'churn'*. (Note that, unlike load, require doesn't need the *.rb* at the end of the filename; it can figure it out.)

❸ For the moment, let's ignore what this line means beyond saying that **class**... **end** serves to group the tests. See Chapter 11, *Classes Bundle Data and Methods*, beginning on page 105, for more. 'X' names the file's group or *suite* of tests. You can pick any name you want, but it must begin with a capital letter. ChurnTests seems reasonable.

suite

❹ When you run a test file (e.g., ruby churn-tests.rb), Test::Unit executes each method whose name begins with test_. It ignores other methods. The ones it ignores can be used as utilities by the ones it does run.

❺ Each assert_equal message compares its first argument (the expected value) to the second (the actual value produced by the code under test). If they aren't equal, it complains. (You'll see a typical complaint in a minute.)

What would a test for month_before do? A working month is 28 days. So the month before January 29 is January 1. In the script proper,

Joe Asks...

Why Does Ruby Have Both require and load?

require and load do almost the same thing. The important difference is that require remembers the files it's loaded and will load each only once. That behavior is useful when script A.rb uses a method in B.rb and B.rb uses a method in A.rb. If A.rb had load 'B.rb' and B.rb had load 'A.rb', then loading A.rb would load B.rb, which would load A.rb, which would load B.rb. . . .

Given require, why ever use load? Suppose you're writing some code in a file. You require it into irb and try it. Oops, it's wrong. You change the file. If you require it again, you won't get the changed version (because Ruby knows you've already loaded that file). You have to use load to get the new version.

So use require in script files and load in irb.

Time.now is used as the argument to month_before, but the test doesn't have to use a Time that represents the current instant. In fact, it *can't* use that. If it used Time.now, the actual value would change every time the test ran. What would the expected value be?

Fortunately, Time provides methods that construct any arbitrary time: local is the one that constructs Times relative to the local time zone. That means we can ask month_before to pass this test:

`code/churn/snapshots/churn-tests.v1.rb`

```
def test_month_before_is_28_days
  assert_equal(Time.local(2005, 1, 1),
        month_before(Time.local(2005, 1, 29)))
end
```

Let's see that test fail.[2]

Before you can run the test, you'll need to copy it from the snapshots folder. On Windows, you do that like this:

```
prompt> copy snapshots\churn-tests.v1.rb churn-tests.rb
```

---

2. It's common practice to run a test even if you *know* it will fail. I thought that was a silly ritual until the first time I did it and saw no failure. I had put the test in the wrong place, so Test::Unit hadn't run it. If I hadn't tried the test first, I might have written bad code, run the tests, seen no failure, and thought I'd done well. That would have been bad.

On Unix-like systems, it's like this:

```
prompt> cp snapshots/churn-tests.v1.rb churn-tests.rb
```

All the tests assume they're testing churn.rb. Unless you've already created it, do that now by copying churn.v1.rb from the snapshots folder into the current working folder. Be sure to copy it into churn.rb.

Having prepared the test, run it like this:

```
prompt> ruby churn-tests.rb
Loaded suite churn-tests
Started
E
Finished in 0.002627 seconds.

  1) Error:
test_month_before_is_28_days(ChurnTests):
NoMethodError: undefined method 'month_before' for #<ChurnTests:0x32f8f0>
    churn-tests.rb:9:in 'test_month_before_is_28_days'

1 tests, 0 assertions, 0 failures, 1 errors
```

The test correctly tells us that there's no method named month_before yet. Let's define it. But where?

The test will requirechurn.rb. That means Ruby will ignore the body of the if $0 == __FILE__ check. (See Section 5.7, *Prelude to the Exercises*, on page 46.) So it should be above the **if**.

In order to see a more typical failure, let's define month_before wrong:[3]

`code/churn/snapshots/churn.v2.rb`

```
def month_before(a_time)
end
```

Here's the failure:

```
  1) Failure:
test_month_before_is_28_days(ChurnTests) [churn-tests.rb:9]:
<Sat Jan 01 00:00:00 CST 2005> expected but was
<nil>.

1 tests, 1 assertions, 1 failures, 0 errors
```

An empty method returns nil, which certainly isn't the Time expected. Notice that the failure message identifies both the test that failed

---

3. I usually don't bother running a test that fails because the method isn't defined. I define an empty method before running the test for the first time.

Joe Asks. . .

What's the Difference Between an Error and a Failure?

A Test::Unit test can fail in two ways. Our second test run showed a failure. A *failure* means that what an assertion asserts to be true isn't in fact true. An *error* means that something else went wrong before the assertion was tried. In our first test run, Ruby stopped the script when it discovered there was no such method as month_before and, therefore, no return value for assert_equal to compare against January 1, 2005.

Frankly, I always have to think for a minute when I'm asked which is which. Perhaps that's because I treat both cases the same. I look at the explanation of what went wrong, I go to the line number mentioned, and I fix the problem.

(test_month_before_is_28_days) and the line it failed on (line 9). The latter is useful when there's more than one assertion in a test.

Let's write the right code. To get an earlier Time, you subtract some number of seconds:

```
irb(main):001:0> now = Time.now
=> Mon Aug 29 11:42:19 CDT 2005
irb(main):002:0> now-1
=> Mon Aug 29 11:42:18 CDT 2005
```

So all we have to do is subtract 28 days of seconds:

`code/churn/snapshots/churn.v3.rb`

```
def month_before(a_time)
  a_time - 28 * 24 * 60 * 60
end
```

And it passes:

```
prompt> ruby churn-tests.rb
Loaded suite churn-tests
Started
.
Finished in 0.00247 seconds.

1 tests, 1 assertions, 0 failures, 0 errors
```

It's such a satisfying moment when that happens. Those frequent jolts of pleasure are what makes test-driven scripting so satisfying. You won't believe it until you try it.

Formatting Time

Now that we believe month_before works, we also believe that start_date will name the right object after this assignment:

start_date = month_before(Time.now)

So it makes sense to now write the method, header, that uses the returned Time:

`code/churn/snapshots/churn.v3.rb`

puts header(start_date)

Here are two possible tests:

`code/churn/snapshots/churn-tests.v2.rb`

```
def test_header_format
  assert_equal("Changes since 2005-08-05:",
            header(Time.local(2005, 8, 5)))
end
```

```
def test_header_format
  assert_equal("Changes since 2005-08-05:",
            header(month_before(Time.local(2005, 9, 2))))
end
```

direct test

bootstrapping test

For both, I just copied the expected output from Figure 7.2, on page 60. The difference between the two is how they generate the value given to header. One is a *direct test*: it uses Time.local to make exactly the Time it needs. The other is a *bootstrapping test*: it uses an already-tested method from the script under test to test a new method.

The two types of tests have contrasting advantages. A direct test is usually easier to understand. It's also usually easier to debug if it fails. Suppose that I later change month_before and break it. Then both the direct test_header_format and the test_month_before_is_28_days will fail. I'll have to decide which one to look at. If I look at test_header_format, I have to wonder whether the problem is in header or in month_before. That's hardly a big deal in this case, but it can get cumbersome when you have 200 tests that use month_before. It's even worse if the change to month_before *deliberately* changes its behavior (maybe I want it to return a different kind of object). Then I may have to fix all 200 tests.

The advantage of bootstrapping tests is that they're more realistic and thorough. Suppose it turns out that there's a mismatch between what month_before returns and what header expects. Perhaps month_before returns a Time and header expects a string. A bootstrapping test for header would detect that, but a direct test would not, since the test that header is to pass will use the string it expects.

A second advantage of bootstrapping tests is that they use month_before again. I made sure I tried a different kind of value in the test of test_header_format than I did in the earlier test for month_before. Since, in the previous test, both "now" and the date 28 days earlier are in the same month, this time I picked ones in different months. I have no reason to think that will find a bug, but I've found too many bugs through sheer dumb luck to use the same value twice. On the other hand, figuring out what date to hand to month_before to cause it to hand August 5 to header was more work than the direct test requires. Was it worth it?

Different people have different biases. Mine is toward bootstrapping tests, so I'll use the second version. But if I had a lot of tests to write for header, I'd make only a couple of them bootstrapping. I'd make the rest of them direct so that I didn't face the prospect of changing many tests if I ever change my mind about what month_before should do.

Everyone finds their own balance between testing directly and testing indirectly. You will too.

The only tricky part about implementing header is formatting dates. Ruby's default format (from the scripter-friendly inspect message) is something like "Mon Aug 29 12:20:00 CDT 2005". That's not the format we want. Fortunately, Time objects respond to the gracefully named strftime message. And here's an example of the result:

```
irb(main):002:0> Time.now.strftime('%Y-%m-%d')
=> "2005-08-29"
```

Each character that follows % picks out a piece of the Time and places the result in the string strftime returns. You can find the complete table of format characters either in a Ruby reference like *Programming Ruby* [TH01] or like this:

```
prompt> ri Time.strftime
```

(You can find information about ri in the sidebar on page 111.)

header can just be a more elaborate format string:

```ruby
def header(a_time)
  a_time.strftime("Changes since %Y-%m-%d:")
end
```

The test passes:

```
prompt> ruby churn-tests.rb
Loaded suite churn-tests
Started
..
Finished in 0.006264 seconds.

2 tests, 2 assertions, 0 failures, 0 errors
```

Note that the earlier test still passes. That's good to know.

Formatting Strings

subsystem_line is another method that is about formatting, so let's do that next. Here's a test:

```ruby
def test_normal_subsystem_line_format
  assert_equal('        audit ********* (45)',
         subsystem_line("audit", 45))
end
```

The subsystem name is right-justified in a field fourteen characters wide, followed by a space, followed by nine asterisks and the count of 45.

What does this test tell us about the method we have to write? It will look something like this:

```ruby
def subsystem_line(subsystem_name, change_count)
  # code here...
end
```

subsystem_name's string can be justified with Ruby's rjust method. That works like this:

```
irb(main):002:0> 'audit'.rjust(14)
=> "         audit"
```

Next the output has the row of nine asterisks. I'll put off figuring out how to make that string by assuming there's a method called asterisks_for that converts an integer into the right number of asterisks (nine, the number of changes divided by five). It'll be used like this:

```
def subsystem_line(subsystem_name, change_count)
  asterisks = asterisks_for(change_count)
  # more code here...
end
```

The final bit is the change count, which is passed as an argument and needs only to be plugged into the result.

Given variables subsystem_name, asterisks, and change_count, the return value could be constructed using addition of strings:

```
subsystem_name.rjust(14) + ' ' + asterisks +
    ' (' + change_count.inspect + ')'
```

That's ugly. Not only is it ugly, but it took me three tries to get it right. The first try, I forgot to use inspect to convert the integer named change_count to a string that could be added. The second try, I realized I'd forgotten to add the space after the subsystem_name and before the opening parenthesis.

My rule of thumb for Ruby is anything that's ugly or awkward can probably be done a better way. I'd make fewer mistakes if I didn't have to add strings together and if I could write the output as I want to see it, leaving blanks for Ruby to fill in. Here's what that looks like:

```
"#{subsystem_name.rjust(14)} #{asterisks} (#{change_count})"
```

This is an example of *string substitution*. You can place any Ruby code within the #{} marker. Ruby will evaluate that code, convert it to a string, and insert that string where the marker is. See the sidebar on the following page, for more about string substitution.

string substitution

All that given, here's subsystem_line:

code/churn/snapshots/churn.v3.rb

```
def subsystem_line(subsystem_name, change_count)
  asterisks = asterisks_for(change_count)
  "#{subsystem_name.rjust(14)} #{asterisks} (#{change_count})"
end
```

This method won't pass the test because asterisks_for doesn't work yet. So that's the next thing to write. Here's a starting test:

code/churn/snapshots/churn-tests.v3.rb

```
def test_asterisks_for_divides_by_five
  assert_equal('****', asterisks_for(20))
end
```

String Substitution

Single-quoted and double-quoted strings handle string substitution differently. The different rules make double-quoted strings good for constructing complicated strings in a readable way. Single-quoted strings are good for making strings that contain characters that would otherwise trigger string substitution.

Double-quoted strings allow inline substitution of any Ruby expression with #{}:

```
irb(main):018:0> "1 + 1 = #{1 + 1}"
=> "1 + 1 = 2"
```

Double-quoted strings also use backslash to denote single characters. \n is the line separator character, \s is the space character, and \t is the tab character. The latter two are useful to make it clear whether " " contains five spaces, a tab, or some combination. There are other, less important substitutions—see a more complete Ruby reference.

Any other character that follows a backslash is inserted literally (*without* the backslash). That is, "\d" is the same as "d". More important, \" lets you put a double quote in a double-quoted string, and \\ lets you put in a backslash.

In almost all cases, a single-quoted string contains exactly and only the characters you type. There are two exceptions:

- You can put a single quote in a single-quoted string by preceding it with a backslash:

```
irb(main):001:0> 'I\'m hungry, said the weasel.'
=> "I'm hungry, said the weasel."
```

- Two backslashes in a row are treated as a single backslash. As far as I know, all that's good for is putting a backslash at the end of a string.

```
irb(main):002:0> puts 'three backslashes: \, \\, and \\'
three backslashes: \, \, and \
=> nil
```

If you're like me and use single quotes because they're easier to type, beware of reflexively using \n in a single-quoted string. You probably don't really want a string with a backslash and an "n."

But now I face an annoyance. I want to define an empty asterisks_for, run the test, and see it fail. But if I run all the tests in the latest churn-tests.rb, *two* tests will fail, like this:

```
 1) Failure:
test_asterisks_for_divides_by_five(ChurnTests) [churn-tests.rb:26]:
<"****"> expected but was
<nil>.

 2) Failure:
test_normal_subsystem_format(ChurnTests) [churn-tests.rb:19]:
<"          audit ********* (45)"> expected but was
<"          audit  (45)">.
```

One failure is the test for asterisks_for. That is good, since that is the method we're working on. The other is the test for subsystem_line, which can't pass until asterisks_for is done. That's bad, because it makes it harder for me to see what's happening—it's a little bit of sand in the gears. Fortunately, Test::Unit's *–name* option lets you run one test at a time:

```
prompt> ruby churn-tests.rb --name=/asterisks/
Loaded suite churn-tests
Started
F
Finished in 0.058324 seconds.

 1) Failure:
test_asterisks_for_divides_by_five(ChurnTests) [churn-tests.rb:26]:
<"****"> expected but was
<nil>.

1 tests, 1 assertions, 1 failures, 0 errors
```

Any test matching *–name*'s argument will be run. Notice that you don't have to give the full name.[4] Note also that *–name* starts with two dashes, not one, despite how it might look on this page.

Here is code that passes the test:

code/churn/snapshots/churn.v4.rb

```
def asterisks_for(an_integer)
  '*' * (an_integer / 5)
end
```

---

4. Strictly, *–name*'s argument is a *regular expression*. You'll learn about those in Chapter 9, *Our Friend, the Regular Expression*, beginning on page 91.

It takes advantage of Ruby's string multiplication. Like multiplication of integers, it's just shorthand for adding the same thing multiple times. So '*' * 5 is the same as '*' + '*' + '*' + '*' + '*' and '*****'.

What should happen when the change count is not evenly divisible by five? It should round:

`code/churn/snapshots/churn-tests.v4.rb`

```
def test_asterisks_for_rounds_up_and_down
  assert_equal('****', asterisks_for(18))
  assert_equal('***', asterisks_for(17))
```

That fails:

```
1) Failure:
test_asterisks_for_rounds_up_and_down(ChurnTests) [churn-tests.rb:27]:
<"****"> expected but was
<"***">.
```

It's the first assertion (the one on line 27) that fails.[5] To fix it, we have to deal with an unfortunate fact about computers. To a pocket calculator, it makes absolutely no difference whether you key in 4 or 4.0. That's the case even though the computer that runs the calculator almost certainly makes a distinction between the *integer* 4 and the *floating-point* number 4.0. A calculator hides that fact from you; Ruby, like most programming languages, does not. So when asterisks_for(18) executes, it divides the *integer* 18 by the *integer* 5. In the real world, 18/5 is 3.6. In the computer world, it's 3—that is, computers always round down.

floating-point

We want to round up 18/5 because it's closer to 4 than to 3. There are two steps. First, we need to get the floating point number 3.6. Then we need to explicitly round it up.

To get 3.6, we can't divide 18 by 5. Arithmetic operations involving only integers always produce integers. But if one of the numbers is floating point, the result will also be floating point. So we divide the count, 18, by 5.0:

```
irb(main):001:0> 18 / 5.0
=> 3.6
```

Now the floating-point number can be rounded to an integer:

```
irb(main):002:0> (18/5.0).round
=> 4
```

---

5. After one assertion fails, the method stops. None of the assertions following it runs. The assumption is that they'd fail too, adding no information—just clutter—to the test output.

That suggests this method:

`code/churn/snapshots/churn.v5.rb`

```
def asterisks_for(an_integer)
  '*' * (an_integer / 5.0).round
end
```

Not only does asterisks_for pass the new test, it continues to pass the old one:

```
prompt> ruby churn-tests.rb --name=/asterisks/
Loaded suite churn-tests
Started
..
Finished in 0.002288 seconds.

2 tests, 3 assertions, 0 failures, 0 errors
```

In fact, now that asterisks_for is complete, the test for line_format should pass. *All* tests should pass, and they do:

```
prompt> ruby churn-tests.rb
Loaded suite churn-tests
Started
.....
Finished in 0.00460100000000005 seconds.

5 tests, 6 assertions, 0 failures, 0 errors
```

Using External Programs

Only one method remains: change_count_for. It has to fetch data from Subversion and extract the change count from it. Here's my sketch of that method:

`code/churn/snapshots/churn.v6.rb`

```
def change_count_for(name)
  extract_change_count_from(svn_log(name))
end
```

It's not a massively exciting method. All I've done is split the work into two parts. I've done that to separate what's hard to test with Test::Unit from what's easy. To test extract_change_count_from, we just have to build a string that looks like a Subversion log, pass it to the method, and check that the answer is correct. svn_log is a different kind of beast: it has to communicate with the outside world. An automated test would have to set a Subversion repository to a known state, use svn_log, and check the results. That's a lot of work, and I don't think it's worthwhile. So I'll check that method once, manually.

First, let's get extract_change_count out of the way. It will work on Subversion output like that which we've already seen. Here are its tests:[6]

`code/churn/snapshots/churn-tests.v5.rb`

```
def test_subversion_log_can_have_no_changes
  assert_equal(0, extract_change_count_from("————————————————-\
————————————————\n"))
end

def test_subversion_log_with_changes
  assert_equal(2, extract_change_count_from("————————————————-\
————————————————=——————\nr2531 | bem | 2005-07-01 01:1\
1:44 -0500 (Fri, 01 Jul 2005) | 1 line\n\nrevisions up through ch 3 exer\
cises\n————————————————=————————————-\
-\nr2524 | bem | 2005-06-30 18:45:59 -0500 (Thu, 30 Jun 2005) | 1 line\n\
\nresults of read-through; including renaming mistyping to snapshots\n—\
————————————————-\n"))
end
```

The backslash at the end of the data lines tells Ruby to ignore the immediately following line break, not to include it in the string. I used it to make these lines fit inside this book's margins.

The first test is output from a boundary case I tried: what happens if there have been no changes in a time period? In a way, that's the simplest case the program will have to handle. Often (though not in this case), it's easiest to start by passing the simplest test and then add code to pass harder ones. The second test is more typical output.

It seems fairly easy to calculate the change count: it's the number of dashed lines minus one. Here's code that passes the test:

`code/churn/snapshots/churn.v6.rb`

```
   def extract_change_count_from(log_text)
❶   lines = log_text.split("\n")
❷   dashed_lines = lines.find_all do | line |
❸     line.include?('——————')
     end
❹   dashed_lines.length - 1
   end
```

At ❶, the long string is converted into an array of lines (breaking at the end-of-line marker). Then (at ❷), a previously undescribed method, find_all, is used. It finds all lines for which the block (at ❸) is true and collects them into an array. In this case, the block is true when the line

---

6. If you're working along with the book, you can find sample Subversion output to build your test from in `code/churn/snapshots/subversion-output.txt`. And good for you!

What to Test

You don't need as many tests for code you can see as for code you can't. Consider the tests for asterisks_for. The first test will cause asterisks_for to round up 3.6; the second will cause it to round down 3.4. Numbers that end exactly in 5, like 3.5, are trickier. Under at least some rounding rules, sometimes you should round up, sometimes down. Yet I have no test that exercises such numbers.

The two tests I have suffice to convince me that I'm *using* rounding correctly. Further tests would be checking whether Ruby *implements* rounding correctly. I already believe it does; more to the point, nobody is paying me to test Ruby.

Black-box testing needs to be more exhaustive because you don't know which parts of the product's behavior you can justifiably trust.

Similarly, I'm not worried that the only subsystem_line test I have checks only the case where the number of changes is exactly divisible by five. That convinces me that subsystem_lines uses asterisks_for correctly. (For example, I now believe I haven't left off its argument.) Adding a test with a different number (18, for example) would only tell me two things I already believe: that asterisks_for works and that it's used correctly.

in question includes dashes. (I used only a short run of dashes so that trivial changes to the Subversion output won't break the script.)

Now to get the Subversion data. svn_log has to execute the same command I typed manually in Figure 7.1, on page 60. That's a longish string, so I built it up in parts:

code/churn/snapshots/churn.v7.rb

```
def svn_log(subsystem, start_date)
  timespan = "-revision 'HEAD:{#{start_date}}'"
  root = "svn://rubyforge.org//var/svn/churn-demo"

  `svn log #{timespan} #{root}/#{subsystem}`
end
```

The first lines should look familiar by now. (Notice that I just realized this method needs the start date, so I added it as an argument. I also had to fix change_count_for to use svn_log correctly.) The last line is peculiar. It appears to be a string, built up by the usual string substitution, but the text is enclosed in backticks. Those tell Ruby to take the given string, send it to the command-line interpreter, and return the results as a string. Like this:

```
irb(main):012:0> svn_log('persistence', '2005-06-30')
=> "--------------------------------------------------------
-----------\nr2531 | bem | 2005-07-01 01:11:44 -0500 (Fri, 01 Jul
2005) | 1 line\n\nrevisions up through ch 3 exercises\n---------
---------------------------------------------------------------\n
r2524 | bem | 2005-06-30 18:45:59 -0500 (Thu, 30 Jun 2005) | 1 li
ne\n\nresults of read-through; including renaming mistyping to sn
apshots\n-----------------------------------------------------
----------------\n"
```

Blunder the First

The complete code is shown in Figure 7.4, on page 81. Having written all that code and tested it, the program should now work. But I'm sure you know what's coming. . . .

```
prompt> ruby churn.rb
Changes since 2006-07-10:
subversion/clients/cmdline/main.c:832: (apr_err=205000)
svn: Syntax error in revision argument 'HEAD:{Mon Jul 10 23:15:47 CDT 2006}'
        audit  (-1)
subversion/clients/cmdline/main.c:832: (apr_err=205000)
svn: Syntax error in revision argument 'HEAD:{Mon Jul 10 23:15:47 CDT 2006}'
    fulfillment  (-1)
...
```

What went wrong? The clue is *HEAD:{Wed Aug 03 12:51:38 CDT 2005}*. That comes from line ❶ in svn_log:

```
timespan = "--revision 'HEAD:{#{start_date}}'"
```

I just tested svn_log by hand.[7] Why does it fail now?

When I tested it, I used a string like '2005-08-01' for the start_date argument. But when it's called by the program, that argument is a Time object from month_before. #{} converts that object into a string, using the default formatting, which is not what Subversion expects.

The problem will be easy enough to fix, but first I should think about why I let it happen in the first case. It seems to me it's because my names are bad. Look at line ❷, which I show here again.

```
start_date = month_before(Time.now)
```

---

7. This is the only method I tested manually, but that's not why the problem slipped past. I would have made the same mistake with a Test::Unit test.

One Test or Several?

In both subsystem_line and asterisks_for, I began writing code after writing a single test. I could have waited until I'd written more tests that forced me to make more decisions. For example, I might not have started asterisks_for until I'd written the rounding tests. And I might not have started subsystem_line until I decided what it should do when the subsystem name is too big to fit into the fourteen-character space allotted. (Something I still haven't decided.)

The argument for writing one test, then only the code that passes it, and then the next test is that the knowledge you learn writing the script allows you to write a better next test. It might also let you skip a test because you have high and justified confidence that the code would already pass that next test.

One argument against writing just one test is that knowing too much about how the script already works will bias you, perhaps subtly, causing you to overlook a test you should write. Another argument is that the fifth test might reveal that the code you wrote to pass the first four is just wrong, so you have to throw away that work. It would be better to know everything a method has to do before starting it.

For a long time, I was firmly in the "many tests" camp, but I've drifted away from it in the past four years. I'm not good enough at predicting all the tests I'll need, so I end up rewriting code in either case. Working one test at a time encourages working in small chunks, always making steady progress. That helps keep me from getting overwhelmed by the task. I suspect I miss more bugs working one test at a time, but I also suspect that getting the script done and in use sooner makes up for that.

I do, however, jot down ideas for tests as they come to me, because otherwise I'd forget them. I find pencil and paper the best technology for that purpose.

month_before returns a Time object, but the variable's name declares it to be about a "date." "Date" is an idea from Subversion—it's a year, a month, and a day of the month, all in a particular format. Naming a Ruby Time with start_date was asking for trouble—and the universe answered. Either start_date should be renamed start_time or it should really *be* a date. I choose the latter. I begin by converting month_before's return value into a Subversion-style date string:

code/churn/snapshots/churn.v8.rb

```
start_date = svn_date(month_before(Time.now))
```

That means a test for svn_date:

code/churn/snapshots/churn-tests.v6.rb

```
def test_svn_date
  assert_equal('2005-03-04',
          svn_date(Time.local(2005, 3, 4)))
end
```

The implementation is simple, reminiscent of the implementation of header:

code/churn/snapshots/churn.v8.rb

```
def svn_date(a_time)
  a_time.strftime("%Y-%m-%d")
end
```

I also have to change any methods that previously *correctly* expected start_date to be a Time object. Now they will *incorrectly* expect that, and they have to be made to correctly expect a formatted string. Scanning the tests is a good way to find such methods.

test_header_format reveals that header expects a Time object:

```
def test_header_format
  assert_equal("Changes since 2005-08-05:",
          header(month_before(Time.local(2005, 9, 2))))
end
```

When I tacked on an svn_date to do the conversion, the book's original formatting made the line too long to fit on a page. So I also introduced a variable to save horizontal space:

code/churn/snapshots/churn-tests.v6.rb

```
def test_header_format
  head = header(svn_date(month_before(Time.local(2005, 9, 2))))
  assert_equal("Changes since 2005-08-05:", head)
end
```

```
code/churn/snapshots/churn.v7copy.rb
```

```ruby
def month_before(a_time)
  a_time - 28 * 24 * 60 * 60
end

def header(a_time)
  a_time.strftime("Changes since %Y-%m-%d:")
end

def subsystem_line(subsystem_name, change_count)
  asterisks = asterisks_for(change_count)
  "#{subsystem_name.rjust(14)} #{asterisks} (#{change_count})"
end

def asterisks_for(an_integer)
  '*' * (an_integer / 5.0).round
end

def change_count_for(name, start_date)
  extract_change_count_from(svn_log(name, start_date))
end

def extract_change_count_from(log_text)
  lines = log_text.split("\n")
  dashed_lines = lines.find_all do | line |
    line.include?('————')
  end
  dashed_lines.length - 1
end

def svn_log(subsystem, start_date)
❶    timespan = "–revision 'HEAD:{#{start_date}}'"
  root = "svn://rubyforge.org//var/svn/churn-demo"

  `svn log #{timespan} #{root}/#{subsystem}`
end

if $0 == __FILE__
  subsystem_names = ['audit', 'fulfillment', 'persistence',
                     'ui', 'util', 'inventory']
❷  start_date = month_before(Time.now)

  puts header(start_date)
  subsystem_names.each do | name |
❸    puts subsystem_line(name, change_count_for(name, start_date))
  end
end
```

Figure 7.4: CHURN

Bugs in Tested Code

As I've mentioned, test-driven programming is becoming more popular. People are sometimes too enthused by it, to the point they think it's all the testing that's needed. But it wouldn't have caught Blunder the First. Test-driven programming is good at eliminating bugs where you intend to do something but failed. That's because each intention is described and then checked with a test. But it doesn't prevent you from forgetting to state an important intention. In churn's tests, I never stated my intention that the results of month_before could be used by svn_log.

As another example, I've consistently "forgotten" to worry about handling errors. What happens, for example, if no connection can be made to the Subversion server? (You can see by running churn without Subversion installed or while you're not connected to the Internet.) I'm doing that on purpose—error handling is deferred to Chapter 21, *When Scripts Run into Problems*, beginning on page Chapter 21, *When Scripts Run into Problems*—but it's certainly not unknown for people to do it by accident.

The test fails. Now that it's given a formatted string, header no longer needs to use strftime:

`code/churn/snapshots/churn.v8.rb`

```
def header(an_svn_date)
  "Changes since #{an_svn_date}:"
end
```

The tests pass. I wish I hadn't made this mistake (and I really did make it), but fixing it was an unexciting, straightforward, step-by-step process not much different from writing the methods in the first place.

Blunder the Second

Does the program now work? Let's see:

```
prompt> ruby churn.rb
Changes since 2006-07-11:
      audit * (5)
  fulfillment  (2)
  persistence * (3)
        ui ** (8)
      util * (4)
  inventory  (2)
```

Oh no! I forgot to order the lines in decreasing order of change count! Looking at Figure 7.4, on page 81, what has to be done to fix it? The root problem is that the change count is fetched at ❸, which is too late to affect the order in which things are printed. We'll solve that in the next chapter.

7.3 Where Do We Stand?

I live in a very flat part of the world. Many of the roads are straight and level—you can almost imagine you could point a car down the road, take your hands off the steering wheel, and the car would go exactly where you pointed it. You can't, of course. Even on Illinois roads, driving is a matter of frequent, tiny corrections to your course. And even on these roads, the novice driver will lurch wildly from one overcorrection to its opposite.

Programming, for many, is like forever being a novice driver: periods of calm where things go invisibly wrong, followed by bursts of frantic panic and correction. I sometimes think that the only people who become programmers are ones who can tolerate that environment and that observing programmers struggle is the reason so many other people think programming is too hard for them.

However, programming *can* be much more like driving a car: steady, small corrections on the way to the goal. Test-driven programming is a good way to do that. It makes scripting more accessible.[8]

7.4 Exercises

When working on the exercises, continue to use the churn subfolder of your code folder.

1. Alter header so that its format output looks like "Changes between YYYY-MM-DD and YYYY-MM-DD:" where one of the dates is a month before now and the other is the date the script is run.

2. I'm not fond of the way the output looks in the case of zero or few changes:

```
 inventory  (0)
fulfillment  (2)
        ui *** (15)
```

---

8. The driving metaphor is due to Kent Beck in *Extreme Programming Explained* [Bec00].

Change the script so that a subsystem with no changes prints a dash instead of zero asterisks. Also change it so that one or two changes are *not* rounded down to zero. They should instead print as a single asterisk. I want "changed a little" to be visually distinct from "changed not at all." subsystem_lines should produce lines like this:

```
inventory - (0)
fulfillment * (2)
      ui *** (15)
```

3. Change subsystem_line so that its output is like this:

```
prompt> ruby churn.rb
Changes between 2006-08-05 and 2006-09-02:
audit        (45 changes)  *********
fulfillment  (19 changes)  ****
persistence  (17 changes)  ***
ui           (15 changes)  ***
util         (2 changes)   *
data            -             -
```

Notice two things:

a) Both the subsystem name and the change count are to be left-justified in a field of fourteen spaces.

b) When there are no changes, what used to be printed as *(0 changes)* is to be printed as a dash.

My Story of Shame

Even those who believe in test-driven programming face a life filled with temptation. At the time I was finishing up this book, I was also a web lackey for the Agile Alliance nonprofit (www.agilealliance.org). The Agile Alliance runs an annual conference, and everyone who attends gets a free membership in the organization. Those already members get a one-year extension to their existing membership. One week, I had the task of using conference attendee spreadsheet to update the membership database and mail the affected members the good news.

That required some simple scripts, ones that I knew I'd never use again. (We were about to switch to a completely new system.) I remember thinking that I really ought to test-drive those scripts into existence, because I shouldn't write one thing in this book and do another. But the scripts were *so* simple. . . .

You can guess the rest. I made a stupid mistake that led to a bad script. It would give existing members duplicate memberships instead of extensions. I *did* manually test the scripts before putting them into production; as best I can figure, the lag between running the script and getting the confirmation emails caused me to mistake one kind of confirmation for another. (I was in a hurry, which is always the best time to slow down.)

I ran the bad script in production. Shortly thereafter, I had to send an embarrassed email to 267 people who might have otherwise thought I know something about preventing bugs from escaping into production.

I tell this story not because I want even more potential clients to lose confidence in me but to drive home that you're better off testing first, even when you think that can't possibly do anything but slow you down. Many of the chapters in this book talk only about the final scripts, not the tests that drove their creation. Even though the exercises often have you changing the tests, I worry that the importance of disciplined testing won't stick. I hope my sad story makes it stickier.

Chapter 8

Ruby Facts: Booleans

Ruby has two boolean values, true and false, and three boolean operators: **not**, **and**, and **or**. The negation of a false expression is true, and vice versa. **and** and **or** work like this:

left	right	left **or** right	left **and** right
true	true	true	true
true	false	true	false
false	true	true	false
false	false	false	false

8.1 Other Boolean Operators

People who come to Ruby from other programming languages are used to a different way of writing boolean operators. Ruby supports that alternate notation:

not x	is the same as	!x
a **or** b	is the same as	a || b
a **and** b	is the same as	a **&&** b

This alternate notation is much more common than the more human-readable one I've used so far, so I'm going to use it henceforth.

8.2 Precedence

Which of the following expressions always produce the same result, no matter what the values of a and b?

```
a || b && c
a || (b && c)
(a || b) && c
```

The first and second do. In jargon, **&&** has higher *precedence* than ||.   *precedence*

Which of these three expressions mean the same thing?

```
!a || b
(!a) || b
!(a || b)
```

Again, it's the first and second. Negation has a higher precedence than the other two boolean operators.

Except in simple cases, I recommend you use parentheses to make it absolutely clear what you mean. Just because the computer under-stands doesn't mean someone else reading your script will.

Here's something I hesitate to mention because I think it's more con-fusing than useful. The precedence rules are *different* for the two ways of writing boolean operators. The first difference is that **and** does not bind more strongly than **or**. That is, in the following:

```
a or b and c
a or (b and c)
(a or b) and c
```

it's the first and the *third* that have the same value.

not binds more strongly than **and** and **or**, so these two expressions mean the same thing:

```
not a and b
!a && b
```

However, **not** binds *less* strongly than **&&** and **||**. That means the follow-ing mean the same thing:

```
not a && b
! (a && b)
```

If I *ever* catch you taking advantage of that, I'll crawl out of this page and make you suffer. If you want to risk that, here is the complete list of precedence rules, in decreasing order of precedence:

```
    !
   &&
   ||
   not
or and
```

All kidding aside, take advantage of language quirks only if they're widely known. For example, the idiom shown in Section 8.4, *Boolean Expressions Can Select Objects*, on the next page, is hard to figure out if you first see it without an explanation, but it's so widely used that it will quickly become second nature.

8.3 Every Object Is a Truth Value

In all the examples earlier in the chapter, I let you assume that the variables must name either true or false. In fact, they may name any Ruby object.

To see why that's useful, recall that a Ruby array will produce nil when asked for an element beyond the boundary of its size. That's a pretty common convention: if you can't return what was desired, return "nothing." That would imply that Ruby code must be scattered with tests like this:

```
if something == nil ...
```

It's not, because nil counts as false. So the previous can be more conveniently written like this:

```
unless something ...
```

All objects other than nil and false count as true. So instead of this:

```
if not object == nil ...
```

you can write

```
if object ...
```

8.4 Boolean Expressions Can Select Objects

I've also let you assume that boolean expressions will return either true or false. In fact, they can return any object.

That is useful behavior, especially because Ruby supports *short-circuiting evaluation*. Consider a && b. Suppose a is false. Ruby need not evaluate b to know that the whole expression must be false, so it doesn't. The same is true of a || b; Ruby won't evaluate b if a is known to be true.

short-circuit

This behavior is often used to pick one of two values. Here's a typical example:

```
file = ARGV[0] || "default.txt"
```

If the script is given command-line arguments, ARGV[0] is the first one (some string). Otherwise, it's nil.

Suppose ARGV[0] is a string. Any string counts as true, so Ruby doesn't check the right side of the ||-expression. It just returns the string, which becomes file's value.

Suppose ARGV[0] is nil. Then Ruby must evaluate the right side to find the value of the whole ||-expression. Since "default.txt" counts as true, it is that value, and file is set to *"default.txt"*.

So file always names a string, either the one given or some default. That's the same result as the following, only more compact:

```
if ARGV[0]
  file = ARGV[0]
else
  file = "default.txt"
end
```

## Chapter 9

Our Friend, the Regular Expression

In Chapter 7, *The Churn Project: Writing Scripts without Fuss*, beginning on page 59, we ended with a problem: output lines were being generated in the wrong order. In this chapter, we'll look at a venerable problem-solving strategy: build the wrong thing, and then make it right by brute force. We'll generate churn's output lines in no particular order and then order them. Here's a sketch of the code:

`code/churn/snapshots/churn-re.rb`

```
if $0 == __FILE__
  subsystem_names = ['audit', 'fulfillment', 'persistence',
                     'ui', 'util', 'inventory']
  start_date = svn_date(month_before(Time.now))

  puts header(start_date)
❶  lines = subsystem_names.collect do | name |
    subsystem_line(name, change_count_for(name, start_date))
  end
❷  puts order_by_descending_change_count(lines)
end
```

At ❶, the original each is changed to a collect. The lines aren't made and printed; they're made and saved in an array. That array will then be put right at ❷ and printed.

To make order_by_descending_change_count work, we need some way of extracting the change count from a string. That's where regular expressions come in.

9.1 Regular Expressions Match Strings

Regular expressions *Regular expressions*, often abbreviated "regexps," are a tool used to check whether strings have the right form. Here's an example:

```
irb(main):001:0> /match/ =~ "does this have a match?"
=> 17
```

The result, 17, marks the position where the match occurs. Like every value in Ruby other than false and nil, 17 counts as true, allowing you to write code like this:

```
irb(main):002:0> puts 'got one!' if /match/ =~ "match here?"
got one!
=> nil
```

Here is an example of a match that fails:

```
irb(main):003:0> /no match/ =~ "not match"
=> nil
```

You might not have noticed that those expressions use a new operator, =~. (The second character is a tilde, sometimes called "twiddle.") =~ looks a little like ==, but it checks for a regular expression match instead of exact equality. If you accidentally use == instead, you'll find that *no* regular expression is equal to *any* string:

```
irb(main):004:0> /match/ == "match"
=> false
```

After all, they're different kinds of objects.

Just as double-quoted strings can contain characters that are interpreted specially, so can regular expressions. In this chapter, I'll explain only the ones we need for this script. See Chapter 10, *Ruby Facts: Regular Expressions*, beginning on page 99, for more.

The special character + says that the preceding character must be repeated one or more times to match:

```
irb(main):005:0> /ab+c/ =~ "matches 'abbc'?"
=> 9
irb(main):006:0> /ab+c/ =~ "matches 'abc'?"
=> 9
irb(main):007:0> /ab+c/ =~ "matches 'ac'?"
=> nil
```

The two-character sequence \d matches only digits:

```
irb(main):008:0> /\d time/ =~ "he was arrested 3 times"
=> 16
irb(main):009:0> /\d time/ =~ "we had some fine old times"
=> nil
```

We can put those two together to match lines that look like churn.rb output:

```
irb(main):010:0> /\d+/ =~ "    ui ** (13)"
=> 14
```

We now know that this line's change count starts at character 14. If we knew where it ended, we could pluck it out of the string and use it to order the output lines. However, that regular expression is too simple. Suppose we created another subsystem called ui2. The regular expression would match the 2:

```
irb(main):011:0> /\d+/ =~ "    ui2 ** (13)"
=> 9
```

You can tell that it matched the 2, not the 13, by counting characters. Alternately, you can make the wrongness more obvious by pulling out everything from the match on:

```
irb(main):012:0> line = "    ui2 ** (13)"
=> "    ui2 ** (13)"
irb(main):013:0> /\d+/ =~ line
=> 9
irb(main):014:0> line[9..-1]
=> "2 ** (13)"
```

Strings are indexable, like arrays, so you can use the different variants of [] to pull out substrings.

Since we got the wrong match, we need a regular expression to match only numbers inside parentheses.[1] It seems like this should work:

```
irb(main):015:0> /(\d+)/ =~ "    ui2 ** (13)"
=> 9
```

If you look closely, you'll see that it didn't. The return value is 9, indicating that it matched the 2 again. That's because parentheses are special, like \d is. You'll see what they do in the next section. To get *real* parentheses in the regular expression, you have to *escape* them by preceding them with a backslash:

escape

```
irb(main):016:0> /\(\d+\)/ =~ "    ui2 ** (13)"
=> 14
```

You will notice that regular expressions can get hard to read pretty quickly. For that reason, I usually put all but the simplest inside well-named methods like has_parenthesized_number. That also lets me easily test them, because complicated ones are as hard to get right as they are to read.

---

1. I'm going to assume there won't be a subsystem named ui(2).

9.2 Dissecting Strings with Regular Expressions

Regular expressions can also be used to pick out pieces of a string. There's more than one way to do that. We'll use the match message. It works much like =~:

```
irb(main):017:0> /a/.match('this is a string')
=> #<MatchData:0x326d04>
irb(main):018:0> /a/.match('not one here')
=> nil
```

When there is a match, match returns a MatchData object. That object acts like an array. Its zeroth element is the first matching string. Here's an example:

```
irb(main):019:0> match = /\(\d+\)/.match("     ui2 ** (13)")
=> #<MatchData:0x326390>
irb(main):020:0> match[0]
=> "(13)"
```

That's pretty close to being the change count, which is what we want. Using the to_i (for "to integer") method and string slicing, we could produce the count:

```
irb(main):021:0> "(13)"[1..-2].to_i
=> 13
```

Given that, here's the whole story about extracting the change count:

```
irb(main):022:0> match = /\(\d+\)/.match("     ui2 ** (13)")
=> #<MatchData:0x334738>
irb(main):023:0> match[0][1..-2].to_i
=> 13
```

group

In order to explain another regexp feature, I'll get the count a different way. In regular expressions, parentheses that are *not* preceded by backslashes surround a *group*. Each group identifies a part of a match, and each part is accessible through the MatchData object. Here's an example of matching a simple arithmetic equation:

```
irb(main):024:0> match = /(\d)+(\d)=(\d)/.match("1+1=2")
=> nil
```

Hold on ... why'd that happen? (Can you see?)

It's because I forgot to escape the plus. The previous reads "one *or more* digits, followed by a digit, followed by an equal sign, followed by a digit," not the intended "*one* digit, followed by a plus sign, followed by a digit ...." Here's the right regexp:

```
irb(main):025:0> match = /(\d)\+(\d)=(\d)/.match("1+1=2")
=> #<MatchData:0x319118>
irb(main):026:0> "#{match[1]} plus #{match[2]} equals #{match[3]}"
=> "1 plus 1 equals 2"
```

After the zeroth element (the whole match), the rest of the elements of
a MatchData are the grouped matches, in left to right order. We can use
a group to get the number without the parentheses by putting the real
parentheses outside the parentheses that mark a group:

```
irb(main):027:0> match = /\((\d+)\)/.match("      ui2 ** (13)")
=> #<MatchData:0x1af280>
irb(main):028:0> match[1]
=> "13"
irb(main):029:0> match[1].to_i
=> 13
```

Now that we know what we're doing, let's write a test and its method:

`code/churn/snapshots/churn-tests-re.rb`

```
def test_churn_line_to_int_extracts_parenthesized_change_count
  assert_equal(19, churn_line_to_int("      ui2 **** (19)"))
  assert_equal(9, churn_line_to_int("      ui ** (9)"))
end
```

`code/churn/snapshots/churn-re.rb`

```
def churn_line_to_int(line)
  /\((\d+)\)/.match(line)[1].to_i
end
```

9.3 Reordering an Array

Our goal, remember, is to reorder an array of lines according to their
embedded change counts. Now that we can extract change counts from
a line, we need to do that.

The sort method, when received by an array, produces a new array with
a new order. In order to do that, it has to be able to know when one
element should go in front of another. Some objects, like integers and
strings, have that knowledge built in. Behind the scenes, sort accesses
that knowledge with something called the *spaceship operator*. (It looks   *spaceship operator*
a little like a flying saucer.) Here it is in use:

```
irb(main):030:0> 1 <=> 2
=> -1
irb(main):031:0> "a" <=> "b"
=> -1
```

The -1 return value means that the objects are in the correct order. When they're in the wrong order, the return value is 1:

```
irb(main):032:0> 2 <=> 1
=> 1
irb(main):033:0> 'b' <=> 'a'
=> 1
```

When the left and right sides are equal, the return value is 0.

Because of the spaceship operator, sort needs no extra information to put some arrays in order:

```
irb(main):034:0> [3, 1, 2].sort
=> [1, 2, 3]
irb(main):035:0> ['a', 'round', 'shell', 'rolled'].sort
=> ["a", "rolled", "round", "shell"]
```

But we want the strings in descending order of change count, not in alphabetical order. So we can't implicitly use the built-in knowledge. Instead, we have to give sort a block that uses the spaceship operator, like this:

code/churn/snapshots/churn-re.rb

```
def order_by_descending_change_count(lines)
  lines.sort do | one, another |
❶   one_count = churn_line_to_int(one)
❷   another_count = churn_line_to_int(another)
❸   - (one_count <=> another_count)
  end
end
```

sort will pass pairs of lines to the block. The first two Ruby statements in the block extract the change counts from the lines, and the last one compares them. Since the spaceship operator assumes ascending order and we want descending, the last line reverses its result. To be specific:

- Suppose the line named one has a change count of 3 and the line named another has a change count of 5. We'll want another to come first in the sorted list, which will happen if the block returns -1.
- The value of 3 <=> 5 is 1, meaning that 5 comes after 3 in the built-in ordering.
- If the block returned that 1, sort would interpret it as an instruction to put one in front of another—the opposite of what we want.
- So we negate the result of <=> to convert the 1 into -1, telling sort to put the line named another first.

sort will use the block to compare many pairs of lines, enough for it to determine the right order for all of them. (There are an amazing number of ways to sort an array, but they all involve comparing pairs of elements.)

And here's the final output:

```
prompt> ruby churn-re.rb
Changes since 2006-07-11:
          ui ** (8)
       audit * (5)
        util * (4)
 persistence * (3)
 fulfillment  (2)
   inventory  (2)
```

The order is now correct.

9.4 Where Do We Stand?

Scripting languages are traditionally better at handling text than other programming languages. That means two things: lots of built-in string operations and good support for regular expressions.

9.5 Exercises

There's a new assertion you may find useful in these exercises, which is assert_match. It uses =~ instead of == (like assert_equal does).

1. Recall that the find_all message produces a new array containing every element that causes the given block to be true. (It was used in Section 7.2, *Using External Programs*, on page 75.) Using it, change churn-re to show only lines that have at least one asterisk. Use a regular expression. Ignore the possibility that the subsystem name might contain an asterisk. (That's pretty unlikely.)

   Note: an asterisk has a special meaning in a regular expression. It means "match zero or more repetitions." Given strings "ac", "abc", and "abbc", /ab*c/ matches all of them, whereas /ab+c/ matches only the last two. Because of this, you have to escape an asterisk if you want to search for it explicitly. For example, /**/ means "zero or more asterisks," whereas /**/ will only make Ruby complain that the regular expression is invalid.

2. It turns out that the convention on your project is to end certain subsystem names with an asterisk. Change the previous exercise's solution so that it's not fooled by such names. Continue to base your solution on asterisks, not on the change count.

You may assume that asterisks can appear only at the end of a subsystem name.

Hint: look carefully at the differences between these two lines from subsystem_line:

```
irb(main):001:0> load 'exercise-1.rb'
=> true
irb(main):002:0> subsystem_line('ui*', 0)
=> "          ui*  (0)"
irb(main):003:0> subsystem_line('ui*', 5)
=> "          ui* * (5)"
```

word character

3. Within a regular expression, \w signifies a *word character*, which is any alphabetic character A through Z, in uppercase or lowercase, plus the digits, plus underscore. Using it, write a method, rearrange, that passes this test:

code/exercise-solutions/churn-regexp/exercise-3-tests.rb

```
def test_rearrange_with_middle_name
  assert_equal("Dawn E. Marick",
          rearrange("Marick, Dawn Elaine"))
end
```

That is, it converts a *lastname, firstname middlename* format into a *firstname middleinitial lastname* format.

4. Extend rearrange to pass this test *in addition to* the previous one:

code/exercise-solutions/churn-regexp/exercise-4-tests.rb

```
def test_rearrange_without_middle_name
  assert_equal("Paul Marick", rearrange("Marick, Paul"))
end
```

Now rearrange will work even if there's no middle name.

Note: the last two tests are Anglocentric. Unless you're vastly lucky, the resulting code will not be suited for Adolpho de la Huerta, briefly president of Mexico, much less the more recent President Ernesto Zedillo Ponce de León. Worse, it's not even *properly* Anglocentric: it doesn't handle Gordon Matthew Thomas Sumner, not even under his stage name, Sting. But handling the immense variety of possible names would take us far beyond a mere introduction to regular expressions.

## Chapter 10

Ruby Facts: Regular Expressions

/abc/ =~ "abc" ↪ 0	Regular expressions ("regexps") match strings. When a match is successful, the return value is the position of the first matching character.
puts 'match' if /abc/ =~ "abc" ↪ match	An **if** construct will count a successful match as true.
/abc/ =~ "cbaabc" ↪ 3	The matching substring can be anywhere in the string.
/abc/ =~ "ab!c" ↪ nil	When the string doesn't match, the result is nil.
/abc/ =~ "abc and abc" ↪ 0	There may be more than one match in the string. Matching always returns the index of the first match.
/cow/ =~ "Cow" ↪ nil	Case matters.
"foofarah" =~ /foo/ ↪ 0	The regular expression doesn't have to be on the left.

10.1   Special Characters

/^abc/ =~ "!abc" ↪ nil	You can **anchor** the match to the beginning of the string with ^ (the caret character, sometimes called "hat").
/abc$/ =~ "abc!" ↪ nil	You can also anchor the match to the end of the string with a dollar sign character, often abbreviated "dollar." Special characters like the caret and dollar are what make regular expressions more powerful than something like "string".include?("ing").

\d   Any digit

\D   Any character except a digit

\s   "whitespace": space, tab, carriage return, line feed, or newline

\S   Anything except whitespace

\w   A "word character": [A-Za-z0-9_]

\W   Any character except a word character

Figure 10.1: CHARACTER CLASSES

/a.c/ =~ "does abc match?" ↪ 5	A period ("dot") matches any character.
/ab*c/ =~ "does abbbbc match?" ↪ 5	The asterisk character ("star") matches any number of occurrences of the character preceding it.
/ab*c/ =~ "does ac match?" ↪ 5	"Any number" includes zero.
/ab+c/ =~ "does ac match?" ↪ nil	Frequently, you'll want to match one or more occurrence but not zero. That's done with the plus character.
/ab?c/ =~ "does ac match?" ↪ 5	The question mark character matches zero or one occurrences but not more than one.
/a.*b/ =~ "a ! b ! i j k b" ↪ 0	Special characters can be combined. The combination of a dot and star is used to match any number of any kind of character.
/[0123456789]+/ =~ "number 55" ↪ 7	To match all characters in a **character class**, enclose them within square brackets.
/[0-9][a-f]/ =~ "5f" ↪ 0	Character classes containing alphabetically ordered runs of characters can be abbreviated with the dash.
/[.]/ =~ "b" ↪ nil	Within brackets, characters like the dot, plus, and star are not special.
/\[a\]\+/ =~ "[a]+" ↪ 0	Outside of brackets, special characters can be stripped of their powers by "escaping" them with a backslash.
/^[\[=\]]+$/ =~ '=]=[=' ↪ 0	To include open and close brackets inside of brackets, escape them with a backslash. This expression matches any sequence of one or more characters, all of which must be either [,], or =. (The two anchors ensure that there are no characters before or after the matching characters.)

/[^ab]/ =~ "z" ↪ 0	Putting a caret at the beginning of a character class causes the set to contain all characters *except* the ones listed.
/=\d=[x\d]=/ =~ "=5=x=" ↪ 0	Some character classes are so common they're given abbreviations. \d is the same character class as [0-9]. Other characters can be added to the abbreviation, in which case brackets are needed. See Figure 10.1, on the preceding page, for a complete list of abbreviations.

10.2 Grouping and Alternatives

/(ab)+/ =~ "ababab" ↪ 0	Parentheses can group sequences of characters so that special characters apply to the whole sequence.
/(ab*)+/ =~ "aababbabbb" ↪ 0	Special characters can appear within groups. Here, the group containing one a and any number of b's is repeated one or more times.
/a|b/ =~ "a" ↪ 0	The vertical bar character is used to allow alternatives. Here, either a or b match.
/^Fine birds|cows ate\.$/ =~ "Fine birds ate seeds." ↪ 0	A vertical bar divides the regular expression into two smaller regular expressions. A match means that either the *entire* left regexp matches or the entire right one does. This regular expression does *not* mean "Match either 'Fine birds ate.' or 'Fine cows ate.'" It actually matches either a string beginning with *"Fine birds"* or one ending in *"cows ate."*
/^Fine (birds|cows) ate\.$/ =~ "Fine birds ate seeds." ↪ nil	This regular expression matches only the two alternate sentences, not the infinite number of possibilities the previous example's regexp does.

10.3 Taking Strings Apart

re = /(\w+), (\w+), or (\w+)/ s = 'Without a Bob, ox, or bin!' match = re.match(s) ↪ #<MatchData:0x323c44>	Like the =~ operator, match returns nil if there's no match. If there is, it returns a MatchData object. You can pull information out of that object.
match[0] ↪ "Bob, ox, or bin"	A MatchData is indexable. Its zeroth element is the entire match.
match[1] ↪ "Bob"	Each following element stores the result of what a group matched, counting from left to right.

"#{match[3]} and #{match[1]}" ↪ "bin and Bob"	Groups are often used to pull apart strings and construct new ones.
match.pre_match ↪ "Without a "	pre_match returns any portion of the string before the part that matched.
match.post_match ↪ "!"	post_match returns any portion of the string after the part that matched. match.pre_match, match(0), and match.post_match can be added together to reconstruct the original string.
str = "a bee in my bonnet" /a.*b/.match(str)[0] ↪ "a bee in my b"	The plus and star special characters are **greedy**: they match as many characters as they can. Expect that to catch you by surprise sometimes.
/a.*?b/.match(str)[0] ↪ "a b"	You can make plus and star match as few characters as they can by suffixing them with a question mark.
"has 5 and 3"[/\d+/] ↪ "5"	You can use a regular expression to slice a string. The result is the first substring that matches the regular expression.

10.4 Variables Behind the Scenes

re = /(\w+), (\w+), or (\w+)/ s = 'Without a Bob, ox, or bin!' re =~ s [$1, $2, $3] ↪ ["Bob", "ox", "bin"]	Both =~ and match set some variables. All begin with $. Each parenthesized group gets its own number, from $1 up through $9. You might expect $0 to name the entire string that matched, but it's already used for something else: the name of the program being executed.
$& ↪ "Bob, ox, or bin"	$& is the equivalent of match[0].
$` + $' ↪ "Without a !"	These two variables are used to store the string before the match and the string after the match. (The first is a backward quote / backtick; the second a normal quote.)

These variables are probably most often used to immediately do something with a string that's "equal enough" to some pattern. Like this:

```
if name =~ /(.+), (.+)/
  name = "#{$2} #{$1}"
end
```

10.5 Regular Expression Options

/a.*b/ =~ "az\nzb" ↪ nil	Normally, the period in a regular expression does not match the end-of-line character. Therefore, .* or .+ matches won't span lines.

/a.*b/m =~ "az\nzb" ↪ 0	Adding the m (**multiline**) option makes a period match end-of-line characters, so the regular expression match can span lines.
/[cC][aA][tT]/ =~ "Cat" ↪ 0	This is a far too annoying way to do a case-insensitive match.
/cat/i =~ "Cat" ↪ 0	The i (**insensitive**) option is a better way.

10.6 Wait, There's More. . .

There's even more you can do with regular expressions. Please consult a complete Ruby reference such as *Programming Ruby* [TH01] or a book on regular expressions such as *Mastering Regular Expressions* [Fri97].

10.7 Exercises

1. Return to exercise 2 in Section 9.5, *Exercises*, on page 97. Assume that the subsystem name can contain *anything*. In particular, it might be like the bizarre subsystem name of this test:

```
code/exercise-solutions/regexp/exercise-1-tests.rb
def test_interesting_lines_subsystem_can_have_asterisk_anywhere
  weird_but_boring = subsystem_line('+ and *** (3) and -', 0)

  original = [weird_but_boring]
  expected = []

  assert_equal(expected, interesting(original))
end
```

Make this test (and previous tests) pass. The presence of asterisks continues to be what makes a line interesting. (Don't extract the change count and check its value.)

Hint: you now know about anchors.

2. Return to exercises 2, 3, and 4 in Section 9.5, *Exercises* on page 97. Using what you now know, solve the problem using only a single regular expression.

Hint: the person's middle name has to occur zero or one times.

Hint: You can have a group in a regular expression that doesn't participate in the match. In that case, its entry in the MatchData object is nil:

```
irb(main):001:0> match = /(.)(.)?/.match('a')
=> #<MatchData:0x5e6d9c>
irb(main):002:0> match[2]
=> nil
```

## Chapter 11

Classes Bundle Data and Methods

As it stands, our churn script is just a pile of methods without any particular organization. That's great for a small script, but it would get out of hand if we kept adding features. If churn kept growing, we'd at some point feel the need to group related methods. One way would be to put them in a file of their own. All the methods responsible for communicating with a Subversion repository could be in repository.rb, and all the ones responsible for formatting output could be in formatting.rb. churn.rb could require those files.

A fine solution, but there's an alternative. A Subversion repository has a cohesive identity. It's a unique thing out there on the network, so it might make sense to make it a unique thing—an object—in the Ruby universe. Then all the methods that work on Subversion repositories would be reached by messages sent to such objects.

Ruby *classes* let you gather methods that have related responsibilities. *classes*
Let's create the simplest possible Subversion repository class:

```
irb(main):001:0> class SubversionRepository
irb(main):002:1> end
=> nil
```

Later, we'll put methods within it. But there are a few things we can do with it even now.

instance

We can create an *instance* of SubversionRepository:

```
irb(main):003:0> repository = SubversionRepository.new
=> #<SubversionRepository:0x326548>
```

new is a common way of asking a class to create a new instance. You haven't seen it before now because many of the built-in classes have easier ways of creating instances. You *could* create an array using something like this. . .

```
irb(main):004:0> a = Array.new
=> []
irb(main):005:0> a.push(1)
=> [1]
irb(main):006:0> a.push(2)
=> [1, 2]
irb(main):007:0> a.push(3)
=> [1, 2, 3]
```

. . . but it's an awful lot easier to type this:

```
irb(main):008:0> a = [1, 2, 3]
=> [1, 2, 3]
```

Behind the scenes, Ruby does the Array.new for you.

Classes are objects. So what happened in irb previously is that the new message was being sent to an object named SubversionRepository. That object constructed a new object, which we say is *a* SubversionRepository or *an instance* of SubversionRepository. That instance responds to all messages that SubversionRepository defines, which seems to be no messages at all.

Not quite. Every object, just by virtue of being an object, responds to some messages. One of them is class, which asks the object to return the class that created it and describes it:

```
irb(main):009:0> repository.class
=> SubversionRepository
```

Another predefined method is respond_to?, which asks whether an object responds to a particular method:

```
irb(main):010:0> repository.respond_to?("class")
=> true
irb(main):011:0> repository.respond_to?("new")
=> false
```

repository does not respond to new because it's not itself a class. Only classes respond to new.

Talking About Classes and Instances

Ideally, everyone would be precise about classes and instances in both speech and writing. People would refer to "*the* Time class" and "*a* Time instance."

But people aren't precise; they use shorthand. "Let's use Time" refers to the Time class, whereas "We need a Time" refers to a Time instance. (It's the "a" that gives it away.) People will also say "We need a Time object" despite the fact that both classes and instances are objects.

Again, the "a" distinguishes between the two possibilities.

How does a class define a method? The same way as always, except the **def**. . . **end** appears within the **class**. . . **end**:

```
irb(main):012:0> class SubversionRepository
irb(main):013:1>   def hello
irb(main):014:2>     'hi!'
irb(main):015:2>   end
irb(main):016:1> end
=> nil
irb(main):017:0> repository.hello
=> "hi!"
irb(main):018:0> repository.respond_to?('hello')
=> true
```

What we just did shows two Ruby conveniences:

- When you add to a class, the new method is immediately available to existing instances of that class.

- We added on to SubversionRepository by naming it again in a **class**. . . **end** construct. You can always add to a Ruby class. You can even add to a predefined class. Try it: add the hello method to class String. After you do that, you should be able to tell any string to "hello itself":

```
irb(main):030:0> "a string".hello
=> "hi!"
```

Enough background. Let's change churn.

11.1 Classes Define Methods

Take a look at your latest version of churn. Which methods do you think are concerned with details about Subversion?

My answer is svn_date, change_count_for, extract_change_count_from, and svn_log. That means my class definition should look something like this:

```
class SubversionRepository
  def svn_date(a_time)...
  def change_count_for(name, start_date)...
  def extract_change_count_from(log_text) ...
  def svn_log(subsystem, start_date) ...
end
```

The two names prefixed with "svn" are kind of silly, though. Given that svn_date is a SubversionRepository method, do I really need to say that it returns a "svn" date? What other kind would it return? I'll remove the prefixes. Other than that, the methods are completely unchanged, just moved inside the class. See Figure 11.1, on the facing page. How would these moved methods be used?

```
irb(main):037:0> require 'churn-classes.v1'
=> true
irb(main):038:0> repository = SubversionRepository.new
=> #<SubversionRepository:0x325d14>
irb(main):039:0> repository.date(Time.now)
=> "2005-11-17"
```

The bottom of the script needs to be changed to use the class. That means changing only three lines, numbered here:

```
code/churn/snapshots/churn-classes.v1.rb
if $0 == __FILE__
  subsystem_names = ['audit', 'fulfillment', 'persistence',
                     'ui', 'util', 'inventory']
❶ repository = SubversionRepository.new
❷ start_date = repository.date(month_before(Time.now))

  puts header(start_date)
  lines = subsystem_names.collect do | name |
    subsystem_line(name,
❸            repository.change_count_for(name, start_date))
  end
  puts order_by_descending_change_count(lines)
end
```

```
code/churn/snapshots/churn-classes.v1.rb
class SubversionRepository
  def date(a_time)
    a_time.strftime("%Y-%m-%d")
  end

  def change_count_for(name, start_date)
    extract_change_count_from(log(name, start_date))
  end

  def extract_change_count_from(log_text)
    lines = log_text.split("\n")
    dashed_lines = lines.find_all do | line |
      line.include?('————')
    end
    dashed_lines.length - 1
  end

  def log(subsystem, start_date)
    timespan = "–revision 'HEAD:{#{start_date}}'"
    root = "svn://rubyforge.org//var/svn/churn-demo"

    `svn log #{timespan} #{root}/#{subsystem}`
  end
end
```

                                    churn/snapshots/churn-classes.v1.rb

Figure 11.1: BUNDLING RELATED METHODS INTO A CLASS

11.2 Objects Contain Data

Right now, SubversionRepository can be used for exactly one repository because log always uses a hard-coded URL. (See Figure 11.1.) That's a little like being able to open only the file named old-inventory.txt: not awfully flexible. Let's pull the URL out of SubversionRepository and have it be given to the instance when it's created with new. Here's how the new version of new would be used:

```
code/churn/snapshots/churn-classes.v2.rb
root="svn://rubyforge.org//var/svn/churn-demo"
repository = SubversionRepository.new(root)
start_date = repository.date(month_before(Time.now))
```

When the class object named SubversionRepository receives new, what happens? The first thing that new does is create a new SubversionRepository instance. It then sends the newborn method the initialize message, handing over whatever arguments were given to new. To see that happening, let's make initialize just print its argument:

```
irb(main):040:0> class SubversionRepository
irb(main):041:1>   def initialize(root)
irb(main):042:2>     puts "The root is '#{root}'."
irb(main):043:2>   end
irb(main):044:1> end
=> nil

irb(main):045:0> SubversionRepository.new(svn://blah.blah.blah')
The root is 'svn://blah.blah.blah'.
=> #<SubversionRepository:0x33285c>
```

The repository root is given to method new and hence to initialize, but it's log that needs it. Something needs to hang onto the root until log uses it. The way we've always held onto objects for later use is by naming them with variables. We'll continue to do that, but we can't use the same kind of variables as in earlier chapters. Those are *local variables*. They are not visible outside of their method. Here's an example:

local variables

```
irb(main):001:0> class SubversionRepository
irb(main):002:1>   def initialize(root)
irb(main):003:2>     saved_root = root
irb(main):004:2>   end
irb(main):005:1>
irb(main):006:1*   def log
irb(main):007:2>     puts saved_root
irb(main):008:2>   end
irb(main):009:1> end
=> nil
irb(main):010:0> repository = SubversionRepository.new('the root')
=> #<SubversionRepository:0x31a57c>
irb(main):011:0> repository.log
NameError: undefined local variable or method 'saved_root' for
#<SubversionRepository:0x31a57c>
        from (irb):7:in 'log'
        from (irb):11
```

The variable saved_root in log is a completely different one than the one in initialize, just as the word "Dawn" in my house refers to a different person than it would in Dawn Baker's house in California. Local variables won't work, but *instance variables* will. Those are variables that can be seen by each of an object's methods and so are used for communication between them. Here's an example:

instance variables

```
irb(main):017:0> class SubversionRepository
irb(main):018:1>   def initialize(root)
irb(main):019:2>     @root = root
irb(main):020:2>   end
irb(main):021:1>
irb(main):022:1*   def log
irb(main):023:2>     puts @root
irb(main):024:2>   end
irb(main):025:1> end
```

```
=> nil
irb(main):026:0> repository = SubversionRepository.new('the root')
=> #<SubversionRepository:0x329ea0 @root="the root">
irb(main):027:0> repository.log
the root
=> nil
```

Instance variables always begin with @; local variables never do.

Instance variables cannot be seen outside of their object:

```
irb(main):028:0> repository.@root
SyntaxError: compile error
(irb):28: syntax error
        from (irb):28

irb(main):029:0> repository.root
NoMethodError: undefined method 'root' for
    #<SubversionRepository:0x329ea0 @root="the root">
        from (irb):29
```

If you want the outside to have access to the object named by an instance variable, you can define a method that returns it:

```
irb(main):030:0> class SubversionRepository
irb(main):031:1>   def root
irb(main):032:2>     @root
irb(main):033:2>   end
irb(main):034:1> end
=> nil
irb(main):035:0> repository.root
=> "the root"
```

If you have two objects of the same class, their instance variables are completely distinct. In the following, creating a new SubversionRepository with a different root has no effect on the old one:

```
irb(main):036:0> different = SubversionRepository.new('different')
=> #<SubversionRepository:0x30d4a8 @root="different">
irb(main):037:0> different.root
=> "different"
irb(main):038:0> repository.root
=> "the root"
```

In short, objects share methods, but they do not share variables. One way to think of an object is as a bundle of private variables surrounded by methods that work with them. Figure 11.2, on page 113, shows a finished SubversionRepository that uses an instance variable, created at ❶ and used at ❷.

Ruby Documentation: ri

String and the other "core" Ruby classes have documentation available through the command line. Suppose you *know* there's some String message that does exactly what you want, but you've forgotten its name. You can remind yourself with this:

```
prompt> ri String
...
Instance methods:
------------------
    %, *, +, <<, <=>, ==, =~, [], []=, capitalize, capitalize!,
    casecmp, center, chomp, chomp!, chop, chop!, concat, count,
    crypt, delete, delete!, downcase, downcase!, dump, each,
    each_byte, each_line, empty?, eql?, gsub, gsub!, hash, hex,
    include?, index, initialize_copy, insert, inspect, intern,
    length, ljust, lstrip, lstrip!, match, next, next!, oct,
    replace, reverse, reverse!, rindex, rjust, rstrip, rstrip!,
    scan, size, slice, slice!, split, squeeze, squeeze!, strip,
    strip!, sub, sub!, succ, succ!, sum, swapcase, swapcase!,
    to_f, to_i, to_s, to_str, to_sym, tr, tr!, tr_s, tr_s!,
    unpack, upcase, upcase!, upto
```

ri displays its information a page at a time. When you hit the end, you may need to quit with q̄. (On some systems, it exits automatically.)

If you've forgotten what a method's arguments are, you can get more detail:

```
prompt> ri String.center
-------------------------------------------- String#center
    str.center(integer)   => new_str
------------------------------------------------------------
    If _integer_ is greater than the length of _str_, returns
    a new +String+ of length _integer_ with _str_ centered
    between spaces; otherwise, returns _str_.

      "hello".center(4)   #=> "hello"
      "hello".center(20)  #=> "       hello        "
```

`code/churn/snapshots/churn-classes.v2.rb`

```ruby
class SubversionRepository

  def initialize(root)
❶   @root = root
  end

  def date(a_time)
    a_time.strftime("%Y-%m-%d")
  end

  def change_count_for(name, start_date)
    extract_change_count_from(log(name, start_date))
  end

  def extract_change_count_from(log_text)
    lines = log_text.split("\n")
    dashed_lines = lines.find_all do | line |
      line.include?('——')
    end
    dashed_lines.length - 1
  end

  def log(subsystem, start_date)
    timespan = "–revision 'HEAD:{#{start_date}}'"

❷   `svn log #{timespan} #{@root}/#{subsystem}`
  end

end
```

churn/snapshots/churn-classes.v2.rb

Figure 11.2: THE FINISHED SUBVERSIONREPOSITORY CLASS

11.3 Where Do We Stand?

Classes are a way of organizing chunks of code by grouping related
data with methods that manipulate it. Classes aren't the only organizing principle. Modules are another. You'll learn about modules in Section 19.3, *Avoiding Class Name Clashes Using Modules*, on page 179;
Chapter 20, *Ruby Facts: Modules*; and Section 23.3, *Modules Instead of
Superclasses*, on page 240.

11.4 Exercises

When writing the tests in this chapter, you may find assert_equal and assert_match limiting. Test::Unit has other assertions; see Figure 11.3, on page 116.

1. Suppose you wanted to gather all of churn's methods that format output into a Formatter class. Which would you choose to put there? Which would you choose to leave out of the class? Why?

2. How will the tests have to change to make use of your new class? (Use churn-tests-classes.rb as a guide.)

3. Make a Formatter class that passes the tests.

4. The following code shows how churn would be changed to make use of the new Formatter class.

```
code/exercise-solutions/churn-classes/exercise-3.rb
if $0 == __FILE__
  subsystem_names = ['audit', 'fulfillment', 'persistence',
                     'ui', 'util', 'inventory']
  root="svn://rubyforge.org//var/svn/churn-demo"
  repository = SubversionRepository.new(root)

  start_date = repository.date(month_before(Time.now))

  formatter = Formatter.new

  puts formatter.header(start_date)
❶ lines = subsystem_names.collect do | name |
    formatter.subsystem_line(name,
              repository.change_count_for(name, start_date))

  end
  puts formatter.order_by_descending_change_count(lines)
end
```

client

That's really rather horrible, though. At ❶, the Formatter's *client* (the code that sends it messages) is having to hold onto all the lines the Formatter creates. Shouldn't that be the Formatter's job?

Absolutely, it should. Let's change Formatter so that churn can be written as shown here:

```
code/exercise-solutions/churn-classes/exercise-5.rb
if $0 == __FILE__
  subsystem_names = ['audit', 'fulfillment', 'persistence',
                     'ui', 'util', 'inventory']
  root="svn://rubyforge.org//var/svn/churn-demo"
```

> ### \|// Joe Asks...
>
> #### What About Local Variables That Aren't in a Method?
>
> The rule is that local variables are visible only in their method. But we've seen local variables outside a method in irb sessions or in the lines at the end of churn.rb. What about them? Consider them to be inside an unnamed, invisible method, and then the same rule applies:
>
> ```
> irb(main):012:0> local = 5
> => 5
> irb(main):013:0> def print_local
> irb(main):014:1>   puts local
> irb(main):015:1> end
> => nil
> irb(main):016:0> print_local
> NameError: undefined local variable or method 'local' for
>   main:Object
>       from (irb):14:in 'print_local'
>       from (irb):16
> ```

```
    repository = SubversionRepository.new(root)
    start_date = repository.date(month_before(Time.now))

    formatter = Formatter.new
❶   formatter.use_date(start_date)
    subsystem_names.each do | name |
❷     formatter.use_subsystem_with_change_count(
          name, repository.change_count_for(name, start_date))
    end
❸   puts formatter.output
  end
```

The theme of the change is that we hand the formatter data to hang onto. It gets the date at ❶ and a subsystem's name and change count at ❷. Notice that I've changed the names to be more exact about what responsibilities I want the methods to take on. I changed header to use_date and subsystem_line to use_subsystem_with_change_count. By sending the previous names, clients were proclaiming decisions about formatting: there will be a header (but no footer) that contains a date, and each subsystem will be on its own line. The new names isolate decisions about what the output looks like where it belongs, in the Formatter.

assert(*value*)

> claims that value is logically true. The test will fail if it's either false or nil. Values like 5 or *"hello"* don't cause a failure because they're logically true.

assert_not_equal(*disallowed,actual*)

> claims that actual is not equal to disallowed.

assert_match(*/regexp/,actual*)

> claims that the regular expression regexp matches actual.

assert_no_match(*/regexp/,actual*)

> claims that the regular expression regexp does not match actual.

Notes:

- All Test::Unit assertions can take an extra argument, a string that's to be printed if the assertion fails.
- This is not a complete list of assertions. See [TFH05] for more.

Figure 11.3: MORE TEST::UNIT ASSERTIONS

The client gives the Formatter the data it needs, and the Formatter decides what to do with it.

Once we've given the Formatter all the data, we ask it for the complete output, which we print (❸).

For this exercise, write tests for the three new methods (use_date, use_subsystem_with_change_count, and output). Hints:

- The new methods use some other methods in the class, methods that already have tests. Don't repeat yourself in the new tests. Say only what the new methods add to the methods they use.

- The output is printed with puts. puts prints an array like ['line1', 'line2'] exactly like it prints "line1\nline2", so when you write output's tests, you get to choose whether output should return an array of strings or a string with embedded line separators. Which is more convenient? Which is more flexible? (I suggest you try it both ways.)

  Here's how to convert a string with embedded line separators into an array:

  ```
  irb(main):005:0> "123\n124\n".split("\n")
  => ["123", "124"]
  ```

```
irb(main):006:0> "123\n124".split("\n")
=> ["123", "124"]
```

Notice that split allows you not to care about whether the last line ends with a line separator.

5. Write the code for use_date. Hint: you'll probably want an instance variable.

6. Write the code for use_subsystem_with_change_count. Hint: what will you add the change count *to*?

7. Write output. If you chose to have output's return value be a string (rather than an array of strings), you'll want to know about join, which converts arrays of strings into single strings:

```
irb(main):001:0> ["line1", "line2"].join("\n")
=> "line1\nline2"
```

join concatenates all the strings, separating them with its argument.

8. Some silliness has crept into the code. You can see it here:

`code/exercise-solutions/churn-classes/exercise-7.rb`

```
start_date = repository.date(month_before(Time.now))

formatter = Formatter.new
formatter.use_date(start_date)
```

We get the current Time from Ruby and then calculate the Time that's a month before. We turn it into the format that Subversion-Repository likes and then hand that off to the Formatter. Why should the Formatter care about SubversionRepository's date format?

In the jargon, there's *coupling* between SubversionRepository and For- *coupling* matter. To use a Formatter, you have to have a SubversionRepository, even if you're formatting information that comes from some completely different version control system.

There's also a form of duplication. The main script knows two ways of talking about instants of time: as Times and as SubversionRepository.dates. There's no gain from that kind of duplication. Worse: as we saw in Section 7.2, *Blunder the First*, on page 78, it causes bugs. Back then, we had no way of isolating knowledge. Now, with classes, we do.

Change the script so that its main code looks like the following. (Changed lines are numbered.) Change the tests accordingly, and make them work.

code/exercise-solutions/churn-classes/exercise-8.rb

```
if $0 == __FILE__
  subsystem_names = ['audit', 'fulfillment', 'persistence',
                     'ui', 'util', 'inventory']
  root="svn://rubyforge.org//var/svn/churn-demo"
  repository = SubversionRepository.new(root)
❶ last_month = month_before(Time.now)

  formatter = Formatter.new
❷ formatter.report_range(last_month, Time.now)
  subsystem_names.each do | name |
    formatter.use_subsystem_with_change_count(
❸       name, repository.change_count_for(name, last_month))
  end
  puts formatter.output
end
```

Notice that I changed use_date to report_range at line ❷. Two times are relevant to gathering the change data—right now and a month before now. Giving both to the Formatter gives it the responsibility of deciding whether or how to use them. You'll make the decision when you write the tests. Right now, the Formatter uses only the starting date (header's original format). You could leave that as is, have the header say something like "changes in the month before 01-03-2006," or have it use both dates. You could even have both a header and a footer. Go wild.

9. Formatting is still coupled to SubversionRepository: since they're both in the same file, they can't be used independently. Put both of them in their own file, and have churn.rb require it.

Chapter 12

Ruby Facts: Classes (with a Side Order of Symbols)

This chapter describes facts about classes that didn't come up during the previous chapter's changes to churn. I describe an alternative to strings and two more types of variables.

12.1 Defining Accessors

Classes are bundles of named objects manipulated through methods. A method that returns one of the objects without changing it is called a *reader*. The second method shown here is an example of a reader:

reader

```
class MyClass
  def initialize(name)
    @name = name
  end

  def name
    @name
  end
end
```

It's used like this:

```
irb(main):001:0> fred = MyClass.new('fred')
=> #<MyClass:0x3146a4 @name="fred">
irb(main):002:0> fred.name
=> "fred"
```

A method that changes which object an instance variable refers to is called a *writer*. For convenience, Ruby makes writers look like any old assignment to a variable:

writer

```
irb(main):003:0> fred.name = 'Fredrick'
=> "Fredrick"
irb(main):004:0> fred.name
=> "Fredrick"
```

The first line is actually sending the name= message with the single argument *'Fredrick'* to fred. name='s definition shows there's really a method behind the scenes:

```
class MyClass
  def name=(new_name)
    @name=new_name
  end
end
```

accessors

Readers and writers are collectively called *accessors*. It's a crashing bore to have to define accessors explicitly, so Ruby provides shorthand:

```
irb(main):005:0> class MyOtherClass
irb(main):006:1>   attr_accessor :name
irb(main):007:1>
irb(main):008:1*   def initialize(name)
irb(main):009:2>     @name = name
irb(main):010:2>   end
irb(main):011:1> end
=> nil
irb(main):012:0> dawn = MyOtherClass.new('Dawn')
=> #<MyOtherClass:0x32542c @name="Dawn">
irb(main):013:0> dawn.name
=> "Dawn"
irb(main):014:0> dawn.name = 'Dr. Morin'
=> "Dr. Morin"
irb(main):015:0> dawn.name
=> "Dr. Morin"
```

"attr" in attr_accessor is short for "attribute." It's common to speak of objects as having fundamental properties or attributes. Those attributes would be named by instance variables and accessed by accessors. For example, one attribute of a Person might be her name, represented by the variable @name and accessed by name and name=.

symbol

Notice attr_accessor's attribute is named oddly: :name. Text beginning with a colon is a *symbol*. You can think of symbols as a simplified kind of string. In fact, in most places you can use strings in place of symbols. Defining accessors is one of those places:

```
irb(main):016:0> class MyOtherClass
irb(main):017:1>   attr_accessor 'credentials'
irb(main):018:1> end
=> nil
```

```
irb(main):019:0> dawn.credentials = ['DVM', 'MS', 'DACVIM']
=> ["DVM", "MS", "DACVIM"]
irb(main):020:0> dawn.credentials
=> ["DVM", "MS", "DACVIM"]
```

Notice that I didn't have to create the instance variable @credentials in
initialize. It will be created the first time credentials= is used. That raises
a question: what happens if you try to use an instance variable before
ever pointing it at an object?

```
irb(main):023:0* paul = MyOtherClass.new('paul')
=> #<MyOtherClass:0x33c99c @name="paul">
irb(main):024:0> paul.credentials
=> nil
```

Unassigned instance variables have the value nil. That's different from
unassigned local variables, which produce an error:

```
irb(main):025:0> def negate(value)
irb(main):026:1>   -valu
irb(main):027:1> end
=> nil
irb(main):028:0> negate 5
NameError: undefined local variable or method 'valu' for main:Object
      from (irb):10:in 'negate'
      from (irb):12
      from :0
```

Mistyping a local variable produces an immediate failure, one that's easy to find. Mistyping an instance variable tends to produce more subtle problems:

```
irb(main):030:1>   def reverse_credentials
irb(main):031:2>     @credentials = @credentals.reverse
irb(main):032:2>   end
irb(main):033:1> end
=> nil
irb(main):034:0> dawn.reverse_credentials
NoMethodError: undefined method 'reverse' for nil:NilClass
     from (irb):27:in 'reverse_credentials'
     from (irb):30
     from :0
```

The mistyped @credentals produces a nil, instead of the expected array. Reversing a nil fails as shown. You'll spend part of your Ruby life wondering how a particular variable could have gotten the value nil when the problem is actually that it's a mistyping of the variable you meant.

Sometimes you don't want both a reader and a writer. You can define one without the other:

```
irb(main):035:0> class MyOtherClass
irb(main):036:1>   attr_reader :schedule
irb(main):037:1>   attr_writer :weight
irb(main):038:1> end

irb(main):039:0> dawn.schedule
=> nil
irb(main):040:0> dawn.schedule = 'overfull'
NoMethodError: undefined method 'schedule=' for #<MyOtherClass:0x3361f0>
     from (irb):20
irb(main):041:0> dawn.weight = 127
=> 127
irb(main):042:0> dawn.weight
NoMethodError: undefined method 'weight' for #<MyOtherClass:0x3361f0 @weight=127>
     from (irb):22
```

You can define more than one attribute at a time by separating them with commas:

```
irb(main):043:0> class MyOtherClass
irb(main):044:1>   attr_reader :schedule, :salary
irb(main):045:1> end
```

12.2 Self

An object can send a message in three ways:

- It can send a message to another object:

```
irb(main):046:0> class Upcaser
irb(main):047:1>   def some_behavior_on(a_string)
irb(main):048:2>     a_string.upcase
irb(main):049:2>   end
irb(main):050:1> end

irb(main):051:0> Upcaser.new.some_behavior_on("foo")
=> "FOO"
```

- It can send a message to no object, which implicitly sends the message to itself:

```
irb(main):052:0> class Bouncer
irb(main):053:1>
irb(main):054:1>   def some_behavior
irb(main):055:2>     another_behavior
irb(main):056:2>   end
irb(main):057:1>
irb(main):058:1>   def another_behavior
irb(main):059:2>     "another_behavior used"
irb(main):060:2>   end
irb(main):061:1> end

irb(main):062:0> Bouncer.new.some_behavior
=> "another_behavior used"
```

- It can send a message *explicitly* to itself, as shown at ❶:

```
  irb(main):063:0> class AnotherBouncer
  irb(main):064:1>
  irb(main):065:1>   def some_behavior
❶ irb(main):066:2>     self.another_behavior
  irb(main):067:2>   end
  irb(main):068:1>
  irb(main):069:1>   def another_behavior
  irb(main):070:2>     "another_behavior used"
  irb(main):071:2>   end
  irb(main):072:1> end

  irb(main):073:0> AnotherBouncer.new.some_behavior
  => "another_behavior used"
```

self is a variable that always names the object itself. It's not wildly common in scripts, but it does have important uses:

- Suppose you have a class that stores an integer and can do nothing but add one to it:

```
irb(main):074:0> class Adder
irb(main):075:1>   attr_reader :value
irb(main):076:1>
irb(main):077:1>   def initialize
irb(main):078:2>     @value = 0
irb(main):079:2>   end
```

```
irb(main):080:1>
irb(main):081:1>   def add1
irb(main):082:2>      @value += 1
irb(main):083:2>   end
irb(main):084:1> end
```

(@value += 1 is a shorthand way of writing @value = @value + 1.)

Further suppose you wanted to add three to one of these objects. You'd have to do this:

```
irb(main):085:0> a = Adder.new
=> #<Adder:0x32b23c @value=0>
irb(main):086:0> a.add1
=> 1
irb(main):087:0> a.add1
=> 2
irb(main):088:0> a.add1
=> 3
```

That's rather verbose. But suppose add1 returned self instead of the result of the addition:

```
irb(main):089:0> class Adder
irb(main):090:1>   def add1
irb(main):091:2>      @value += 1
irb(main):092:2>      self
irb(main):093:2>   end
irb(main):094:1> end
```

That allows this more succinct form:

```
irb(main):095:0> Adder.new.add1.add1.add1.value
=> 3
```

• Some method names are also special words in the Ruby language. For example, when Ruby sees class, how does it know whether you are sending the class message to self or starting to define a new class? The answer is that it doesn't:

```
irb(main):120:0> class Informer
irb(main):121:1>   def return_your_class
irb(main):122:2>      class
irb(main):123:2>   end
irb(main):124:1> end
SyntaxError: compile error
(irb):123: syntax error
```

You can prevent the error with self:

```
irb(main):125:0> class Informer
irb(main):126:1>   def return_your_class
irb(main):127:2>     self.class
irb(main):128:2>   end
irb(main):129:1> end
=> nil
irb(main):130:0> Informer.new.return_your_class
=> Informer
```

- When you leave parentheses off messages with no arguments, what you have looks just like a local variable. Consider the following:

```
irb(main):131:0> class M
irb(main):132:1>   def start
irb(main):133:2>     1
irb(main):134:2>   end
irb(main):135:1>
irb(main):136:1>   def multiplier
irb(main):137:2>     start = start
irb(main):138:2>     start * 30
irb(main):139:2>   end
irb(main):140:1> end
```

❶

At ❶, is the start to the right of the equal sign the *local variable* created on the left, or does it represent sending the message start to self? Let's find out:

```
irb(main):141:0> M.new.multiplier
NoMethodError: undefined method '*' for nil:NilClass
        from (irb):156:in 'multiplier'
        from (irb):161
        from :0
```

Both uses of the word "start" refer to a variable, though the exact sequence of events is a little hard to figure out:

1. Ruby encounters the line at ❶. It's an assignment to a name never been seen before. Ruby creates the new local variable and gives it the value nil.

2. Ruby now looks at the right side of the assignment. There's a reference to . . . what? Ruby guesses it's the local variable start. So Ruby assigns start the value it already has, nil.

3. The next line multiplies nil by 30.

The problem can be avoided by sending the message to self. . .

```
start = self.start
```

. . . or by using parentheses:

```
start = start()
```

It's a good idea to get in the habit of doing one or the other. I favor using self, for no good reason.

12.3 Class Methods

Classes are objects. Like all objects, they have methods that respond to messages. One such message is new:

```
irb(main):142:0> fred = MyClass.new('fred')
=> #<MyClass:0x3146a4 @name="fred">
irb(main):143:0> fred.name
=> "fred"
```

class method

instance method

It's useful to distinguish between the methods belonging to a class and the methods belonging to its instances. So, in the case of MyClass, we say that new is a *class method* and name is an *instance method*. You can define your own class methods like this:

```
irb(main):144:0> class AnyOldClass
irb(main):145:1>   def self.class_method
irb(main):146:2>     "I am a class method."
irb(main):147:2>   end
irb(main):148:1> end
```

The self indicates that the method is to be defined for the class itself, not for instances. Here's how that new class method would be used:

```
irb(main):149:0> AnyOldClass.class_method
=> "I am a class method."
```

The class method is not available to instances:

```
irb(main):150:0> AnyOldClass.new.class_method
NoMethodError: undefined method 'class_method' for #<AnyOldClass:0x31f248>
    from (irb):11
```

One common use for class methods is to provide more descriptive names than new. For example, both Time.now and Time.new create an object representing the current instance, but the former is clearer about exactly what Time will be created.

Here's how to create such a synonym. I'll use right_now since now is already taken. It will be used like this:

```
irb(main):151:0> require 'class-facts/more-time'
=> true
irb(main):152:0> Time.right_now
=> Thu Sep 14 12:33:14 CDT 2006
```

Here's the method:

`code/class-facts/more-time.rb`

```
class Time
  def self.right_now
    new
  end
end
```

For the first time in this book, new wasn't explicitly sent to a class object. Instead, it was implicitly sent to self, which names the same class object that Time does. That is, within right_now, all three of these lines are interchangeable:

```
new
self.new
Time.new
```

Time.right_now is just a synonym (a more convenient name) for Time.new. You can also write class methods that do more than new does. For example, suppose you often want to create Time objects representing yesterday (exactly twenty-four hours ago). Following scripting by assumption, you'd write the script as if Ruby already had the appropriate message. Where would you expect to find it? I'd expect it to be a class method of Time. So let's create it there:

`code/class-facts/more-time.rb`

```
class Time
  def self.yesterday
    right_now - 24 * 60 * 60
  end
end
```

```
irb(main):153:0> # Reload because I just added a new method.
irb(main):154:0* load 'class-facts/more-time.rb'
=> true
irb(main):155:0> Time.now
=> Thu Sep 14 12:36:28 CDT 2006
irb(main):156:0> Time.yesterday
=> Wed Sep 13 12:36:31 CDT 2006
```

Note that yesterday uses new indirectly, via right_now. It could also use new or now, since they all mean the same thing. (Try it and see.)

Class methods don't have to use new at all. Consider the predefined method Symbol.all_symbols:

```
irb(main):200:0> Symbol.all_symbols
=> [:floor, :HISTORY, :TkMOD,: @input, :ARGV, :rjust, :size,
    ...
    :Context, :keys, :delete, :gsub, :bind, :update]
```

This doesn't create any new symbols, but it does list all the symbols Ruby knows about. Because of what it does, it's appropriate to associate all_symbols with the object Symbol.

Since classes are objects, they have instance variables that can be used in class methods. Consider a class that records how many instances it has created in the method counted_new. It can use an instance variable to hold the count:

```
code/exercise-solutions/classes/exercise-1.v1.rb
class Counter
  def self.counted_new
    @count = 0 if @count.nil?
    @count += 1
    new
  end

  def self.count
    @count
  end
end
```

The first line of Counter.counted_new sets the count to 0 the first time the message is received. (Remember that instance variables start out as nil.) The second line increases the count by one. The third line creates and returns the instance.

Notice that a reader named Counter.count is defined explicitly instead of with attr_reader. attr_reader defines a method for all Counter *instances*, not for Counter itself.

Here's the result:

```
irb(main):220:0> Counter.counted_new
=> #<Counter:0x30aa00>
irb(main):221:0> Counter.count
=> 1
irb(main):222:0> Counter.counted_new
=> #<Counter:0x1ba974>
irb(main):223:0> Counter.count
=> 2
```

12.4   Class Variables and Globals

In addition to local and instance variables, Ruby also has class and global variables.*Class variables* begin with **@@**. They're not much used, *Class variables* so I'll describe them only briefly. A class variable is visible in all methods of *all* objects of a class, as well as in class methods. (Contrast this to a class's instance variables—as on the preceding page—which are visible only in class methods, not visible to an instance at all.) Many consider class variables a bad idea. I wouldn't go that far, but I think you can live a rich and fulfilling life without ever using one.

Global variables don't have anything in particular to do with classes, *Global variables* but they're the last kind of variable left, and I have to describe them somewhere. Globals begin with **$**. A global variable is visible everywhere, in every method of every object of every class. Globals have more legitimate uses than class variables, but they can get out of control. When you have a larger script with many globals, any change might affect anything anywhere. If you restrict yourself to local and instance variables, you don't need to look at as much code to figure out what's going on and what's safe to change.

12.5   Exercises

1. Write a test that demonstrates Counter's behavior. If you find any bugs, fix them.

2. There's going to be a problem when we add another test. You can see it by duplicating your existing test (but with a new name). Now run both tests. I bet one of them fails. The reason is that the first one that ran left the count set to some value, and the second started the count with that value rather than 0.

   You could change the second test so it starts where the first left off, but there are two problems with that:

   a) That way lies madness. Innocent rearrangements of the tests will break things all over the place. No, tests should be independent of each other.

   b) It won't work, anyway. Tests aren't guaranteed to run in any particular order. Even if you get the tests ordered just so today, that might be the wrong order tomorrow.

   Can you think of a workable solution to the problem?

3. Let's have each instance of Counter know whether it was the first one created, the second one, etc. To start, add accessors for an instance variable called @birth_order.

Remember, the accessors are for the *instance*, not Counter itself. Here's a sample usage:

```
Counter.counted_new.birth_order
```

At this point, Counter doesn't tell its instance what its order is, so birth_order will return nil. (Why?)

4. Change Counter.counted_new to tell each new instance its birth order. (Don't forget to start with tests.)

Part III

Working in a World Full of People

## Chapter 13

Scraping Web Pages
with Regular Expressions

Here's what happens when you use a web application: you poke at a browser to make it send an HTTP command to a server. That server is full of nice tidy arrays, strings, and other objects—just the sort of things a script would like to work with. In response to the command, the server converts some of that data into vast masses of HTML. If you want your script to work with the results, you have to *un*convert the HTML into nice tidy arrays, strings, and other objects.

It's enough to drive one mad.

Mad or sane, you'll spend some of your scripting life "scraping" information out of the HTML that web applications deliver to your computer. In this chapter, we'll build a script that scrapes information from a page and prints it to a screen in a human-friendly form. In Chapter 15, *Working with Comma-Separated Values*, beginning on page 153, the script will be made more useful by having it create a comma-separated value (CSV) file for import into a spreadsheet.

For this part's example, I need to use a web interface that's universally available, that's from a company that won't go out of business soon, and that contains information that's likely to still be available in version 834 of the interface. I chose Amazon book listings. To make the problem more interesting, I'll have the app print an *affinity trip*. Amazon's page about a book tells you about other books purchased by people who bought it. An affinity trip follows the first such link, finds the same links on the next book's page, follows that..., printing what it finds

affinity trip

```
prompt> ruby affinity-trip.rb 0974514055
Programming Ruby: The Pragmatic Programmers' Guide, Second Edition
Agile Web Development with Rails : A Pragmatic Guide (The Facets of  ↩
Ruby Series)
Ajax in Action
Foundations of Ajax (Foundation)
DHTML Utopia Modern Web Design Using JavaScript & DOM
The CSS Anthology : 101 Essential Tips, Tricks, and Hacks
The Zen of CSS Design : Visual Enlightenment for the Web (Voices Th  ↩
at Matter)
Web Standards Solutions: The Markup and Style Handbook (Pioneering  ↩
Series)
Bulletproof Web Design : Improving flexibility and protecting again  ↩
st worst-case scenarios with XHTML and CSS
DOM Scripting: Web Design with JavaScript and the Document Object M  ↩    ,
odel
```

Figure 13.1: AN AFFINITY TRIP FOR A BOOK

along the way. Figure 13.1 shows the trip that starts with the ISBN[1] of *Programming Ruby*.

We're going to cover a lot of ground in this chapter, so here's how the trip is organized:

1. We first have to know how to *fetch a web page into a string*.

2. An important tactic for dealing with vast amounts of text is to use regular expressions to *restrict the focus to part of the page*.

3. *Extracting the title and authors* requires further use of regular expressions.

4. That different information needs to be *bundled together for future use*. A new kind of object, the *hash*, is handy for that.

hash

5. Finally, it all has to be orchestrated with a method that *takes the affinity trip*.

13.1   Treating Web Pages Like Files

Copy this into the address bar of your browser: http://www.amazon.com/ gp/product/0974514055. After you go to that page, view the page source

---

1.   Each book has a unique ISBN.

> **Mysterious Failures**
>
> There are several reasons the examples in this chapter might fail when you try them:
>
> - You might be behind a proxy server. Until you tell Ruby about it, connections will be blocked.
>
> - You might have a firewall that will let only an officially blessed browser use HTTP.
>
> - Amazon is constantly changing the format of its book pages. I've tried to make the regular expressions used in this chapter resilient in the face of change, but an Amazon change may still break them.
>
> When you see a mysterious failure, go to http://www.pragmaticprogrammer.com/titles/bmsft/ for help.

(that option is probably in your browser's View menu). I just did that, and the page was 6,692 lines of HTML source. Somewhere in there is the information we need. One way we could get at it with Ruby is to save the text to a file, open the file, read it in, and use string searches or regular expressions to find what we need.

The open-uri library, written by Tanaka Akira, does the first part of that for us. After requiring it, an open message that's available everywhere can open both local files and URLs.[2] Here's an example:

```
irb(main):001:0> require 'open-uri'
=> true
irb(main):002:0> url = 'http://www.amazon.com/gp/product/0974514055'
=> "http://www.amazon.com/gp/product/0974514055"
irb(main):003:0> page = open(url)
=> #<File:/tmp/open-uri2897.0>
```

Once the page is opened, its contents can be read:

```
irb(main):004:0> text = page.read; nil
=> nil
```

The ; nil at the end is a trick to prevent irb from shoving all 6,692 lines in your face. Normally, Ruby statements are on separate lines, but you

---

2. It works with URLs by fetching a page, putting it in a temporary file, and opening that file. It also arranges for the temporary file to be deleted when irb or the script finishes.

```
<div class="buying"><b class="sans">Programming Ruby: The Pragmatic P  ↩
rogrammers' Guide, Second Edition (Paperback)</b><br />by         ↩


<a href="/exec/obidos/search-handle-url/index=books&field-author-exac  ↩
t=Dave Thomas&rank=-relevance,+availability,-daterank/002-4184610-544  ↩
0038">Dave Thomas</a>, <a href="/exec/obidos/search-handle-url/index=  ↩
books&field-author-exact=Chad Fowler&rank=-relevance,+availability,-d  ↩
aterank/002-4184610-5440038">Chad Fowler</a>, <a href="/exec/obidos/s  ↩
earch-handle-url/index=books&field-author-exact=Andy Hunt&rank=-relev  ↩
ance,+availability,-daterank/002-4184610-5440038">Andy   Hunt</a>     ↩


</div>
```

Figure 13.2: BOOK INFORMATION INSIDE HTML

---

can put several on one line if you separate them with semicolons. Given multiple statements, irb will print the value of only the last one (nil, in this case).

I'll search for something interesting in the text, just to check that it looks like an Amazon page:

```
irb(main):016:0> text.scan(/Customers.*also/)
=> ["Customers who bought this  also", "Customers interested in this
title may also", "Customers who viewed this  also"]
```

scan is a handy method that returns all substrings that match a regular expression. Notice that two of these strings contain more than one space between adjacent words. That's extremely common in HTML documents, so beware of putting spaces in regular expressions. Instead, you should write them like this: /Programming\s+Ruby/.

13.2   Restricting Attention to Part of the Page

Somewhere inside those 6,692 lines is the author and title information for the book. It in fact appears in several places. I want to pick a place that's easy to locate with a regular expression and also not likely to change soon. (Having to change scripts to keep pace with page changes is *the* bane of screen scraping.) I'll choose the first visible use of the information on the page, which looks something like Figure 13.2.

When faced with searches through huge strings, the first step I take is to restrict the text I'm working with to a small chunk containing the data I want. That way, I don't risk having a regular expression match something that happens to be earlier in the file. I also avoid the problem of "greedy" regular expressions accidentally matching huge swaths of text that extend far beyond my expected end. That happens when you have a regular expression like /BEGIN.*END/. If there are three copies of END in the text, it will match all the way through the third. You can make it match only through the first by using the question mark: /BEGIN.*?END/. That causes the match to stop at the first END. That's fine, but what if you want to match through the second, stopping at neither the third (greedy) nor the first (nongreedy)? Then you have to restrict the regular expression's attention by chopping off the third END and using a greedy match.

In this case, I want to restrict attention to the block of text that looks like this:

```
<div class="buying"><b
  ...
</div>
```

I have to include the start of the *<b>* tag because there are earlier blocks of text that begin with <div class="buying">, and I don't want to match them.

Here is a regular expression that matches the beginning of that text:

```
/<div class="buying"><b/,
```

That's fragile, though. Because HTML is relaxed about where its author can put whitespace, it's quite plausible that someone someday will decide to put a space between the *<div>* tag and the *<b>* tag. I want my script to be robust against such changes, so I'll allow whitespace anywhere it's legal. Here's a regular expression that does that:

```
/<div\s+class\s*=\s*"buying"\s*>\s*<b/
```

That does make the regular expression harder to read, which is a shame.

To match the end of the block, we can use this:

```
%r{</div\s*>}
```

That's odd looking—where are the beginning and ending slashes? Instead of slashes, you can surround a regular expression with %r{}. That's useful when the regular expression will have to contain slashes itself, which is often the case with HTML. In this case, there's only one slash, so I could have just put a backslash in front of it, but I think this variant is clearer.

I can write a general-purpose method to pull out an area defined by the beginning and ending regular expressions:

`code/affinity-trip/affinity-trip.rb`

```
def restrict(html, starting_regexp, stopping_regexp)
  start = html.index(starting_regexp)
  stop = html.index(stopping_regexp, start)
  html[start..stop]
end
```

index returns the number of the first character of the first match of the regular expression. That's the same number returned by =~. The advantage of index is that it takes a second argument that says where the search should start. That way, we can look for the first *<div>* after starting_regexp, not one of the many that appear before it. After we have the starting and stopping regular indices, we can just pull out the substring with an indexing message (brackets).

13.3 Plucking Out the Title and Authors

Once the script's attention is focused on part of the page, finding the title and author is a straightforward use of regular expressions. Here's the HTML for another book's title:

```
<div class="buying"><b class="sans">Cell: A Novel (Hardcover)
```

```
</b><br />by
```

Why, in this case, is the closing of the *<b>* tag on a different line? (On *Programming Ruby*'s page, it wasn't.) And why all the blank lines? I don't know. That kind of variation in the data is what makes scraping with regular expressions annoying. Just after you think you've gotten the expression right, you see an example that shows that it's wrong. These kinds of programs tend to take a while to get good at their job. (I expect this one isn't yet.)

Here's code that handles that HTML:

`code/affinity-trip/affinity-trip.rb`

```
def scrape_title(html)
  %r{<b.*?>(.*?)</b\s*>}m =~ html
  clean_title($1)
end
```

Notice the **m** at the end of the expression. That tells Ruby to match across multiple lines. My first try at this regular expression didn't have it, but the *Cell: A Novel* page taught me I needed it.

The actual title is between the bold markers. The regular expression's first group (denoted $1) contains it. clean_title strips off the trailing *(Paperback)* or *(Hardcover)* that Amazon puts on book titles. It uses— once again—regular expressions to do the work.

The code that scrapes out the author names is a bit more complicated because it must return an array of authors:

`code/affinity-trip/affinity-trip.rb`
```
def scrape_authors(html)
  author_anchor = %r{<a.*?href=".*?field-author-exact.*?".*?>(.+?)</a\s*>}m
  html.scan(author_anchor).flatten.collect do | author |
    clean_author(author)
  end
end
```

- Each author is stored within an HTML anchor (<a>) tag. (See Figure 13.2, on page 136, for an example.) The regular expression on the first line is the best one I found to pluck the author out without accidentally matching nonauthor anchors.

- scan, first seen on page 136, returns an array of matches. In our earlier example, the matches were just strings, but scan behaves specially when the regular expression has groups in it, as this example shows:

```
irb(main):008:0> "1a b2 3c ".scan(/(\d)(\S)/)
=> [["1", "a"], ["3", "c"]]
```

That regular expression matches a digit followed by a nonspace character. In this particular string, *1a* and *3c* match. Because the regular expression contains groups, scan doesn't return an array of matching strings. It still returns an array, but each element of the array is itself an array containing each group's matches.

In scrape_authors's regular expression (the first line), there's one group, intended to match one author's name. So the result will be something like this:

```
[ ["Dave Thomas"], ["Chad Fowler"], ["Andy  Hunt"] ]
```

In order to convert that into a simple array of author names, there are two issues to solve:

- First we have to get rid of the nested arrays. The flatten method does that:

```
irb(main):001:0> [["Dave Thomas"], ["Chad"], ["Andy  Hunt"]].flatten
=> ["Dave Thomas", "Chad", "Andy  Hunt"]
```

- Next we have to deal with possible spurious blanks (as in *"Andy   Hunt"*). clean_author does that; all we have to do is collect the results of applying it to each author.

13.4 Hashes Store Named Data

We're now able to retrieve a book title and author list from an Amazon page. Later we'll need to pull out titles and associated URLs from the page's affinity list. Usually such pairs—or larger clumpings—of values are gotten at the same time and always used together, so they should travel through the script together from the moment of creation to the moment of use. How to do that? We could refer to them with distinct variables:

```
title = find_title(html)
url = find_url(html)
next_step(title, url)
...
```

That's a good way to confuse yourself: the variables that ought to go together get separated, one gets changed without updating the other, and so on. No, variables that are used together should be bundled into *composite object* a *composite object*. But how? One way is to put them into an array:

```
info_array = find_book_info(html)
next_step(info_array)
...
```

The problem is that now you have to remember whether the title is info_array[0] or info_array[1]. It would be better if you could name the elements of an array so that you could refer to info[:title] or info[:url]. Unsurprisingly, you can. Not with arrays, but with *hashes*.[3] You create a hash *hashes* like you create an array, just using different brackets:

```
irb(main):002:0> hash = {}
=> {}
```

---

3. The word "hash" is meaningless. It's derived from "hash table," an implementation technique. Other languages call them "dictionaries" or "associative arrays." You'll occasionally hear Rubyists use those terms.

You put something into a hash much like you put it into an array, except that instead of using an integer as a index, you can use any object as a *hash key*:

```
irb(main):003:0> hash[:title] = "book"
=> "book"
```

You can probably guess how to extract a *hash value*:

```
irb(main):004:0> hash[:title]
=> "book"
```

Like an array (again), you can create a hash already filled with values:

```
irb(main):005:0> hash = {:title => 'title', :url => 'www.book.com' }
=> {:url=>"www.book.com", :title=>"title"}
```

The following shows a typical use of hashes. scrape_book_info should return both a title and an author. It creates an empty hash, finds the author and title in turn, puts them into a hash, and returns it.

> code/affinity-trip/affinity-trip.rb

```
def scrape_book_info(html)
  retval = {}
  html = restrict(html,
             /<div.+class\s*=\s*"buying".*?>\s*<b/,
             %r{</div\s*>})
  retval[:title] = scrape_title(html)
  retval[:authors] = scrape_authors(html)
  retval
end
```

For more about hashes, see Chapter 16, *Ruby Facts: Hashes*, beginning on page 161.

13.5 Taking the Trip

The following is a first draft of the method that actually takes the trip:

> code/affinity-trip/affinity-trip.rb

```
❶ def trip(url, steps=10)

❷   steps.times do
      page = fetch(url)
      book_info = scrape_book_info(page)
      puts format_output(book_info)

      next_book = scrape_affinity_list(page)[0]

      url = next_book[:url]
    end
end
```

The first interesting fact about that method is the argument list (❶). The second argument is defined with a default value. If the method is not given enough values to fill out the argument list, it uses the defaults. For example:

```
irb(main):039:0> def flip(url, steps=10, another=[])
irb(main):040:1>   "#{url}/#{steps}/#{another.inspect}"
irb(main):041:1> end
=> nil
irb(main):042:0> flip('url')
=> "url/10/[]"
irb(main):043:0> flip('url', 1)
=> "url/1/[]"
irb(main):044:0> flip('url', 8, [33])
=> "url/8/[33]"
```

optional arguments

These kind of arguments are *optional arguments*. They're useful when almost all of a method's clients will want to use the same value. Rather than force each of them to give it, the duplication is removed by putting the value in one place: the method's argument list.

You can learn more about optional and other special kinds of arguments in Chapter 17, *Ruby Facts: Argument Lists*, starting on page 165.

The second interesting fact is the times method (❷). It's sent to an integer to repeat a block that number of times. The block fetches the URL, scrapes the information out, prints it, scrapes out the affinity list, and repeats it all with the url updated to be the first book in the affinity list.

If you're having trouble following what the different messages trip sends actually do, I suggest you require affinity-list.rb and try the individual methods yourself. Judiciously placed puts statements can also help.

A Better Trip

As I write, the first title in *Programming Ruby*'s affinity list is *Agile Web Development with Rails*. As it happens, *Programming Ruby* is in *Agile Web Development with Rails*'s affinity list. In fact, it's first. The version of trip shown previously will show only those two books, alternating.

It would be better if trip remembered what books it has already visited. If the top of an affinity list is somewhere it has already been, it should instead go to the second book in the list. Here's a version to do that:

```
def trip(url, steps=10)
❶  so_far = []

  steps.times do
    page = fetch(url)
    book_info = scrape_book_info(page)
    so_far << book_info[:title]
    puts format_output(book_info)

❷   next_book = scrape_affinity_list(page).find do | possible |
      not so_far.include?(possible[:title])
    end

    url = next_book[:url]
  end
end
```

Variable so_far (❶) names an array that stores URLs visited so far. At ❷ the entire affinity list is searched for a book that hasn't already been used.

13.6 Exercise Yourself

It takes practice to get good at regular expressions. One way to practice is to extend the script to pluck out different information from Amazon pages. For example, an Amazon page also has a "what do customers ultimately buy after viewing items like this?" affinity list. Can you scrape that list instead? Or perhaps it would be useful to include the price in the output. A fun one would be to include the average star ranking. (In that case, you'd have to pull out an <img> tag and convert names like stars-4-5.gif into appropriate numbers.)

Rather than work with affinity-trip.rb, which runs slowly because it contacts Amazon five times, you may want to model your scripts after isbn-to-affinity-list and isbn-to-title.rb. Each of those pulls out one bit of information about one book.

Alternately, you could look at pages that surprised me when I was developing affinity-trip.rb. For example, the original version of the scrape_authors regular expression didn't use href=".*?field-author-exact.*?" in it. What is it about professional-ajax-amazon-page.html that requires it? Can you find a better way to pluck out the author? (I wouldn't be surprised.)

There's at least one bug in trip: what happens if it can't find a next book? If you want to fix this bug, you'll find the **return** keyword useful. It's described on page 238. You'll probably also want to pull the search for a next book out into its own (testable) method.

Tests

As you exercise yourself, you'll want to write and run tests. You're starting with two kinds of tests. affinity-trip-tests.rb are tests that work on local data files like professional-ajax-amazon-page.html. On my rather slow computer, they run in 0.11 seconds. affinity-trip-slowtests.rb are tests that reach out over the network and actually take affinity trips. They take 151 seconds.

When you work on the code, you'll want to run the fast tests frequently. You'll add a fast test, run it to see it fail, change code, run it and other fast tests until the code passes, add another fast test, run it. . . . Test-driven programming thrives on that fast feedback loop.

It's important to *keep fast tests fast*. If you start adding slower tests to them, you'll run them less often, which will allow confusion and broken code to build up before a test tells you of it. But it's also important for fast tests to be complete enough that you can make changes with confidence that the fast tests will tell you when you err. Part of the skill of test-driven programming is knowing how to break your script into pieces that can be tested quickly, isolating the inherently slow bits like network access. (We saw an example of that with churn, where the code that spoke to Subversion was in a method that did nothing else.)

What's the role of slow tests? They test some script behavior that simply can't be tested fast (like communication with a Subversion server). They also act as a safety net: even if each piece of a script has been tested individually, it's nice to see a test of the whole thing, end to end.

In this particular case, the slow tests have the advantage that they work with the real pages that Amazon delivers today, not the pages it delivered sometime in 2005. I guarantee the Amazon page format has changed since then; the slow tests check whether it has changed in a way that breaks affinity-trip.rb.

You may end up with several files of fast tests and several of slow tests. A Ruby script named test-all.rb makes it a bit easier to run different sets of tests. Here are the three ways to use it:

```
prompt> ruby test-all.rb fast
affinity-trip-tests.rb
Loaded suite test-all
Started
.........
Finished in 0.096975 seconds.

9 tests, 18 assertions, 0 failures, 0 errors

prompt> ruby test-all.rb slow
affinity-trip-slowtests.rb
Loaded suite test-all
Started
....
Finished in 140.487732 seconds.

4 tests, 6 assertions, 0 failures, 0 errors

prompt> ruby test-all.rb
affinity-trip-slowtests.rb
affinity-trip-tests.rb
Loaded suite test-all
Started
.............
Finished in 148.029845 seconds.

13 tests, 24 assertions, 0 failures, 0 errors
```

You might want to peek inside test-all.rb to see how it works. ri File.glob
will help you understand it.

## Chapter 14

Other Ways of Working with Web Applications

In the previous chapter, I showed you how to use open-uri and regular expressions to scrape a web page. That approach has some disadvantages:

- open-uri can only get to pages that have a fixed URL. It will have problems with applications that use cookies or certain kinds of forms. It's also no help when testing JavaScript within web pages, something that is becoming increasingly important.

- It's hard to write regular expressions that will survive changes to the page structure.

In this chapter, I'll sketch some other approaches you can use when working with web applications. I give only a brief sketch, just enough for you to know what's available and how it works.

14.1 Handling XHTML

The more structure text has, the easier it is for a script to pick it apart. When text is less structured, you need pages and pages of code to do better than regular expressions.

HTML is only semistructured. Worse, browsers have traditionally contained pages and pages *and pages and pages* of code that let them successfully display even web pages that violate HTML's rules. There's a lot of lousy HTML out there, and you should expect to have to scrape it. That's why the previous chapter relies on regular expressions.

XHTML is an increasingly popular variant of HTML with a stricter structure that's more often enforced. Even better, XHTML is a specialized dialect of the general-purpose "markup language" XML, so most every language—including Ruby—comes with a lot of built-in support.

Amazon's web pages don't use XHTML, but the organization responsible for web standards does. (It's the World Wide Web Consortium, or W3C.) I've saved a snapshot of its front page in code/scraping-alternatives/www.w3.org.html. If you browse it, you'll see there are a large number of links to technologies the W3C works with. Each of them has this format (which I've indented for clarity):

```
<li>
  <a href="/XML/" class="navlink" shape="rect">
   <abbr title="Extensible Markup Language">
    XML
   </abbr>
  </a>
</li>
```

parser

Suppose I wanted to check that XML was one of the technologies covered. With regular expressions, I'd have to worry about the */XML/* in the <a> tag. That might lead to contorted regular expressions. Instead, though, I can use Ruby's built-in XML *parser*, REXML.[1] A parser converts structured text into a collection of interlinked objects. In the case of an XHTML document, each tag and block of text becomes an object. The previous snippet of XHTML would become this structure:

The gray boxes represent Element objects, and the white one is a Text object. An object below another is contained within it. Notice that the

---

1. REXML was written by Sean Russell.

text looks odd—that's because it contains all the characters from the opening of the *<abbr>* tag to its close, which includes whitespace and line breaks.

Suppose I told you to check manually whether XML was a technology the W3C covers. You might conceive of the task as finding all the lines with an *<abbr>* inside an *<a>* inside an *<li>*. When you find one, you'd look at the text. Is it *XML*, possibly surrounded by whitespace? If so, the answer is yes.

The following test follows almost the same steps, except that I find all the matching tags before I check for *XML*:

`code/scraping-alternatives/xhtml.rb`

```
def test_xhtml_included_in_document
  page_text = IO.read("www.w3.org.html")
  document = Document.new(page_text)
  topics = XPath.match(document, '//li/a/abbr')
  assert(topics.find { | topic | topic.text.strip == "XML" })
end
```

❶ IO.read is the shortest way to convert an entire file into a single string.

❷ The Document object is the gateway to the entire collection of objects resulting from parsing the page.

❸ This line produces an array of all the *<abbr>* tags that are nested as desired. The second argument to match is an XPath expression. XPath is a standardized way of referring to parts of XML documents. It's complicated and powerful.

❹ Each *<abbr>* tag contains a Text object. This line finds the first one that contains *XML* (and possibly whitespace). Notice that find and its associated block are all inside the parentheses that surround assert's single argument. It's not unusual to see that in Ruby when the block is small enough (in which case you surround the block with { and } instead of **do** and **end**).

There's a good deal more information on XML in the forthcoming *Working with XML and XPath* supplement.

14.2 Driving the Browser

Rather than driving the server directly, testers who are doing end-to-end tests often write scripts that ask a browser to do the work. At this writing, the two most popular tools among Ruby scripters are Watir (http://wtr.rubyforge.org/) and Selenium (http://www.openqa.org/selenium/). Both are open source and have enthusiastic user communities. Both allow you to test the JavaScript within web pages, and that's impossible to do without driving the browser.

Here is an example of driving Internet Explorer with Watir:

```
code/scraping-alternatives/watir.rb
def test_marick_vanity
  ie = IE.new     # Launch Internet Explorer

  ie.goto('http://www.google.com')

  # If you view the HTML source, you can see that Google
  # names the search field 'q'.
  ie.text_field(:name, "q").set("scripting for testers")

  # 'btnI' is the name of the "I'm Feeling Lucky" button.
  ie.button(:name, "btnI").click

  # Case-insensitive search for my name.
  assert(ie.contains_text(/marick/i))
end
```

As you write tests that drive the browser, be especially vigilant about duplicate code. Suppose you have 1,000 tests that start like this:

```
ie.goto(START_PAGE)
ie.text_field(:name, "login").set("marick")
ie.text_field(:name, "password").set("not the real one")
ie.button(:name, "login").click
```

You're in big trouble when the names of fields change, the authentication rules change to require that all passwords contain numbers and capital letters, or two-factor authentication is added. For your own sake, create utility methods such as standard_login to contain what would otherwise be duplicated.

14.3 Direct Access to Underlying Protocols

open-uri is built on top of classes that give more direct access to the network. You can avoid its restrictions by working directly with those classes. I'll show that by testing this exciting web application:

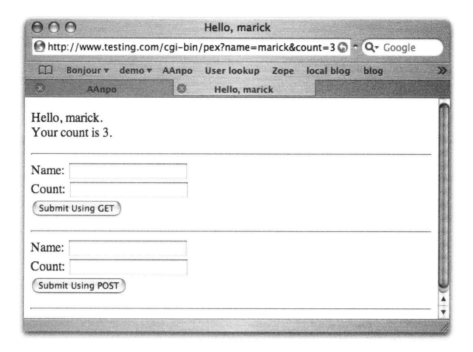

It accepts two parameters, name and count, and echoes them back. You can see those parameters in the address bar's URL.

Putting parameters in a URL is called an HTTP GET request, and open-uri would have no problem "opening" that URL. However, parameters can also be sent separately in what's called an HTTP POST request. Forms that change an application's state often use POST requests, reserving GET for requests that read—but don't modify—data.

open-uri cannot send POST requests, so it cannot generate the request produced by clicking the lower button. To do that, we'd need lower-level code like this:

code/scraping-alternatives/http.rb

```
def test_echoing
❶    HTTP.start('www.testing.com') do |server|
❷      name = CGI.escape("Brian Marick")
       count = CGI.escape("3")
❸      params = "name=#{name}&count=#{count}"
❹      response = server.post('/cgi-bin/post-example', params)
❺      assert_match(/Brian Marick/, response.body)
       assert_match(/count is 3/, response.body)
     end
   end
```

❶ start opens a connection to the web server. Within the block, server names that connection. You can learn more about this style of using blocks in Section 15.2, *Using Blocks for Automatic Cleanup*, on page 154.

❷ In your life using the Web, you may have noticed that URLs never have spaces. Where you'd expect spaces, they have plus signs. You might have also noticed oddities like &21 in URLs. That's because characters like spaces and exclamation points aren't allowed in POST or GET data, so they have to be converted (in this case, to plus signs and &21). CGI.escape does that conversion.

CGI.escape isn't needed on the next line, since 3 is a perfectly valid character, but it can't hurt.

❸ The ampersand-separated format is the way parameters are sent to a web server, regardless of whether the request is a GET or POST. The difference is whether the parameters are put into the URL or sent along via a different route.

❹ The opened server connection and the two post arguments together make up the URL you're used to seeing in a browser's address bar. The only part that's missing is the question mark that normally precedes the options (as you can see in the previous picture of the browser).

❺ An HTTP response contains a whole pile of information. The body is the HTML that a browser would normally display.

Chapter 15

Working with
Comma-Separated Values

In Chapter 13, *Scraping Web Pages with Regular Expressions*, beginning on page 133, the output was ordinary human-readable text. In this chapter, I'll describe how affinity-trip can also produce comma-separated values. Here's what that looks like:

```
prompt> ruby affinity-trip.rb --csv
"Programming Ruby: The Pragmatic Programmers' Guide, Second Edition", ←
"Dave Thomas, Chad Fowler, Andy Hunt"
Agile Web Development with Rails : A Pragmatic Guide (The Facets of R ←
uby Series),"Dave Thomas, David Hansson, Leon Breedt, Mike Clark, Tho ←
mas Fuchs, Andrea Schwarz"
Ajax Patterns and Best Practices (Expert's Voice),Christian Gross
...
```

Each line has two fields, separated by a comma. The first is the title; the second is a comma-separated list of authors. Notice that the CSV output surrounds a field with quotes when the content contains a comma.

This chapter also covers three other topics:

- Finding packages like CSV and their documentation.

- A better way of working with files than the File.open you're familiar with.

- How to use messages as nouns as well as verbs. You can do more than just send messages; you can grab hold of them with variables and decide what to do with them later.

15.1 The CSV Library

To use the CSV library, you have to require it:

```
irb#1(main):001:0> require 'csv'
=> true
```

Once you've done that, you can write CSV files, read them into arrays, or generate individual CSV structures for use by your script. We'll start with writing. Here's one way to do it:

```
irb(main):001:0> writer = CSV.open('test.csv', 'w')
=> #<CSV::BasicWriter:0x8cfa4 @rs=nil, ...>
irb(main):002:0> writer << [1, 5.3, 'dawn']
=> #<CSV::BasicWriter:0x8cfa4 @rs=nil, ...>
irb(main):003:0> writer << [2, 5.5, 'paul']
=> #<CSV::BasicWriter:0x8cfa4 @rs=nil, ...>
irb(main):004:0> writer.close
=> nil
```

That should look familiar. Opening a CSV file looks like opening any other file: you give open the filename and, if the file is to be written, *'w'*.

The values to write are given by arrays. They're "pushed" onto the output with <<, which should remind you of pushing values onto arrays or strings.

The last line fixes some sloppiness I've indulged in. An open file consumes some operating system resources. close frees them. If a script keeps opening files and not closing them, eventually the operating system will get fed up and stop letting it open files. However, since all of the scripts we've been using open only one or two files, I've just been letting the operating system close them for us when the script exits.

15.2 Using Blocks for Automatic Cleanup

The close method is annoying because you have to remember to call it. For that reason, the following is more idiomatic Ruby:

```
CSV.open("test.csv", 'w') do | writer |
  writer << ['sophie', 9, 75.0]
  writer << ['brian', 46, 175.4]
end
```

The file is automatically closed when the block finishes. As far as I know, all the classes that have an open method support either version. More generally, most any method that lets you do something you later have to undo has such a variant. You'll see how to write one in Chapter 21, *When Scripts Run into Problems*, beginning on page 199.

The result of either of the previous snippets is a file containing something like this:

```
sophie,9,75.0
brian,46,175.4
```

15.3 More CSV Operations

A CSV object's **<<** performs two tasks:

1. It converts an array into a string: converting all nonstring elements into strings and surrounding strings with commas in them with quotes.

2. It writes the resulting line to an open file.

If you want to do only the first of those tasks, you do it like this:

```
irb(main):006:0> CSV.generate_line(['title', 'author, author', 34.95])
=> "title,\"author, author\",34.95"
```

A CSV file can be read in like this:

```
irb(main):026:0> s = CSV.readlines('test.csv')
=> [["sophie", "9", "75.0"], ["brian", "46", "175.4"]]
```

Notice that all the values are strings. You have to convert them to other classes yourself. Here's a way to do that for integers and floating-point numbers using the built-in conversion methods to_i and to_f:

```
irb(main):028:0> s.collect do | row |
irb(main):029:1*    [row[0], row[1].to_i, row[2].to_f]
irb(main):030:1> end
=> [["sophie", 9, 75.0], ["brian", 46, 175.4]]
```

15.4 Applying It All to affinity-trip.rb

With all that given, here's the method in affinity-trip.rb that produces CSV output:

`code/affinity-trip/affinity-trip.rb`

```
def csv_string(book_info)
  title = book_info[:title]
  authors = book_info[:authors].join(', ')
  CSV.generate_line([title, authors])
end
```

Rather than printing the line itself, it just creates a string for its caller to print. All those strings are printed with puts.

That output goes to the screen, but you can *redirect* it into a file like this:

prompt> ruby affinity-trip.rb --csv > file.csv

If you then start Excel (or some other spreadsheet) and open that file, you'll see the titles in one column and the authors in another. (Warning: in at least some versions of Excel, asking the open dialog to show you "All Readable Documents" won't allow you to select file.csv. Ask it to show you "All Documents.")

It's polite to let the user of the script decide whether to read it on the screen or redirect into a file.

15.5 Discovering and Understanding Classes in the Standard Library

How did I even know that Ruby had a CSV class? You can buy both a hard copy and PDF copy of *Programming Ruby* [TH01]. When I'm working in Ruby, I always have the PDF copy a couple of keystrokes away. When I'm wondering whether Ruby can do something, I scan down the list of classes in the PDF's table of contents to see what catches my eye. If that fails, I search the Web for something like "ruby csv files."

The next step is to move from knowledge that something exists to knowledge of what it does. The classes delivered with Ruby fall into two classes: the *core* and the *standard library*. The core are those classes you can use without requiring them. The standard library classes have to be required. There's another important difference, though: *Programming Ruby* is only 800 pages long. That's enough to describe every method of the core classes but only to devote a page or two to each of the standard library classes.

To find more documentation on standard library classes, go to http://www.ruby-doc.org/stdlib/. All of CSV's methods are described there in the format shown in Figure 15.1, on the next page. Along the top, the leftmost pane describes files in the package. If you click a filename, documentation for it appears in the bottom pane. Often, there's only one file, and its documentation often contains an overview and examples. The center top pane lists classes. When you click on one, the lower pane fills with an alphabetical list of its methods (and a clickable table

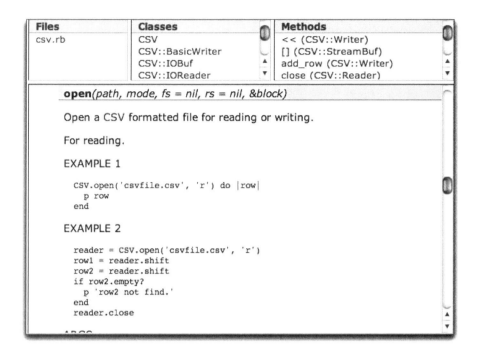

Figure 15.1: COMMA-SEPARATED VALUES

of contents at the top). The right-top pane is an alphabetical list of all the methods in all the classes.

ri doesn't contain documentation for much of the standard library. However, it's a convention that the documentation be part of the source as comments that can be turned into the files ri displays. Figure 15.2, on the following page, shows how you could create such a file for CSV, assuming that Ruby is installed at /usr/local/lib/ruby/1.8. (You'll learn more about where Ruby source is stored in the "Joe Asks" sidebar on page 173.) Note that there are two dashes in front of *ri*.

You can also create a local copy of the HTML view of the package documentation:

```
prompt> rdoc --op csv --fmt html /usr/lib/ruby/1.8/csv.rb
...
prompt> ls csv
classes/            fr_class_index.html      index.html
created.rid         fr_file_index.html       rdoc-style.css
files/              fr_method_index.html
```

```
prompt> ri CSV
Nothing known about CSV
prompt> rdoc --ri /usr/local/lib/ruby/1.8/csv.rb


    csv.rb: ccc..c..........c.....c........c..c....
          c......c...c...........c....
Generating RI...


Files:   1
Classes: 12
Modules: 0
Methods: 54
Elapsed: 8.832s


prompt> ri CSV
---------------------------------------------------------- Class: CSV
    This program is copyrighted free software by NAKAMURA, Hiroshi. You
    can redistribute it and/or modify it under the same terms of Ruby's
    license; either the dual license version in 2003, or any later
    version.


----------------------------------------------------------------------



Class methods:
-------------
    foreach, generate, generate_line, generate_row, open, parse,
    parse_line, parse_row, read, readlines
...
```

Figure 15.2: MAKING YOUR OWN STANDARD LIBRARY DOCUMENTATION

That command produced HTML and put it in the csv subfolder. Point your browser at the index.html file to see the documentation.

You can also look at the Ruby source itself. The comments that rdoc works from are pretty easy to read directly. That's what I usually do.

15.6   Replacing Code with Data

affinity-trip.rb produces two different kinds of output—comma-separated values or plain titles—depending on the presence or absence of the *–csv* command-line option. That option is processed here:

code/affinity-trip/affinity-trip.rb

```
if $0 == __FILE__

  if ARGV[0] == '-csv'
    FORMAT_STYLE = :csv_string
    ARGV.shift
  else
    FORMAT_STYLE = :normal_string
  end

  starting_isbn = ARGV[0] || '0974514055'
  trip(url_for(starting_isbn))
end
```

FORMAT_STYLE records what kind of output is desired. Since it begins with a capital letter, it's a constant. A constant is really just a variable except that Ruby will complain if you try to change it after you've set it the first time.

That constant could be used in code like this:

```
def format_output(book_info)
  if FORMAT_STYLE == :csv_string
    csv_string(book_info)
  else
    normal_string(book_info)
  end
end
```

That's annoying, though. We already used an **if** to decide which kind of formatting the user wanted (when we set FORMAT_STYLE), and now we have to do it *again*. Making the same decision twice is duplication, and duplication is bad. How do we get rid of it?

By a remarkable coincidence, the formatting methods have the same name as the two possible values of FORMAT_STYLE. What's this code doing in terms of objects and messages? *If FORMAT_STYLE names :csv_string, send the message csv_string to self. Otherwise, send normal_string to self.* If a symbol could somehow represent a message, we could simplify that rule to *send the message named by FORMAT_STYLE to self.* As it happens, both symbols and strings can name messages, and they can be sent using the send message. Like this:

code/affinity-trip/affinity-trip.rb

```
def format_output(book_info)
  self.send(FORMAT_STYLE, book_info)
end
```

The first argument to send is the name of the message to send; whatever comes after is sent along as the message's arguments. Pretty slick, eh?

One standard programming trick is to replace decision-making code with correctly initialized data. The more advanced the language, the more kinds of code you can "grab" and turn into something that can be named by a variable. In this case, we grabbed the idea of a message being sent. It's also possible to grab the idea of the execution of a block, a method, and even the entire rest of the script's execution at any point. You'll see only the first of these in this book (Chapter 21, *When Scripts Run into Problems*, beginning on page 199).

## Chapter 16

Ruby Facts: Hashes

Hashes are collections of named data. Here's a hash that stores information about a product in a store:

```
{ :name=>"Suse Cereal",
  :price=>233,
  :code=>"1234211234",
  :type=>"food",
  :quantity=>10 }
```

h = {} ↪ {}	Curly brackets are used to create empty hashes.
h = { :one => 1, :two => 2 } ↪ {:two=>2, :one=>1}	They can also be started with a set of **key/value pairs**. Notice that the order in which pairs are printed is unpredictable.
h[:three] = 4 ↪ 4	New pairs can be added using an array-like notation.
h[:three] = 3 ↪ 3	You can change an existing value.
h[:three] ↪ 3	Values are fetched using the same notation.
h['four'] = 'four' ↪ "four"	Hash keys can be any object, and the values can be as well. Symbols are the most common class of key.
h ↪ {:two=>2, :one=>1, :three=>3, "four"=>"four"}	Hashes don't care if some keys are strings and some are symbols, and they don't care whether all the values are of the same class. Mix and match however you like.
h[1000] ↪ nil	nil is returned if there's no matching key in the hash. It's the **default hash value**.

h.fetch(1000, 'not found') ↪ "not found"	fetch lets you tell the hash to use a different value than the default if the key is not found.
h.default = 'forever not found' h[1000] ↪ "forever not found"	You can also tell the hash to use a particular default from now on.
h.delete(:three) ↪ 3	You can delete a key/value pair from a hash.
h.empty? ↪ false	You can ask whether a hash is empty...
h.clear ↪ {}	...and you can make sure it's empty.
h = {:one => 1, :two => 2 } h.has_key?(:one) ↪ true	You can ask whether a hash contains a particular key...
h.has_value?(1) ↪ true	...or a particular value.
h.keys ↪ [:two, :one]	You can ask for an array of all the keys a hash contains...
h.values ↪ [2, 1]	...or an array of all its values.
h.size ↪ 2	You can ask how many pairs a hash has.
merge_me = { 'key' => 'value' } h.merge(merge_me) ↪ {:two=>2, :one=>1, "key"=>"value"}	You can merge two hashes to make a third. The original two are left unchanged.
merge_me[:one] = 'another one' h.merge(merge_me) ↪ {:two=>2, :one=>"another one", "key"=>"value"}	If both hashes contain the same key, the value from the second is used.
h.each_pair do | key, value | h[value] = key # reverse key and value end h ↪ {:two=>2, 1=>:one, 2=>:two, :one=>1}	You can apply a block to each key/value pair.

h.each do | key, value |
   h.delete(key) if value==1
end
h
↪ {:two=>2, 1=>:one, 2=>:two}

each is a synonym for each_pair. . .

h.collect do | key, value |
  [key, value]
end
↪ [[:two, 2], [1, :one], [2, :two]]

. . . which is useful because collect and similar methods work whenever each does.

Chapter 17

Ruby Facts: Argument Lists

17.1 Optional Arguments

Here's how you center a string in a field of 20 spaces:

```
irb(main):001:0> "center me".center(20)
=> "     center me      "
```

And here's how you center a string in a field of 20 dashes:

```
irb(main):002:0> "center me".center(20, '-')
=> "-----center me------"
```

center takes an *optional argument* that tells it what character to use   *optional argument*
when centering. If no second argument is given, it uses a space. How
does center accomplish that? By being defined something like this:

`code/arglist-facts/center.rb`

```
class String
  def center(field_width, padding=" ")
```

Notice on the **def** line that padding is assigned a value. That value is
used if none is provided. (The code that implements center is a bit
tricky because it has to handle several special cases. If you want to
understand it, start with the tests in arglist-facts/center-test.rb.)

A method can have many optional arguments. All of them must follow
all of the required arguments (field_width, in the case of center). Here's
an example:

```
irb(main):001:0> def echo(a, b=1, c=2)
irb(main):002:1>   puts "a=#{a}, b=#{b}, c=#{c}"
irb(main):003:1> end
=> nil
irb(main):004:0> echo('hi')
a=hi, b=1, c=2
=> nil
```

```
irb(main):005:0> echo('hi', 'there')
a=hi, b=there, c=2
=> nil
irb(main):006:0> echo('hi', 'there', 'dawn')
a=hi, b=there, c=dawn
=> nil
```

There's no way to give an explicit value to c without giving one to b.

17.2 Rest Arguments

puts can take any number of arguments:

```
irb(main):008:0> puts 1
1
=> nil
irb(main):009:0> puts 1, 2
1
2
=> nil
```

Here's what the definition of puts might look like:

```
def puts(*args)
  args.each do | arg |
    # something to print the argument
  end
end
```

The asterisk in front of args means that it will name all of the arguments, gathered up into an array. Here's an easy way to see that in action:

```
irb(main):014:0> def arrayish(*args)
irb(main):015:1>   args
irb(main):016:1> end
=> nil
irb(main):017:0> arrayish(1, 2, 3)
=> [1, 2, 3]
```

There can be only one rest argument. It must appear at the end of the argument list, after any required and optional arguments. Here's an example:

```
irb(main):032:0> def all(required, optional='opt', *rest)
irb(main):033:1>   [required, optional, rest]
irb(main):034:1> end
=> nil
irb(main):035:0> all(1)
=> [1, "opt", []]
```

```
irb(main):036:0> all(1, 2)
=> [1, 2, []]
irb(main):037:0> all(1, 2, 3)
=> [1, 2, [3]]
```

The Opposite of Rest Arguments

Rest arguments let you combine multiple arguments into a single array. You can also expand a single array into multiple arguments. Recall that the echo defined on page 165 prints one required argument and two optional arguments. If we have a three-argument array, we can prefix it with an asterisk to give values to each argument:

```
irb(main):043:0> array = ['one', 'two', 'three']
=> ["one", "two", "three"]
irb(main):044:0> echo(*array)
a=one, b=two, c=three
=> nil
```

The asterisk doesn't have to be in front of a variable. What matters is the array, not how you refer to it. Here's an example:

```
irb(main):050:0> echo(*[1, 2, 3].reverse)
a=3, b=2, c=1
=> nil
```

17.3 Keyword Arguments

Section 17.1, *Optional Arguments*, on page 165, justified optional arguments in terms of String's center method. Since you'll almost always want to center in a field of spaces, you want to write "s".center(20), not "s".center(20, ' '). You want to give the second argument only in the uncommon case of centering in a field of something else.

But suppose a small but vocal group of users wanted to both center and "spread" strings. If you spread a string by 1 unit, "foo" would turn into something like " f o o ". A spread of 4 would turn into something like "f   o   o". Now you have a dilemma. Do you define center like this?

```
def center(field_width, padding=' ', spread=0)
```

That would annoy the "spreaders" because they have to give the irrelevant padding string when they always want it to be a blank. In turn, you could reverse the optional arguments:

```
def center(field_width, spread=0, padding=' ')
```

But now the "padders" would be outraged, and they're just as vocal as the spreaders.

Keyword arguments

Keyword arguments are a way to satisfy both. Here is what the spreaders and padders, respectively, could type:

```
"string".center(20, :spread => 2)
"string".center(20, :padding => '-')
```

Ruby's support for keyword arguments is not as convenient as in some languages. What you want is, oh, something like this:

```
def center(field_width, spread => 0, padding => ' ')
```

The arrows define spread and padding as keyword arguments and also point to their default values. Instead of that, Ruby bundles all the keyword arguments into a hash that's assigned to the last argument in the argument list. That looks like this:

```
def center(field_width, keys={})
```

(The default value for keys is to handle the case where no keyword arguments are given.)

Given the hash, the method can assign its values to local variables and give default values for variables not mentioned:

`code/arglist-facts/keyword-example.rb`
```
def center(field_width, keys={})
  spread = keys.fetch(:spread, 0)
  padding = keys.fetch(:padding, ' ')
  # ...
```

Consequences

The way Ruby handles keyword arguments is simple and consistent: when sending a message, arguments of the form key=>value have to come at the end of the argument list. All of them are bundled up and treated as if they'd been in a single hash argument all along. The following two lines of Ruby mean *exactly* the same thing:

```
center(20, :spread => 1, :padding => "-")
center(20, {:spread => 1, :padding => "-"})
```

That behavior lets you interpret any method that takes a hash as its last argument as having keyword arguments, which is sometimes convenient, but it means that keyword arguments don't work well with other optional arguments or rest arguments. Experiment with the two following methods—you'll probably find the behavior surprising.

```ruby
def receiver(req, opt=2, keys={})
  # Is the second argument really optional?
  puts "#{req}/#{opt.inspect}/#{keys.inspect}"
end

def receiver(req, keys={}, *rest)
  # Can you give both keywords and extra arguments?
  puts "#{req}/#{keys.inspect}/#{rest.inspect}"
end
```

## Chapter 18

Downloading Helper Scripts and Applications

Hundreds of Rubyists in the world are busily working on software packages to make your life easier. Most such packages are libraries of classes and methods you can require into your scripts. Others contain entire applications. To use packages, you need to find them, download them, install them, and understand them. That's what this chapter is about.

18.1   Finding Packages

Commonly called "the RAA," the Ruby Application Archive is the largest index of Ruby software. You can find it at http://raa.ruby-lang.org/. In early 2006, it contained nearly 1,400 different packages. Almost 900 of them were libraries, and more than 400 were complete applications.

The RAA lets you search for packages by keyword (such as "XML"). Once you've found a listing, you can follow links to its home page or a download page.

Many Ruby projects are hosted at http://www.rubyforge.org. News about changes to those projects is available via an RSS feed. If you subscribe to that feed and glance over the changes each day, you'll learn what's available. Part of being a good scripter is being able to say, "oh, I remember someone has a package that does something like what I need. . ." and then find it through the RAA or a search engine.

One warning about RubyForge: the page layout is misleading. Toward the top, there's a tab that says "Docs." There's almost always nothing there. The real description of, and documentation for, a project is probably further down the page, under "Project Home Page." You'll have to scroll to see it.

18.2 Using setup.rb

The simplest way for you to install packages is through a tool named RubyGems. That's not the easiest way for a package author to distribute the package, though, so many have their own installation scripts. One of these is RubyGems itself (since you can't install RubyGems with RubyGems until you have RubyGems). It uses setup.rb, as do many many Ruby packages.

Since you'll want RubyGems, install it now unless you already have it. (More and more Ruby distributions are starting to include it.) Do that like this:

```
prompt> $ gem --version
0.8.11
```

If you see a version number like the previous one, rather than an error message, finish reading this section—you'll still want to know how to use setup.rb—but don't bother typing the commands to your computer. You can find RubyGems through the RAA, or you can use the version in the code folder.

Your search for RubyGems might have landed you on one of several RubyForge pages. No matter where you are, look for a link named **download**. You'll be given a choice of three types of files: a zip file (ending in .zip), an archive compressed in a different way (.tgz), or a gem file (.gem). Download one of the first two, and unzip it.

Once you have a RubyGems folder, look inside. Every distributed package should have a file named README, INSTALL, or something similar. It should tell you how to install the package. As is common, RubyGems is installed with a script named setup.rb. If you are logged in with administrator privileges (common on Windows), you install it like this:

```
prompt> ruby setup.rb all
```

On Unix-like systems, it's unusual to run with installation privileges turned on. To get them, type this:

```
prompt> sudo ruby setup.rb all
```

> ## Joe Asks...
> ### Where Are Packages Installed?
>
> *Windows:* Unless you installed Ruby in a nonstandard location, its "root" is C:\ruby\lib\ruby. Ruby's own libraries are in 1.8 beneath that. setup.rb will install libraries into site_local\1.8. Gems will be installed into gems\1.8.
>
> Executable scripts go in C:\ruby\bin.
>
> *Unix:* Ruby will typically be in either /usr/lib/ruby (if it came with the operating system) or /usr/local/lib/ruby (if you installed it). Ruby's own libraries are in the 1.8 folder below that. setup.rb will install libraries into site_local/1.8. Gems will be installed into gems/1.8.
>
> Executable scripts go in /usr/bin or /usr/local/bin.

If you can't get administrator privileges, you'll have to install RubyGems in your home folder. For instructions, see this book's support site, http://www.pragmaticprogrammer.com/titles/bmsft/, or the RubyGems documentation site, http://docs.rubygems.org.

18.3 Using RubyGems

To practice using gems, install a tool named rake (which will be elucidated in Section 19.6, *The rakefile*, on page 185). Go somewhere other than your code folder.[1] Type the following (prefixing it with sudo on Unix):

```
prompt> gem install rake
Attempting local installation of 'rake'
Local gem file not found: rake*.gem
Attempting remote installation of 'rake'
Successfully installed rake-0.7.1
Installing RDoc documentation for rake-0.7.1...
```

This example doesn't show a handy feature of RubyGems. If rake had depended on packages X, Y, and Z, RubyGems would have downloaded and installed them first.

---

1. Why?—because that file contains rake-0.7.1.gem. gem would prefer that file to one found on the network. I want to show you automatic downloading.

You can also download a local copy and install that. For example, you can type this in your downloaded code folder:

```
prompt> gem install xml-simple-1.0.8.gem
Attempting local installation of 'xml-simple-1.0.8.gem'
Successfully installed xml-simple, version 1.0.8
```

If you've installed a package, you can uninstall it:

```
prompt> gem uninstall xml-simple
Attempting to uninstall gem 'xml-simple'
Successfully uninstalled xml-simple version 1.0.8
```

Notice that both the install and uninstall commands report a version number. When you install a newer version of a package, it doesn't wipe out the old one; they both stay around until explicitly uninstalled. That means it's always safe to install a newer version of a package. If it breaks a script that used to work, just uninstall it; Ruby will revert to the older version.

Helping Ruby Find Gems

environment variable

You have to tell Ruby that you're using RubyGems in order to have require and load find gems automatically. Do that by setting the RUBYOPT *environment variable* to rubygems. (An environment variable is a name/value pair that's available to every program.)

Setting Environment Variables on Windows

Type this:

```
prompt> echo %RUBYOPT%
```

If you see *rubygems*, there's no need to do anything more. Otherwise:

1. In the Control Panel, open System.

2. On the Advanced tab, click Environment Variables.

3. Add a new environment variable RUBYOPT with the value *rubygems*.

Changes to environment variables don't immediately become available everywhere. irb won't see them until you restart it. If you use SciTE to run scripts with F5, you'll need to restart it before those scripts will see the change.

Setting Environment Variables on the Mac and Other Unix Derivatives

Type this:

```
prompt> echo $RUBYOPT
```

If you see *rubygems*, there's no need to do anything more. Otherwise:

1. At a command prompt, type *cd*. That guarantees you're in your home folder.

2. Type *echo $SHELL*. If you see one of /bin/bash, /bin/sh, or /bin/ksh, edit a file named .profile. If you see /bin/tcsh or /bin/csh, edit .cshrc. (Note that each of those filenames begins with a period; that makes it invisible to casual viewers.)

3. If you're editing .profile, add a line like this to the end:

   export RUBYOPT=rubygems

   If you're editing .cshrc, add a line like this to the end:

   setenv RUBYLIB rubygems

4. For the change to take effect, you need to start a new command line. If you're using an editor that can run scripts with a keypress, you'll need to restart the editor before those scripts will see the change.

18.4 Understanding What You've Downloaded

Most packages contain documentation, often in a subfolder named doc. (It's often the same as what's available on the project's home page.) There may also be a folder full of examples. Failing that, the package's tests (most likely in test) can often serve as examples. For packages installed with setup.rb, you can find those subfolders wherever you unzipped the package.

For gems, look where gems are installed. (See the "Joe Asks" sidebar on page 173.) RubyGems puts the documentation in the doc folder under that. Each separate package has its own folder of documentation.

What you're most likely to see is class and method information, most often in HTML form. You can navigate your browser to the package's folder and find an index.html file. For example, see the rake documentation in gems/1.8/doc/rake-0.7.1/rdoc/index.html.

Packages installed with gems have an easier path to documentation. You can create a web documentation server like this:

```
prompt> gem_server
[2006-04-26 14:44:58] INFO  WEBrick 1.3.1
[2006-04-26 14:44:58] INFO  ruby 1.8.2 (2004-12-25) [powerpc-darwin8.0]
[2006-04-26 14:44:59] INFO  WEBrick::HTTPServer#start: pid=1307 port=8808
```

Thereafter, you can use your browser to visit http://localhost:8808/. That page will show you all the gems installed on the machine, a link to the local class and method documentation (if any), and a link to where the gem came from (which sometimes contains links to documentation that's not part of the downloaded package).

You may need to do some digging for documentation. If there's no class and method information, that doesn't mean you might not find some documentation in the package's gem folder. If there's no documentation there, there might be some on the package's website. If there's none there, your favorite search engine may be able to find some somewhere else.

If you have done a dutiful search and still failed to find the answer you need, you can ask on the Ruby mailing list, which you can find on the page at http://www.ruby-lang.org/en/20020104.html. The mailing list has high traffic, but it's friendly and people will answer well-formulated questions quickly.

Chapter 19

A Polished Script

Up to this point, to run programs like churn.rb or affinity-trip.rb, you've had to know which folder they're in. That's annoying. It would be better if you installed your projects or packages (the terms are synonymous) using setup.rb. After you do, you can execute your scripts like this:

```
prompt> ruby -S my-script.rb
```

The **-S** tells Ruby to look for the script in all the places the command line usually looks for programs.

In most installations, there's an even simpler alternative:

```
prompt> my-script.rb
```

The system figures out that the file is a Ruby script and uses Ruby to run it.

In addition to making your life easier, using setup.rb lets co-workers install your packages on their machines without you having to give them any special instructions.

Accomplishing all this requires a bit of extra work because setup.rb expects your project to have a particular folder structure. This chapter extends that structure to minimize the chance that your work will clash with someone else's. Because it would be silly to make you create the structure yourself, it also provides a script to do it for you. It further shows you how you can have one version of the package installed on your machine, be working on an improved version in your own "sandbox," and not have the two versions interfere with each other.

19.1   The Load Path

You can arrange for ruby -S to find your scripts without knowing anything about the mechanism. That's not all you want, though. You also
want your scripts to be able to require files you've written without knowing where, exactly, those files are. To make that work right, it helps to
load path   know about Ruby's *load path*. It's an array of strings that looks something like this:

```
["/usr/local/lib/ruby/site_ruby/1.8",
 ...
 "/usr/local/lib/ruby/1.8",
 "/usr/local/lib/ruby/1.8/powerpc-darwin7.8.0"
 ...
 "."]
```

Each of those entries is a folder. The first is where libraries not part of
the Ruby distribution should be stored, the second is where the Ruby
distribution's Ruby files are stored, the third is where the Ruby distribution's machine- and operating system-specific files are stored, and
the last is the current working folder.

That first folder is where libraries you install go. I'll call it "the site_ruby
folder" from now on.

Both require and load search for the file they're loading in the load path's
folders, starting with the first one and continuing until the file is found.
Note that means that a library you install takes precedence over any
with the same name in the standard Ruby distribution.

Subfolders are not searched, so if you want to load a file named
site_ruby/subfolder/myfile.rb, the argument to load or require will have to
be *"subfolder/myfile.rb"*. (You've seen examples of this in tests that
requiredtest/unit.)

The global variable $: always points to the load path. You can change
the path at will, but it's unlikely you'll need to do so. Instead, I'll provide
templates for your scripts that do the work for you.

19.2   Avoiding Filename Clashes

Suppose the product you're working on is the Coaxial Straightener. You
might have a library full of Ruby methods and classes that are useful
in testing it. Even though you're in the Coaxial Straightener Validation
team, it would be unwise to name your library csv.rb. As we've seen,

there's already such a name in the Ruby distribution, but it deals with comma-separated values. Although it's true that the ordering of load path entries means that require 'csv' would pick up your library, not Ruby's, you've now lost the ability to use comma-separated values in any of your testing. A name like cs-valid.rb would be better.

To avoid accidental name clashes, you can use a little script I wrote, called clash-check.rb. It's in the code/clash-check folder, and you can install it with setup.rb. It works like this:

```
prompt> ruby -S clash-check.rb csv cs-valid
DANGER: A library named csv already exists.
```

Notice that clash-check.rb prints nothing about names that are safe, only about names that clash. No news is good news.

clash-check.rb is a simple script, but it uses a Ruby feature not explained until Chapter 21, *When Scripts Run into Problems*, starting on page 199.

Even with clash-check.rb, you don't want to put too many files where they could clash—it will keep getting harder and harder to find clash-free names. The usual solution is for your library to be installed as a single file and a folder. The folder would be named cs-valid. It would contain all the Ruby files that do the work. Suppose one of those files were tension.rb. A script that required it would contain this:

```
require 'cs-valid/tension'
```

For convenience, the Ruby file cs-valid.rb in the site_local folder requires all the subfolder files:

```
require 'cs-valid/tension'
require 'cs-valid/torsion'
require 'cs-valid/traction'
...
```

A program that wanted the entire cs-valid library would simply say this:

```
require 'cs-valid'
```

19.3 Avoiding Class Name Clashes Using Modules

Avoiding clashing filenames is not enough. Suppose that your library contains a class Reader. What if you require another class that *also* has a class named Reader? There needs to be a way to distinguish yours from that one.

One way would be to give all of your classes a prefix. For example, your reader could be named CsValidReader. But it would be boring to have to type that all the time.

module

Ruby offers a better solution, which is to include all your package's classes in a *module*. That would look like this:

```
module CsValid
  class Reader...
  class Writer...
end
```

fully qualified

Now no code outside the CsValid module can see any of the classes inside it unless it uses a *fully qualified* name, like this:

```
reader = CsValid::Reader.new
```

unqualified names

However, code within the module can use *unqualified names*:

```
reader = Reader.new
```

Including Modules

including

If you're writing a script that uses a module heavily, you may want to use unqualified names. You do that by *including* the module. A script that used your CsValid library would include it like this:

```
include CsValid
```

Note that include uses the actual module, not a string (as require and load do).

The effects of inclusion depend upon where it happens. For now, I'll explain only the two cases that are by far the most common. See Chapter 20, *Ruby Facts: Modules*, beginning on page 193, for the third, uncommon, case.

If you include a module *outside any module*, any place in the script can refer to classes using unqualified names. That would look like Figure 19.1, on the next page. Run it to see that it works.

"Any place in the script" means within any class within any module within any file you require. If some library you use has a class with a clashing name, you may have problems.

The safe alternative is to include a module only within a class. In that case, only an "including" class can use unqualified names to refer to the module's classes. Figure 19.2, on page 182, shows a class in someone else's package using CsValid in this conservative way.

```
code/module-facts/top-level-include.rb
require 'cs-valid'
include CsValid     # A top-level inclusion

# CsValid's Reader class can be seen everywhere:
puts Reader.new.hello

module MyModule
  class Viewer
    def hello
      "I can see Reader too: " + Reader.new.hello
    end
  end
end

puts MyModule::Viewer.new.hello
```
                                    module-facts/top-level-include.rb

Figure 19.1: MAKING MODULE CONTENTS AVAILABLE EVERYWHERE

Which alternative should you use? I suspect it doesn't much matter. My experience has been that class name clashes don't happen often, especially once you learn the names within modules you use often. When clashes do happen, good testing discipline should catch them: if you have a set of tests that work, you run all of them (or a big subset) frequently, you include a new module for some purpose, and old tests fail mysteriously in the next test run... it shouldn't be too hard to work backward to the cause.

19.4   A Script to Do the Work for You

In a book about using scripting to make your life easier, it would be absurd to stop now and expect you to set up the right folder and module structure. It should be done for you.

Change to your downloaded code workspace, and type the following, answering each question with Enter:

```
prompt> ruby s4t-utils/bin/make-s4t-project.rb
In what folder do you want the project?
(By default, it's the current one.)
[.] =>
What name will a client require to load the project library?
(The name of a Ruby file without the ending '.rb'.)
[default-project] =>
```

`code/module-facts/class-include.rb`

```
require 'cs-valid'

module MyModule
  class Viewer
    include CsValid      # A class-level inclusion

    def hello
      "I can see Reader: " + Reader.new.hello
    end
  end

  class Oblivious
    # "This class does not include CsValid."
    # "So the following method, if used, will fail:"
    def hello
      "I can see Reader too... or can I?" + Reader.new.hello
    end
  end

end

puts "Reader can be seen within Viewer:"
puts MyModule::Viewer::new.hello

puts "Reader can't be seen outside the class..."
puts "...so the following will fail if uncommented:"
# puts Reader.new.hello

puts "So will this class that didn't include CsValid:"
# puts MyModule::Oblivious.new.hello
```

module-facts/class-include.rb

Figure 19.2: MAKING MODULE CONTENTS AVAILABLE EVERYWHERE

If a client wants to include the library, what module name will she use?
[DefaultProject] =>
=> You will need to edit README.txt.
=> You will need to edit lib/default-project.rb.
=> You can use test/test-skeleton as a template.
=> You can use bin/bin-skeleton as a template.
=> You can use lib/default-project/lib-skeleton as a template.

Now would be a good time to put the project under version control.

You now have a default-project folder with lots of files and folders in it.
See Figure 19.3, on the next page.

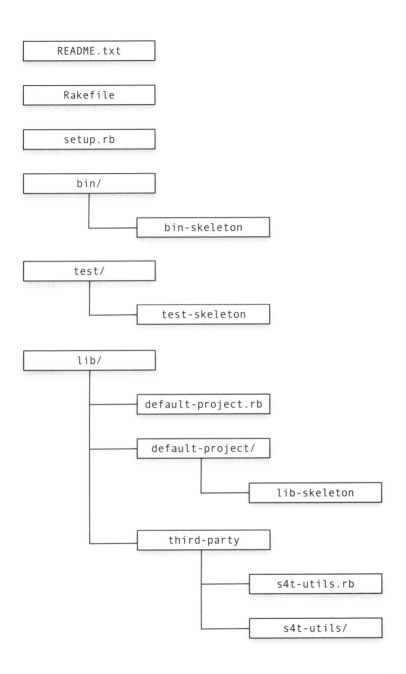

Figure 19.3: THE STANDARD SCRIPT FOLDER STRUCTURE

README.txt is where you describe your package. (Instructions for installing it with setup.rb are already included.) The rakefile makes it easier to do tasks like run tests. See Section 19.6, *The rakefile*, on the facing page, for more.

bin is where to put complete scripts that you run from the command line. test is for tests, and lib is for all the other Ruby files in your project (ones that are required by a bin script or other Ruby file).

lib contains a file and a folder. setup.rb will install both of them in the site_ruby folder. To load all of the files in the project, use require 'default-project'. To load any particular file, use require 'default-project/file'.

Within lib, you'll find another folder third-party. Use it when you're about to distribute your script to others. Suppose your package requires three libraries that don't come with Ruby. You could say to your users, "before you can use my wonderful package, you have to install this, and that, and the other." They'll find it more convenient if you put those libraries into the third-party folder. They'll only have to install your package to be ready to use it. Your scripts will automatically change the load path to automatically pick up the third-party libraries—and pick them up in preference to any in the user's site_ruby folder. That way, your script won't break because they're using a different version of the same utility library.

Each third-party folder starts out with s4t-utils, which are some methods and classes I've found useful when working on this book. You use it with require "s4t-utils". Don't delete that library even if you use nothing in it: the behind-the-scenes load-path–setting code needs it.

19.5 Working Without Stepping on Yourself

Suppose you're spending part of your time working with a stable version of your package and part of the time making a new version. If you're running tests on the new version, you don't want require to find the old version's files. The same is true if you run one of the scripts in the bin folder. "Skeleton" files in the test and bin folders are set up to avoid that. Copy them to create your own files.

bin-skeleton ensures that a script you run finds the correct versions of its files, no matter where you run it from. The test-skeleton requires you to run the tests in the test folder. rake relaxes that requirement.

Installing Into a Package's Third-party Folder

If your package is to be self-contained, you need to install everything it uses into the lib/third-party folder. How do you do that?

- If you're using a gem, install it like this:

  prompt> gem install extensions --remote --install-dir gems

  If you're in the third-party folder of your package, that installs the extensions gem into the gems subfolder. It will now automatically be found by require.

- If you're using a package also created with make-s4t-project.rb, I assume that both packages (the one you're creating now and the one you're using) are contained in the same folder. In that case, go to the package you want to use and type this:

  prompt> rake install-into peer='s4t-inform'

- If the library you want is normally installed with setup.rb, you'll find that installer is rather insistent about the folder structure it creates. The easiest thing to do is have it create its structure in a temporary folder:

  prompt> ruby setup.rb install --prefix=/temp

  Then navigate down to the location where the actual files are, which will be something like /temp/opt/local/lib/ruby/site_ruby/1.8, and copy the files from there into your package.

19.6 The rakefile

rake, written by Jim Weirich, is a Ruby tool that lets you describe simple tasks in a file, the *rakefile*. You can also describe dependencies *rakefile* between tasks so that, for example, the task to install a new version of your package won't start unless the task to run the tests finishes successfully.

You installed rake in Section 18.3, *Using RubyGems*, on page 173. To see what the rakefile can do for you, type the following in your new default-project folder. Take care to type two dashes in front of "tasks".

prompt> rake --tasks

Your Own Utility Library

One of the annoying things about the universe is that a net long-term benefit often has a net short-term costs. One of the annoying things about me—and probably you—is that it's hard to work up the energy to pay the short-term cost when I have so much else to do.

You will be a much better scripter if, whenever you find yourself writing similar code for the second time, you put it in a separate utilities library. Over time, many scripting tasks that are hard now will be easy—just reach in your toolbox and pull out what you need. But there's a short-term cost to that.

The way I convince myself to pay that cost is to make a rule that I *must* spend around twenty minutes at the end of every two-hour, half-day, or full-day task making myself more productive in some way. That might be adding a class to my own private library, cleaning up a script and learning from mistakes I fix, reading some documentation, or seeing what some package on the Net does.

If you're lucky, you can avoid adding something to your utility library because you never needed to write it in the first place. Instead, you found it in someone else's library and used that. So if it seems that *someone* must have already written code like what you want, check for it in the Extensions (http://rubyforge.org/projects/extensions/) and Facets (http://facets.rubyforge.org/) projects. Currently, the Facets library is much larger but has more items without documentation (and the volume can make it hard to find what you want).

Here are descriptions of some of what you'll see.

rake test

> This runs both the fast and slow tests. Fast tests must end in *"-tests.rb"* and slow tests in *"slowtests.rb"*. Tests must be in the test folder or in its subfolders.

> This is the default task, so you can omit the "test" from the command line.

> You can run the tests (and any other rake task) from anywhere in your project, not just in the test directory. The rakefile arranges the load path appropriately.

rake fast

> This runs only the fast tests.

rake install

> This is the safe way to install. It runs the tests first and then runs setup.rb.

rake increment-version

> When someone finds a problem in your package, almost the first question you'll want to ask is "what version are you using?" This book has the convention of putting version numbers in a lib/package/version.rb file. They look like this:

```
code/s4t-utils/lib/s4t-utils/version.rb
module S4tUtils
  Version = '0.2.0'
end
```

> A 00 in the first slot conventionally means "I don't think I'm done with this yet," while a 1 or greater means "it's a complete package." (Note: it has been widely noted that Rubyists often take forever to declare their packages ready to be version 1.)

> The number in the second slot changes when you announce the availability of a significant new zip file or gem to others. It's common for even numbers to be considered stable and odd numbers experimental. For a long time, the stable version of Ruby was 1.6 and the adventurous people used 1.7. At some point, 1.7 was stable enough to be declared 1.8.

> The final number changes much more frequently whenever you have reached some personal milestone and are ready to move on to something else. It's this number that rake increment-version changes.

rake commit

> Commits or checks in changed files to your version management system. Right now, it works only with Subversion, which is the one I use and recommend. If the files aren't under version control, this does nothing.

rake install-into peer=NAME

> If you want to use one package as a third-party library in another, you use this command. The *NAME* is expected to be in the same folder as your project. For example, to install the user-choices library into default-project, you'd do this:

```
prompt> cd user-choices
prompt> rake install-into peer=default-project
```

If you're using Subversion, the installed files will be put under version control.

rake update-peers

Inevitably, just after you install a package into thirty-seven other packages, you'll find a bug. After you fix it, you have to update all thirty-seven packages. Use this command. For example, when I update-peers in the s4t-utils folder, rake looks through all other packages in the code folder that use s4t-utils.

When it finds them, it adds new files or folders, replaces changed ones, and deletes files or folders no longer used. It also tells Subversion of the changes if a peer is under version control.

rake rdoc

This will process the Ruby files and turn comments into HTML with class and method definitions.

rake move-on

I use this when I've finished a task and am ready to move on to something else. It runs the tests, increments the version, commits (if the project is using Subversion), and updates peers.

19.7 Location-independent Tests

Before running its tasks, rake changes the current working folder to the one containing the rakefile. That means that's the current working folder when running rake test. But if you're running an individual test with ruby some-test.rb, you're likely running it in the test subfolder. Normally, you don't care about that difference because tests based on the test-skeleton arrange the load path so that the location doesn't matter.

However, if your test opens a file or uses a script in the bin folder, the location *does* matter. For example, consider test code like this:

```
IO.read('programming-ruby-amazon-page.html')
```

That code assumes the test that contains it is running in the folder that contains the data. That can't always be true when the rakefile is outside that folder. Therefore, the S4TUtils module contains some utility methods to make tests location independent. They are as follows:

> ### Distributing with Gems
>
> RubyGems is a superior distribution method, built on top of
> setup.rb. The big advantage of RubyGems is that each gem
> knows its dependencies. When you install it, all the depen-
> dencies will be fetched too. There's no need for a third-party
> folder.
>
> I've chosen not to use RubyGems in this book's template
> project because I expect that most of your packages will
> depend on at least one in-house library. RubyGems can auto-
> matically install dependencies only if it can find them. That
> means you'd have to run a gems server on a machine in your
> company or put your gems on the http://rubyforge.org site. The
> first might be more work than you want to do, and the second
> is probably prohibited by your company.
>
> If you do want to distribute with gems, see http://docs.rubygems.
> org.

test(name)

> The correct name of file *name* in the test folder. It's typically used
> like this:
>
> ```
> IO.read(test('datafile'))
> ```

test_data(name)

> The correct name of file *name* in a data folder within the test folder.
> I like to separate the data from the tests, and putting them in a
> subfolder is a simple way to do it.

script(name)

> The correct name of file *name* in the bin folder. It's often used like
> this:
>
> ```
> title = 'ruby #{script('isbn-to-title.rb')} 0743292332'
> ```

Since these utilities have such common names, I worried that including
them whenever you includedS4tUtils would lead to name clashes. So I put
them in a nested module S4tUtils::TestUtil.[1] You can use its methods in
three ways:

---

1. You can find out about nested modules in Section 20.1, *Nested Modules*, on page 194.

```
include S4tUtils::TestUtil
... script('name') ...

include S4tUtils
... TestUtil.script('name') ...


... S4tUtils::TestUtil.script('name') ...
```

The utilities work wherever you use them because they depend on the constant PACKAGE_ROOT. It always names the folder that contains the rakefile (and the test folder). You can use that constant to write your own utilities.

19.8   Exercises

1. Add some Ruby files to default-project.

    a) Create a test file by copying test-skeleton. Remember that fast tests are expected to end in "tests.rb" and slow tests should end in "slowtests.rb". You'll need to decide whether your test should require only the file it's testing (a file within lib/default-project) or all the files (by requiring lib/default-project.rb). You'll also need to decide whether to include your module in the test class or spell out names fully (as DefaultProject::Thing). The skeleton shows you where to make those decisions.

    b) Type rake, and watch the test fail.

    c) Create a file in lib/default-project that will pass the test. You can use lib-skeleton as a model.

    d) If you want that file available to those who require the whole library, add the new file's name to lib/default-project.rb.

    e) Type rake again. (Note that you can type it in the lib folder; rake will still find the tests.) If the test doesn't pass, fix the code.

    f) In the bin folder, make a command-line script. You can use bin-skeleton as a template. As with the tests, you'll have to decide whether you want to include your module.

    g) Does the script work?

    h) Try typing this:

        prompt> rake install
        prompt> cd ..
        prompt> ruby -S your-command.rb

The cd is so that Ruby can't find the command by looking in the current folder. It has to search for the installed version.

i) Add a few lines of comment just before your new code in your new lib/default-project file. Type rake rdoc. Then, with your browser open doc/html/index.html. How does it look?

2. Convert the existing affinity-trip project into this new format. The easiest way to do that is to create a fresh project and start moving files into the appropriate places. My solution is in the s4t-affinity-trip folder in your workspace.

As usual, it's probably easiest to start with tests.

Put the new library code within an AffinityTrip module. Don't forget that you'll need to modify the test files to use that module.

In the implementation you're copying from, all the methods are inside the executable affinity-trip.rb script. You should move those out into the lib folder.

The old implementation has comments in it like these:

```
### Fetching Amazon book pages
### Scraping information out of Amazon book pages
### How to print
```

Making a note that the next group of methods are all related is one of the weaker grouping mechanisms. It's easy to put new methods in the wrong group. Putting the groups in separate files is stronger. Putting them all in a class is stronger still. Consider whether you want to split the single library file into two or more.

## Chapter 20

Ruby Facts: Modules

Names refer to Ruby objects. For example, ARGV names an array, String names a class, and puts names a method. A *namespace* is a collection of names. The *global namespace* is the one that contains all the usual Ruby names like ARGV, String, and puts.

namespace

global namespace

You can create another namespace within the global namespace with a module. The module in Figure 20.1, on the next page, contains four new names. They are the name of a class, the name of a string, the name of a *module method*, and the name of a *mixin method*. Module and mixin methods should remind you of the class and instance methods of Section 12.3, *Class Methods*, on page 126. (You'll find out about their connection, and why mixin methods are so named, in Section 23.3, *Modules Instead of Superclasses*, on page 240.)

module method

mixin method

When the four new names are created, they're not placed inside the global namespace. The name of the module is, though, and most of its interior names can be reached through its name.

To use a name within the module, you must *qualify* it with the name of the module:

qualify

```
irb(main):001:0> require 'some-module'   # run irb in code/module-facts
=> true
irb(main):002:0> SomeModule::Constant
=> "I am a constant."
irb(main):003:0> SomeModule::SomeClass.new.hello
=> "hi"
```

You can qualify the names of module methods in the same way:

```
irb(main):004:0> SomeModule::speak
=> "I am a module method."
```

code/module-facts/some-module.rb

```
module SomeModule

  class SomeClass
    def hello
      "hi"
    end
  end

  Constant = "I am a constant."

  def self.speak
    "I am a module method."
  end

  def speak
    "I am a mixin method."
  end

end
```

module-facts/some-module.rb

Figure 20.1: FOUR KINDS OF NAMES WITHIN A MODULE

Because that looks a bit odd, you can also use the dot notation to say, in effect, "send the speak message to SomeModule":

```
irb(main):005:0> SomeModule.speak
=> "I am a module method."
```

You cannot use the dot notation with constants or class names because a dot always means sending a message. So SomeModule.Constant would mean "send the message Constant to module SomeModule." That will fail because there's no method named Constant to receive the message.

The name of the mixin method cannot be reached from outside the module.

20.1 Nested Modules

You can place modules inside other modules, as in Figure 20.2, on the facing page. (Note that, as with classes, the second definition of a module just adds onto the first, so we're still working with the same SomeModule as before.)

```
code/module-facts/some-module.rb
module SomeModule
  module InnerModule
    Constant = "I am an inner constant."

    def self.speak
      "I am an inner module method."
    end

    def speak
      "I am an inner mixin method."
    end

    def SomeClass
      def hello
        "an inner hello"
      end
    end
  end
end
```
                                            module-facts/some-module.rb

Figure 20.2: NESTING MODULES

InnerModule makes no change to the global namespace. However, it does add itself to SomeModule's namespace. Objects inside it can be reached with doubly qualified names:

```
irb(main):006:0> SomeModule::InnerModule::Constant
=> "I am an inner constant."
```

20.2   Including Modules

When you include a module, you make some of its names available in the current namespace:

```
irb(main):007:0> include SomeModule
=> Object
irb(main):008:0> Constant
=> "I am a constant."
irb(main):009:0> speak
=> "I am a mixin method."
irb(main):010:0> SomeClass.new.hello
=> "hi"
irb(main):011:0> InnerModule
=> SomeModule::InnerModule
```

Notice that speak now refers to the mixin method, not the module method. You continue to get to the module method in the old way:

```
irb(main):012:0> SomeModule.speak
=> "I am a module method."
```

Although InnerModule is now in the namespace, its names are not. They need to be qualified with its name (but not with SomeModule):

```
irb(main):013:0> InnerModule::Constant
=> "I am an inner constant."
```

Name Clashes

Having included SomeModule, we can include another one, such as SomeModule::InnerModule. But notice that they share names. What happens?

```
irb(main):014:0> include InnerModule
=> Object
irb(main):015:0> Constant
=> "I am an inner constant."
irb(main):016:0> speak
=> "I am an inner mixin method."
```

The new names *silently* override the old ones. That could cause considerable confusion. Having a thorough test suite helps. If you run your tests frequently, they pass consistently, and then you add an include to some file and old tests suddenly fail, chances are you've overridden something.

In that case, stick to qualified names.

Nesting Is Different From Inclusion

An internal module has access to all the names in its "parent" module. Here's an example:

```
irb(main):017:0> module NewModule
irb(main):018:1>   Slithy = 'slithy'
irb(main):019:1>   module NewInnerModule
irb(main):020:2>     puts Slithy
irb(main):021:2>   end
irb(main):022:1> end
slithy
=> nil
```

However, a nested module *does not* have access to names included in its parent:

```
irb(main):023:0> module IncludedModule
irb(main):024:1>   IncludedConstant = 'hi'
irb(main):025:1> end
=> "hi"
irb(main):026:0> module NewModule
irb(main):027:1>   include IncludedModule  # include into outer module
irb(main):028:1>   module NewInnerModule
irb(main):029:2>     puts IncludedConstant   # This won't work.
irb(main):030:2>   end
irb(main):031:1> end
NameError: uninitialized constant NewModule::NewInnerModule::IncludedConstant
     from (irb):15
```

There's one exception. Names included in the global namespace are available everywhere:

```
irb(main):032:0> include IncludedModule   # include globally
=> Object
irb(main):033:0> module NewModule
irb(main):034:1>   module NewInnerModule
irb(main):035:2>     puts IncludedConstant   # This will now work
irb(main):036:2>   end
irb(main):037:1> end
hi
=> nil
```

20.3   Classes Are Modules

Classes are a kind of module. There are two key differences between them: modules do not respond to new (so you can't make instances), and you cannot include a class. However, the rules about qualifying names apply in the same way:

```
irb(main):038:0> class MyClass
irb(main):039:1>   Constant = "constant in class"
irb(main):040:1>
irb(main):041:1*   def self.reveal_constant
irb(main):042:2>     Constant
irb(main):043:2>   end
irb(main):044:1> end
=> nil
irb(main):045:0> MyClass::Constant
=> "constant in class"
irb(main):046:0> MyClass.reveal_constant
=> "constant in class"
irb(main):047:0> MyClass::reveal_constant
=> "constant in class"
```

One consequence of this similarity is potential confusion when you follow the rules of Chapter 19, *A Polished Script*, beginning on page 177, and put all of your package's code within a module. There's a temptation to suppose this would work:

```
module MyFinePackage
  include SomeOtherModule

  class FirstClass...
  class SecondClass...
end
```

Since classes are modules, what you learned in Section 20.2, *Nesting Is Different From Inclusion*, on page 196, applies. You cannot use unqualified names within FirstClass and SecondClass to refer to constants and methods named within SomeOtherModule.

You *can* use a qualified name. Suppose SomeOtherModule has a constant Constant. Because all the names in SomeOtherModule have been included in MyFinePackage, code within FirstClass or SecondClass can refer to it as MyFinePackage::Constant. The more common alternative is to include SomeOtherModule in each of the two classes.

The file code/module-facts/inclusion-locations.rb is a compact example of how different inclusion locations affect different naming locations.

Chapter 21

When Scripts Run into Problems

In Section 19.8, *Exercises*, on page 190, you created an executable script from the bin-template. At the end of the script, you might have seen this peculiar code:

`code/error-handling/bin/bin-skeleton`

```
with_pleasant_exceptions do
    # Your program here.
end
```

What's that about? To see, run this script:

`code/error-handling/bin/test-with.rb`

```
with_pleasant_exceptions do
    File.open("no-such-file")
end
```

You should see this:

```
prompt> ruby test-with.rb
No such file or directory - no-such-file
```

That's a reasonable error message. Now delete with_pleasant_exceptions, **do**, and **end**, leaving only the line that tries to openno-such-file. Run it again to see this:

```
prompt> ruby test-with.rb
test-with.rb:26:in 'initialize': No such file or directory - no-such-file  ↩
(Errno::ENOENT)
        from test-with.rb:26:in 'open'
        from test-with.rb:26
```

The method with_pleasant_exceptions somehow reduces a spew of error messages down to just the message about what went wrong. This chapter is about how that happens and why it's a sensible thing to do.

exceptions

In order to understand the "how," you'll need to learn about *exceptions* and learn more about blocks. That material is somewhat advanced; you may want to put it off until you're more familiar with Ruby. Even if you do, you should still read the next two sections, which will tell you how to make good use of with_pleasant_exceptions.

21.1 Use Exceptions to Report Problems

stack trace

After you changed test-with.rb, you saw what's often called a *stack trace*. It shows what methods were in progress at the moment the problem was detected. Figure 21.1, on the facing page, shows the same thing in a picture. Some method somewhere in Ruby sends the open message to the class File, causing the method of the same name to run. That method creates a File instance and sends it the initialize message.

Normally, the initialize method would open the file named by the initialize message's argument list and then return to File.open, which would then return to Ruby. But in this case, the file doesn't exist, so initialize *raises* an *exception*. That's like one of those peculiarities of quantum physics where an electron moves from one place to another without ever being in the space between. The exception goes straight from initialize back to Ruby, not stopping in open. So if open were going to do something after initialize returned, well, tough—that code will never run.

raises

exception

Like an electron (sort of), an exception is an object. In this case, it's an instance of Errno::ENOENT. (You won't be surprised, I bet, to read that the name has been traditional since before Ruby.) It contains two items: a message describing the problem and an array of lines describing the methods on the route to the point of the problem (that is, the stack trace). Ruby prints all that out and exits.

with_pleasant_exceptions interposes itself between Ruby and File.open as shown in Figure 21.2, on page 202. It handles the exception by printing only the message, not the stack trace. Then it returns to Ruby, which never knows an exception happened.

21.2 An Error-handling Strategy

Testers know that error handling is a good place to find bugs. It's hard to write good error-handling code. One difficulty is that the place in the code that raises the exception knows precisely what went wrong, but it doesn't know anything about the context—about *why* it was doing

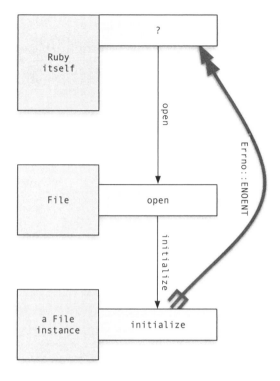

Figure 21.1: AN EXCEPTION BEING RAISED

what it did. It usually doesn't have the information to put things right. It often can't even produce an error message that makes sense to a user.

The code that rescues the exception might know the context, but it lacks details about what went wrong. Without the details, it might not be able to put things right. It often can't produce a helpful error message. Oh, it can say what went wrong in user terms, "sorry, I couldn't print that document," but it can't tell the user why not or what to do about it.

Experience tells us it's extremely hard to get the balance between detail and context right, so I propose you simply wrap the whole program in with_pleasant_exceptions. Don't try to help your user—it's too hard.

There is the matter of helping yourself, though. When you're trying to understand the cause of a problem, the stack trace can be a big help.

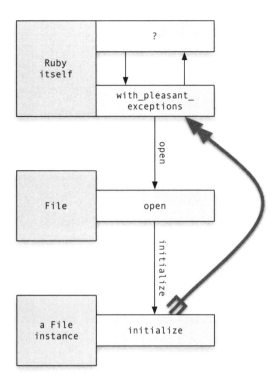

Figure 21.2: AN EXCEPTION BEING HANDLED

If you change the "with" in with_pleasant_exceptions to a "without", you'll get this output:

```
prompt> ruby test-without.rb
Note: exception handling turned off.
test-without.rb:27:in 'initialize': No such file or directory -  ↩
no-such-file (Errno::ENOENT)
    from test-without.rb:27:in 'open'
    from test-without.rb:27
    from test-without.rb:26:in 'without_pleasant_exceptions'
    from test-without.rb:26
```

21.3   Your Exception-handling Options

To understand how with_pleasant_exceptions works, you first need to know how exception handling works. Look at this code:

```
code/error-handling/bin/begin-end.rb
```

```
begin
  File.open("no-such-file")
  puts "You will never see me."
rescue Exception => ex
  puts ex.message
end

puts "End of script"
```

The output looks like that from with_pleasant_exceptions:

```
prompt> ruby begin-end.rb
No such file or directory - no-such-file
End of script
```

Any code between the **begin** and **rescue** markers that raises an exception will have that exception *rescued* by the **rescue** statement. It makes the local variable ex name the Exception object, and then the body of the **rescue** prints the error message. After that, the script continues after the **end**.

rescued

The Scope of an Exception Handler

Just now, I referred to "any code *between* the **begin** and **rescue** markers. . . ." Just what "between" means is a little subtle. It means not only the lines you see between the two markers; it also includes any methods used by those lines, any methods used in turn by *those*, and so on. Here's an example:

```
code/error-handling/bin/nesting.rb
```

```
def level3
  File.open("no-such-file")
end

def level2
  level3
end

begin              # line 11
  level2
rescue Exception => ex   # line 13
  puts ex.message
end
```

That produces the same error message, even though the File.open does not physically appear between line 11 and line 13. It doesn't even have to be in the same file. The net result of this so-called dynamic scoping is that any exception raised anywhere in this script will be rescued by line 13.

Raising Exceptions

Here's the simplest way to raise an exception in your own code:

`code/error-handling/bin/raising.rb`

```
def convert_to_integer(string)
  unless /^-?\d+$/ =~ string
❶    raise "'#{string}' is not an integer."
  end
  string.to_i
end

begin
❷  raise "An argument is required." unless ARGV[0]
  puts convert_to_integer(ARGV[0])
rescue Exception => ex
  puts ex.message
end
```

Exceptions are raised at ❶ and ❷. The string argument to **raise** is what message will return.

If you want, you can name the exception to be raised:

`code/error-handling/bin/raising2.rb`

```
def convert_to_integer(string)
  unless /^-?\d+$/ =~ string
❶    raise RuntimeError.new("'#{string}' is not an integer.")
  end
  string.to_i
end
```

You might notice that we're *raising* RuntimeError but *rescuing* Exception. RuntimeError is a particular kind of Exception. There are other kinds. For example, File.open raised Errno::ENOENT. The rescue Exception statement rescues all kinds of exceptions.[1]

---

1. I'm being deliberately a bit vague in the terminology here. You'll learn about super-classes and subclasses in Chapter 22, *Frameworks: Scripting by Filling in Blanks*, beginning on page 213. Once you've understood that, you'll understand this more exact description: Exception is the superclass for all exceptions. A rescue clause that mentions *SomeExceptionClass* will rescue any exception object that's an instance of that class or any of its subclasses.

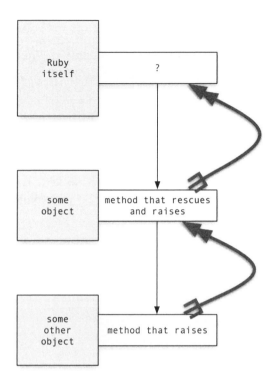

Figure 21.3: AN EXCEPTION BEING RERAISED

Reraising Exceptions

A rescue clause can raise the exception again, or it can raise another exception. That looks like Figure 21.3.

One reason to reraise an exception is when a method somewhere in the middle can do something useful in response to the exception but cannot handle it completely. So it does what it can do and reraises to let some other method handle the rest. For example:

code/error-handling/bin/logger.rb

```
def owned_open(owner, name)
  File.open(name)
rescue Errno::ENOENT => ex
  log(owner, ex)
  raise
end
```

Ensuring Actions

Suppose you were writing a reservation system for test machines. A bit of that code might look like this:

```
machine = reserver.reserve(machine_name)
test_runner.download(tests, machine)
test_runner.run
reserver.release(machine)
```

It would be bad if an exception in the download process caused the program to exit without releasing a reserved machine. You can avoid that like this:

```
begin
  reserver.reserve(machine)
  test_runner.download(tests, machine)
  test_runner.run
ensure
  reserver.release(machine)
end
```

The code between **ensure** and **end** will be executed whether or not an exception was raised.

21.4   Methods That Use Blocks

We keep seeing a pattern:

```
array.each do | element |
  ...
end

File.open(name) do | open_file |
  ...
end

with_pleasant_exceptions do
  ...
end
```

In all cases, we have a method that uses both its arguments (if any) and a block. The block contains code that does some work. The method doesn't know what the work is—it just executes the block, possibly passing in arguments.

Here's the simplest possible example of such a method:

code/error-handling/bin/block-examples.rb

```
def simple
  yield
  puts 'block done.'
end
```

yield simply gives over control to the block. Control returns to simple once the block is done. For, example:

```
irb(main):001:0> require 'block-examples'
=> true
irb(main):002:0> simple do
irb(main):003:1*   puts "In block"
irb(main):004:1> end
In block
block done.
=> nil
```

If yield is given an argument, it's passed along to the block, like this:

code/error-handling/bin/block-examples.rb

```
def with_arg(arg)
  yield arg
end
```

```
irb(main):010:0> with_arg(5) do | given |
irb(main):011:1*   given * given
irb(main):012:1> end
=> 25
```

Notice that **yield** returns whatever the block returns. (In this case, what **yield** returns is then immediately returned by with_arg.)

With what you now know of exceptions and blocks, you're ready to understand the implementation of with_pleasant_exceptions:

code/error-handling/bin/with-pleasant-exceptions.rb

```
def with_pleasant_exceptions
  begin
    yield
❶ rescue SystemExit
    raise
❷ rescue Exception => ex
❸   $stderr.puts(ex.message)
  end
end
```

There are two new bits behind the scenes. Ruby implements the exit method by raising an exception of class SystemExit. The **rescue** statement at ❶ catches that exception before the one at ❷ gets it. It then reraises it. That has the effect of bypassing the code that prints an error message. Otherwise, the program would print an "error message" about exiting, which would not be useful.

stderr

stdout

The other new bit is $stderr at ❸. Programs have two types of output: error output and ordinary output. When people speak of them, they refer to "standard err" and "standard out"; they're often written *stderr* and *stdout*. In Ruby, $stderr refers to the default destination for standard error; $stdout does the same for standard output. By using $stderr, we print exception output to standard error. Normally, stderr and stdout appear mixed together, but it's possible to send them to different places.

21.5 Exercises

Solutions to these exercises are in folder exercise-solutions/error-handling.

1. raising.rb (shown in Section 21.3, *Raising Exceptions*, on page 204) complains when no arguments are given, but not when there are too many. Change it so it complains about both, and consolidate all the error checking in a single method, check_args.

   The method you write should pass the tests in exercise-1-tests.rb. That file will show you how to test whether exceptions are raised.

2. Here's an example of Ruby's while method:

```
irb(main):020:0> while count > 0 do
irb(main):021:1*   puts count
irb(main):022:1>   count -= 1
irb(main):023:1> end
5
4
3
2
1
=> nil
```

   Using **while**, add a method my_each to the Array class. It is to duplicate the behavior of each well enough to pass the tests in exercise-solutions/error-handling/exercise-2-tests.rb.

3. In this exercise, you'll change a script that pretends to reserve a machine for testing. Here's the output from a test failure:

```
prompt> ruby exercise-3-start.rb
Reserved Mycroft.
Downloading test1 to Mycroft...
Downloading test2 to Mycroft...
Downloading test3 to Mycroft...
Running test1...
Running test2...
Running test3...
Test failure: network down
Released Mycroft.
```

Here's a failure to reserve the machine:

```
prompt> ruby exercise-3-start.rb any-old-arg-will-do
Test failure: Could not reserve Mycroft.
```

Here is the current script:

```
code/exercise-solutions/error-handling/exercise-3-start.rb
begin
  machine = reserver.reserve('Mycroft')
  test_runner.download(tests, machine)
  test_runner.run
rescue Exception => ex
  puts "Test failure: #{ex.message}"
ensure
❶  reserver.release(machine) if machine
end
```

That should look familiar except for the trailing **if** on line ❶. If an exception is raised in reserver.reserve, machine will be nil. If so, there's nothing to release.

For this exercise, convert that code so that the following works when executed with the same command-line commands as previously.

```
code/exercise-solutions/error-handling/exercise-3.rb
reserver.reserve('Mycroft') do | machine |
  test_runner.download(tests, machine)
  test_runner.run
end
```

In other words, move the exception handling and use of release into reserve.

Part IV

The Accomplished Scripter

Chapter 22

Frameworks:
Scripting by Filling in Blanks

In this chapter, we'll look at a watchdog script that tells you about the results of long-running tests and programs. It's named watchdog.rb. Figure 22.1, on the next page, shows you an instant message from it, and Figure 22.2, on page 215, shows a mail message.

It happens that the heart of watchdog—the sending of alerts via various routes—is pretty simple. We create instances of classes other people wrote, we send them the right messages with the right arguments, and they do all the work. There's not much new there.

There's another way to reuse people's work, though: *frameworks*. A framework is usually a collection of partially completed classes. You make your script by defining methods to complete the classes. Since most of the work is done already, frameworks let you easily write scripts that you'd otherwise not attempt. This chapter is mostly about the Ruby mechanisms that let you use frameworks.

frameworks

Frameworks are not without their problems. They can be hard to learn. They force you to look at a solution in a certain way, which may not be appropriate for your task. They can make understanding the program harder, because so much happens behind the scenes—the actual script is a collection of snippets without any obvious connective tissue linking them together.

Fortunately, the same Ruby mechanisms frameworks rely on are also useful when you want to make small extensions to your old scripts, so they're well worth learning on their own.

Figure 22.1: A WATCHDOG INSTANT MESSAGE

22.1 Using the watchdog Script

You install watchdog in the usual way: ruby setup.rb all. You'll notice that watchdog comes with a vast array of third-party files. They do almost all the actual work.

By default, watchdog is configured to print its results to the terminal, mail them, and send them to a Jabber instant message service.[1] As delivered, it's not configured for your Jabber or email server, so only the first will work. If you try watchdog, you'll see results like those in Figure 22.3, on page 217. (The actual error messages will probably differ.)

---

1. Jabber is one of several instant message services. It's a good one to use for software development because you can run a Jabber server within your corporate network. A variety of free Jabber servers are available. I use Wildfire (http://www.jivesoftware.org/wildfire/) because it has a nice administrative interface and is extremely easy to set up, provided you already have Java on your machine.

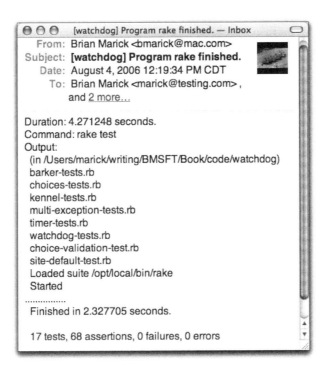

Figure 22.2: A WATCHDOG MAIL MESSAGE

Configuring watchdog

To get use out of watchdog, you'll need to configure it to match your environment. One (silly) way to do that would be use command-line arguments:

```
prompt> ruby -S watchdog.rb --no-mail --no-terminal ↩
--jabber-account  watchdog@mobile-marick.local/bark ↩
--jabber-to marick@mobile-marick.local/iChat ↩
--jabber-password password rake test
```

That instructs watchdog to use only Jabber, and it tells watchdog everything it needs for communication with the Jabber server. Even more command-line options are needed before watchdog can send email.

You can find a complete list of options with the --help option. (You'll find that many Ruby scripts respond to --help.)

```
prompt> ruby -S watchdog.rb --help
```

Command-line options usually override defaults set elsewhere. One place to set defaults is in a configuration file in your home folder.[2] On Windows, the configuration file is named watchdog.xml. On Unix-like systems, it's named .watchdog.xml, with a leading period. That hides the file so that it doesn't clutter up your normal folder view. The configuration file equivalent of the previous command-line arguments would be this:[3]

`code/watchdog/share/jabber-only.watchdog.xml`

```
<watchdog>
  <command-line>false</command-line>
  <jabber>true</jabber>
  <mail>false</mail>

  <jabber-account>watchdog@mobile-marick.local/bark</jabber-account>
  <jabber-to>marick@mobile-marick.local/iChat</jabber-to>
  <jabber-password>password</jabber-password>
</watchdog>
```

Given that, the previous command-line invocation can be written as:

prompt> ruby -S watchdog.rb rake test

That's rather more convenient. Again, there are more configuration file options. You can find all of them in code/watchdog/share/all-config-file-choices.xml. If you have a team of people who'll be using watchdog, it may be more convenient still to set up the configuration once and for all, rather than have each person use her own configuration file. You can do that by editing watchdog/lib/watchdog/site-defaults.rb.[4]

---

2. Your home folder is usually named by the HOME or USERPROFILE environment variable. On Unix and Mac OS X, one of those will almost always be set for you. On Windows, the home folder might be identified by two environment variables: HOMEDRIVE and HOMEPATH. If not, set HOME yourself. If watchdog can't find HOME any of those ways, it will guess that it's in / (C:\ on Windows). ruby watchdog.rb -c will tell you where watchdog is looking.

3. The configuration file is written in XML. XML is rather unfashionable in the Ruby world because it's too verbose and cluttered to be easy to read. Ruby scripts are often configured with YAML, an easier-to-read alternative, or in Ruby itself (so that configuring a script is merely a matter of requiring the configuration file). I chose to use XML so I could use the code that reads the configuration file as an example in the *Testing with XML and XPath* supplement.

4. Note that I make no particular attempt to hide passwords from prying eyes. That's because I assume (1) that you're using shared team or company servers, so everyone should know the password anyway, and (2) watchdog will be run from other scripts (like build scripts) where there is no user interaction. If you want to make watchdog ask for a password (and not echo what you type), feel free. You'll want to use the Readline library. That library isn't installed on all systems, though.

```
prompt> ruby -S watchdog.rb rake test
  Program rake finished.
  Duration: 4.072555 seconds.
  Command: rake test
  Output:
    (in /Users/marick/writing/BMSFT/Book/code/watchdog)
    barker-tests.rb
    choices-tests.rb
    multi-exception-tests.rb
    timer-tests.rb
    watchdog-tests.rb
    Loaded suite /opt/local/bin/rake
    Started
    ............
    Finished in 2.327612 seconds.

    13 tests, 54 assertions, 0 failures, 0 errors
Complaint from jabber: Client authentication failed
    (Jabber::AuthenticationFailure)
Complaint from mail: execution expired (Timeout::Error)
```

Figure 22.3: USING WATCHDOG

The UserChoices Framework

watchdog uses a framework that I'll call UserChoices, after its main class. By filling in that framework's blanks, you can let users of your scripts make choices on the command line, make choices in configuration files, or set environment variables. It's that framework that we'll be exploring in this chapter.

But first, you need some background.

22.2 Inheritance

We've actually been using a framework since Chapter 7, *The Churn Project: Writing Scripts without Fuss*, beginning on page 59: Test::Unit. We never wrote any Ruby code to choose tests to run, to run them, to run setup and teardown[5] before and after each of them, or to collect results. It all just happened. All we had to do was fill in Test::Unit's blanks with test methods.

---

5. See Section B.6, *Exercise 2*, on page 274, for a description of setup and teardown.

inheritance

This all works because of *inheritance*. Inheritance lets us point at a class and say, "this class is just like that one, except. . . ." Every one of our tests is in a class defined like this:

`code/inheritance/inheritance.rb`

```
require 'test/unit'

class Inheritor < Test::Unit::TestCase
  def test_announcer
    puts "This class inherits TestCase's behavior."
  end
end
```

It's the less-than sign in the **class** line that tells Ruby Inheritor is just like TestCase except for explicitly specified differences. In this case, the difference is that Inheritor has one test method while TestCase has none.

superclass

People say that one class "inherits from" another, "subclasses" it, "extends" it, or "descends" from it. You can extend any class you want; there's nothing special about how you define the *superclass* (or "parent," or "base class," or. . .). You can even inherit from Ruby classes. If you want a class that's just like a Hash except. . . , just type this:

```
irb(main):001:0> class MyHash < Hash
irb(main):002:1>   def zorch  # I like this better...
irb(main):003:2>     self.clear
irb(main):004:2>   end
irb(main):005:1> end
=> nil
irb(main):006:0> m = MyHash.new
=> {}
irb(main):007:0> m[1] = 2
=> 2
irb(main):008:0> m
=> {1=>2}
irb(main):009:0> m.zorch
=> {}
irb(main):010:0> m
=> {}
```

In fact, every class inherits from the Ruby class Object. That's where a lot of default behavior is defined. Type this:

```
irb(main):012:0> puts Object.instance_methods
```

You'll see a long list of methods, including ones you recognize, such as send, inspect, and ==. Those are all methods that no class need define; it will inherit them.

Overriding Methods

So far, we've only added new behavior. A subclass can also change old behavior by *overriding* a method it would otherwise inherit. It does that by defining a method with the same name.

overriding

For example, TestCase defines a run method that runs all the test methods in the class. We can override it to do something else:

code/inheritance/override.rb

```
require 'test/unit'

class MyNonTest < Test::Unit::TestCase
  def run(*ignore_all_arguments)
    puts "Nothing will be run because I override my ancestor."
  end

  def test_not
    puts "I will not be run."
  end
end
```

Notice that run uses a rest argument. That's because I don't care if it has an argument or how many arguments it has. We've now overridden the whole point of Test::Unit:

```
prompt> ruby override.rb
Loaded suite override
Started
Nothing will be run because I override my ancestor.

Finished in 0.001085 seconds.

0 tests, 0 assertions, 0 failures, 0 errors
```

Augmenting a Superclass

Quite often, you do not want to completely override a superclass's method; you just want to add a little to it. You do that with the **super** sort-of-message. **super** makes Ruby send the same message to the superclass as it sent to this class.

So here's how to augment run:

```
code/inheritance/extend.rb
```

```ruby
require 'test/unit'

class MyExtendedTest < Test::Unit::TestCase
  def run(*args)
    puts "About to run."
    super
    puts "Done running."
  end

  def test_extension
    puts "I will be run verbosely."
  end
end
```

It happens that the superclass's run method takes a single argument, the object that collects test results. When used like this, with no arguments, **super** will hand the superclass version of the method the same arguments as were given to the subclass version.

(That happens no matter how the arguments are defined; the rest argument has nothing to do with it.)

Sometimes, the subclass method will have a different argument list. In that case, **super** should be given an explicit argument list, like ❶ in the following:

```
code/inheritance/super-with-arg.rb
```

```ruby
class Parent
  def arglist_taker(one_arg)
    puts "Parent: I was given #{one_arg}."
  end
end

class Child < Parent
  def arglist_taker(one_arg, another)
    puts "Child: I have two arguments: #{one_arg} and #{another}."
❶    super(one_arg)
  end
end
```

If the subclass method wants to provide *no* arguments to the superclass version, it can't simply use **super** with nothing after it (since that passes on all the arguments).

Instead, it has to follow **super** with an empty pair of parentheses.

code/inheritance/super-no-arg.rb

```
class Parent
  def arglist_taker(*args)
    puts "Parent: I was given #{args.inspect}."
  end
end

class Child < Parent
  def arglist_taker(one_arg, another)
    puts "Child: I have two arguments: #{one_arg} and #{another}."
    super()
  end
end
```

❶

Instance Variables

An instance variable mentioned in a superclass is also available in the subclass. That's because an instance of a subclass is a single object. It happens to be described in two different classes, with different names, but it's still one object being described. So any mention of a particular instance variable, whether it be in the superclass or subclass, must be the same one.

In Figure 22.4, on the following page, we see how instance variables are "shared." It also shows that any particular transaction with an object can be happily oblivious of whether it's using superclass methods or subclass methods.

A TimingNoteTaker is created at ❽. That subclass doesn't define initialize, so the inherited one at ❶ is used. initialize creates the instance variable @commentary and gives it a starting value. When the new object is sent the timestamp message (at ❾), Ruby finds the corresponding method in the subclass (at ❹). Were there one in the superclass, it would be ignored.

The first line of timestamp sends two messages (at ❺). (Those messages are sent to self, as is any message without an explicit receiver.) One, boundary, is defined in the subclass (at ❼). The other, note, is defined in the superclass (at ❷). That doesn't make any difference; Ruby finds them both. Both timestamp and note refer to @commentary, an instance variable of self. That is, both methods use the same variable to update the same array.

When outside code sends the instance the note message, at ❿, Ruby again finds the corresponding method in the superclass.

code/inheritance/instance.rb

```ruby
class NoteTaker
  attr_reader :commentary

❶ def initialize(title)
    @commentary = [title]
  end

❷ def note(notation)
❸   @commentary << "Note: #{notation}"
  end
end

class TimingNoteTaker < NoteTaker

❹ def timestamp
❺   note(boundary('-'))
❻   @commentary << Time.now.to_s
  end

❼ def boundary(character)
    character * 20
  end
end

❽ child = TimingNoteTaker.new("May 1")
❾ child.timestamp
❿ child.note("coffee")
  child.note("bagels")
  child.timestamp
  child.note('email')
  puts child.commentary
```

inheritance/instance.rb

Figure 22.4: SUPERCLASSES AND SUBCLASSES SHARE INSTANCE VARI-ABLES

22.3 Gathering User Choices

watchdog has two jobs: it has to discover a user's choices (from the command line or configuration file), and it has to act on them. Let's start with discovery which uses the four classes shown in Figure 22.5, on the next page. The framework has many classes, but the figure shows only the three a user of the framework has to care about. They're the top ones. The class on the bottom (marked with a dashed border) is a subclass that completes the framework (fills in the blanks).

To understand the subclass, you first have to understand how the Command class orchestrates the discovery of user choices. I'll explain that with the following code. It's an abbreviated version of the real Command class that can be found in code/user-choices/lib/user-choices/command.rb.

```
class Command

  attr_reader :user_choices

  def initialize
    builder = ChoicesBuilder.new
❶    add_sources(builder)
❷    add_choices(builder)
    @user_choices = builder.build
❸    postprocess_user_choices
  end

❹  def add_sources(builder); subclass_responsibility; end
❺  def add_choices(builder); subclass_responsibility; end

❻  def postprocess_user_choices
  end
```

❶   add_sources tells a ChoicesBuilder object where to look for user choices. In watchdog, that's first in the configuration file and then in the command's argument list on the command line.

❷   add_choices tells the builder what user choices a source may contain: what tags may appear in the configuration file and which command-line options are allowed.

❸   As you'll see, the builder does a certain amount of error checking, and it can convert some of the string-valued choices into integers or other classes. postprocess_user_choices is for all the error checking and conversions that the builder can't do.

There's nothing obvious about the message sends at ❶, ❷, or ❸ to tell you that the subclass has to define those methods. The documentation

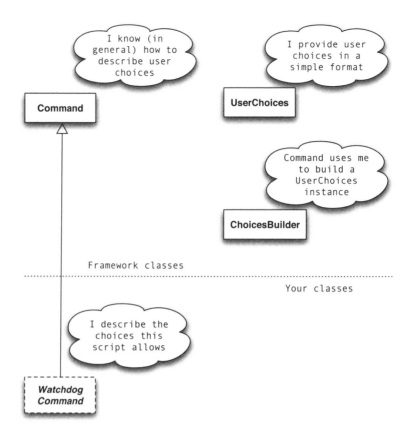

Figure 22.5: CLASSES THAT DISCOVER USER CHOICES

tells you that. I've also made the code give you a broad hint. Lines ❹ and ❺ are defined to use a method, subclass_responsibility, that doesn't exist. If the subclass doesn't redefine add_sources, any attempt to create a new instance will yield an error message like this:

```
NameError: undefined local variable or method 'subclass_responsibility' ↩
for main:Object
```

The mention of "subclass responsibility" is my way of hinting at the underlying problem. I didn't need to define add_sources and add_choices in the superclass. If I had left them out, the attempt to create an instance would yield a similar message:

```
NoMethodError: undefined method 'add_sources' for main:Object
```

I think my way is better because it's more explicit.

At line ❺, postprocess_user_choices is defined a little differently: as a method that does nothing. That means a subclass doesn't have to define that method. If it doesn't, nothing will happen. But the subclass can define it as code that manipulates the @user_choices object that initialize creates.

The Blank-filling Methods

This section will be a brief introduction to how a script uses UserChoices. For more details, I recommend the documentation in the user-choices package (see code/user-choices/doc/html/index.html) and—especially—the examples in the examples folder.

Plugging in is done by subclassing Command and overriding the three choice-handling methods:

```
class WatchdogCommand < Command
  def add_sources...
  def add_choices...
  def postprocess_user_choices...
end
```

add_sources

`code/watchdog/lib/watchdog/choices.rb`

```
def add_sources(builder)
  builder.add_source(PosixCommandLineChoices, :usage,
      "Usage: ruby #{$0} [options] program args...",
      "Site-wide defaults are noted below.",
      "Override them in the '#{RC_FILE}' file in your home folder.")
❶ builder.add_source(XmlConfigFileChoices, :from_file, RC_FILE)
end
```

Each source of configuration information (command line, configuration file, or others) is added to the builder via the builder's add_source method. Each source takes priority over the sources that follow it. So, for example, choices made on the command line take precedence over choices made in the configuration file.

add_source's first argument is a class that processes choices from some source. The second argument is the name of the class method used to create an instance of the class, and remaining arguments are treated as that method's arguments. The builder, then, transforms line ❶ into, in effect, this:

```
XmlConfigFileChoices.from_file(RC_FILE)
```

It then stashes the resulting instance away for later use.

add_choices

`code/watchdog/lib/watchdog/choices.rb`

```
def add_choices(builder)
  builder.add_choice(:jabber,
              :type => :boolean,
              :default => DEFAULT_JABBER) { | command_line |
    command_line.uses_switch('-j', "–jabber",
                  "Control IM notification.",
                  "Defaults to #{DEFAULT_JABBER}.")
  }

  builder.add_choice(:mail,
              :type => :boolean,
              :default => DEFAULT_MAIL) { | command_line |
    command_line.uses_switch('-m', "–mail",
                  "Control mail notification.",
                  "Defaults to #{DEFAULT_MAIL}.")
  }
```

The builder is then told about each possible user choice via a series of add_choice messages. The first, for example, tells the builder that each source should be able to supply the :jabber choice, which is either true or false. If no choice is made in any source, the default from site-defaults.rb is used.

Although XmlConfigFileChoices can figure out for itself that the choice :jabber should be specified with a *<jabber>* tag, the command line requires more flexibility.

For example, it's typical for frequently used choices to have both a long (--jabber) and short (-j) form. The code can't guess which choices are frequently used, so you have to tell it. Further, each choice should provide documentation to be printed when the --help option is given.

The builder handles the add_choice message by passing along appropriately tailored messages to each Choices object, but you don't need to care about that.

postprocess_user_choices

After add_choices returns, the WatchdogCommand asks the builder to spring into action. It asks each source to collect the user's choices, merges the results together, uses defaults if necessary, and converts from Strings to other classes if desired. The resulting UserChoices object (a subclass of Hash) is named by the instance variable @user_choices.

Once @user_choices is ready, postprocess_user_choices does any remaining setup. The bit I show next is something of an aside: if the user selected the --choices command-line option, the program should print a list of the values of all possible choices. (Try it and see).

code/watchdog/lib/watchdog/choices.rb

```
def postprocess_user_choices
  if @user_choices[:choices]
    puts "Choices gathered from all sources:"
    pp @user_choices
    puts "Looking for configuration information in:"
    puts File.join(S4tUtils.find_home, RC_FILE)
  end
```

You can see how @user_choices is treated just like a hash.

Note the useful utility method pp. The name is short for "prettyprint." It prints objects like hashes and arrays in a nicely indented form that makes them easier to read. You need to require 'pp' before using it.

Doing the Work

I didn't choose the name Command for the template class at random. In the jargon, a Command object is one that separates the decision about what should be done from the decision about *when* it should be done. A program creates a Command object (with new) when it knows something should (eventually) be done. It uses the object (by sending it execute) when "eventually" arrives. This separation has a number of advantages in larger programs.[6] This particular script doesn't make use of the potential separation, though. It executes the command as soon as it creates it. (See ❺ in Figure 22.6, on page 229).[7]

---

6. Here's one. Suppose that you want to implement multilevel undo. Make every Command object's execute method record what's needed to undo what it just did. Add an undo method that uses that record. Change the program so that it stores each Command it executes in an array. When the user chooses to undo using a menu item or keystroke, pop the last Command off the array and send it the undo message.

7. I've separated the WatchdogCommand class into two files. watchdog/lib/watchdog/ choices.rb contains the WatchdogCommand code that handles user choices, while watchdog/bin/watchdog.rb contains the WatchdogCommand code that watches programs and informs users. Usually, two sets of methods with completely different responsibilities are a sign that you need two classes, not one. That might be true in this case. That's actually the way I started, but it seemed to work better when I combined them. It would be an interesting exercise to separate them again and see if it works out better now.

The execute method is the one that does the work of the Command. It's defined at line ❶. execute uses a handy method time (defined in watchdog/lib/watchdog/timer.rb) to time the execution of any block. time returns an array of two elements. The first is how long the block took; the second is the result of the block (in this case, the output from the command). Notice (on ❷) that you can assign an array to several variables at once. Each variable gets one of the elements of the array.[8]

The command itself is run using backticks (❸). You saw backticks earlier on page 77, but there's one small addition. A backtick returns only standard output in its string. Standard error will continue to its default destination (usually the terminal window). The notation 2>&1 tells the command line to send standard error to the same place as standard output (so it will appear in the Ruby string).

The @kennel (❹) is an object that was created in postprocess_user_choices. Chapter 23, *Discovery Is Safer Than Creation*, beginning on page 231, explains that creation in detail. Here, it's doing the work of sending results to the selected destinations.

---

8. If there are more elements than variables, the last variable gets an array of all the remaining elements. If there are fewer elements, the extra variables get nil.

```
code/watchdog/bin/watchdog.rb
class WatchdogCommand < Command

  def command_string(command_to_watch =
                  @user_choices[:command_to_watch])
    command_to_watch.join(' ')
  end

  def command_name(command_to_watch = @user_choices[:command_to_watch])
    progname = if command_to_watch[0] == 'ruby'
              command_to_watch[1]
            else
              command_to_watch[0]
            end
    File.basename(progname)
  end

  def message(duration, text)
    [
      "Duration: #{duration} seconds.",
      "Command: #{command_string}",
      "Output:",
      text.indent(2),
    ].join("\n")
  end

❶  def execute
❷    duration, text = Watchdog.time {
❸      `#{self.command_string} 2>&1`
    }
    title = "Program #{self.command_name} finished."
❹    @kennel.bark(title, message(duration, text))
  end

end

if $0 == __FILE__
  with_pleasant_exceptions do
❺    WatchdogCommand.new.execute
  end
end
```

watchdog/bin/watchdog.rb

Figure 22.6: WATCHDOG'S WATCHING CODE

## Chapter 23

Discovery Is Safer Than Creation

The UserChoices framework is a somewhat elaborate one. You may never create one with as many classes as it has. (Most of them are behind the scenes.) You're more likely to create one or two superclasses that you'll use as you adapt your script to new or expanded purposes. This chapter is about how to do that.

Figure 23.1, on the next page, shows a simple framework with two classes, one of which leaves blanks to be filled in with subclasses.[1]

This chapter illustrates my most important advice about frameworks: *be intensely skeptical of any urge to spend time today designing and scripting a framework that will be useful next month.* Instead, write code that solves today's problem. Tomorrow, extend the code to solve tomorrow's problem. With every extension, keep the code clean enough that it's never hard to work with. The main trick is to be ruthless about removing duplication. One way of doing that is to take two related classes and *extract a superclass* from them. When you run into next *extract a superclass* week's problem, perhaps you can solve it with a class that inherits from that superclass. Where the inheritance is awkward, adjust the super-class to make it better. At some point, you'll find that you've evolved one or more superclasses competent to handle everything the world throws at them. Presto! A framework.

---

1. Some would say this is too simple to be a real framework. I'm happy to call it something else. The idea matters more than the name.

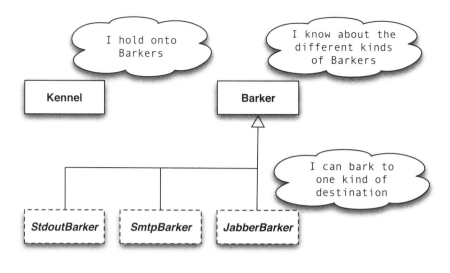

Figure 23.1: THE CLASS STRUCTURE I DISCOVERED

23.1 The Story of Barker

I did not start with any of the classes in Figure 23.1. The WatchdogCommand's execute method at first just called a simple method in the same class. It was named send, and it sent mail to a hard-coded address.

A hard-coded address wouldn't work if I were demoing watchdog on someone else's machine, so I used UserChoices to let people customize choices like the SMTP[2] host. When I added choices, I had to validate them (to check, for example, that there was at least one To address). That seemed to belong in a separate method.

Now I had two methods that were about something—email—that nothing else in the WatchdogCommand class was about. That's often a sign that there's a new class struggling to get out.

Actually, there was something else in the class that was about email. It was inside the execute method:

```
send_email(subject, body) if @user_choices[:mail]
```

---

2. SMTP stands for Simple Mail Transfer Protocol. It defines the rules that one computer uses to send mail to another.

WatchdogCommand knew when email should be sent. If I created a new class for sending email, probably objects of that class should take responsibility for knowing whether the user wants email. So I should move the **if** inside of the send_email method.

I didn't actually make a new class until I finished the code that sent Jabber messages. Now I had three chunks of code with more or less separate responsibilities: one chunk about mail, one about instant messaging, and one about everything else.

So I pulled out the first two chunks of code into their own classes. Because of the name of the script (watchdog), I decided to call them "barkers" and give them a bark method.

They had code in common. For example, to know what the user wanted, they needed a UserChoices object. It was passed into the new method of the two Barker classes:

```
code/watchdog/lib/watchdog/barkers.rb
```
```
def initialize(user_choices = {})
  @user_choices = user_choices
```

Since that code was identical in the two classes, I was inspired to create the Barker superclass and put the initialize method there. initialize also seemed like it would be a good place to initiate validation, so I had it send a validate message to itself:

```
code/watchdog/lib/watchdog/barkers.rb
```
```
def initialize(user_choices = {})
  @user_choices = user_choices
  @errors = self.validate
end
```

The two different subclasses would each implement validate appropriately. At first, there was no version of validate in Barker itself. That made Barker what's called an *abstract superclass.*

abstract superclass

Any attempt to create a Barker would have led to a *no such method 'validate'* error. Later, I created a test subclass of Barker and was surprised by that error. So I created a default version of validate that returns an empty list of errors:

```
code/watchdog/lib/watchdog/barkers.rb
```
```
def validate; []; end
```

> ∖∕∕
> ⸰ᵕ⸰ **Joe Asks...**
> ᵕ
> <u>**You Expect Me to Believe It Went This Smoothly?**</u>
>
> Well, no. This is the general direction I went. I'm leaving out
> the mistaken side trips, the course corrections, and the plain
> stupid mistakes. What matters is that none of those was a
> disaster, because I was moving in small steps, supported by
> tests.

At this point, my WatchdogCommand code used an array of Barkers.[3] It
looked like this:

```
barkers = []
JabberBarker.new(@user_choices).invite_into(barkers)
SmtpBarker.new(@user_choices).invite_into(barkers)
```

Inside invite_into, I had each Barker decide whether it wanted to be in
the list. It would decline the invitation if it had validation errors or the
user didn't want its kind of message. That way, the WatchdogCommand
had no responsibility for knowing which Barkers were being used: it just
went down the barkers list and told each one that had ended up there
to bark.

However, annoyingly, WatchdogCommand still had the responsibility for
knowing which Barkers might be in the list (since it had to know all
their names to invite them). That meant every time I invented a new
kind of Barker, I had to remember to add a single line of code in the
WatchdogCommand. Ick.

Who should have responsibility of keeping track of all the Barkers? How
about the Barker class itself? (After all, don't you have responsibility for
knowing who your own children are?)

After arranging that, the code looked something like this, which will be
explained in Section 23.2, *An Example*, on page 236:

```
barkers = []
Barker::Subclasses.each do | barker_class |
  barker_class.new(@user_choices).invite_into(barkers)
end
```

---

3. Note that when I'm referring to objects that could be either JabberBarkers or SmtpBarkers,
I refer to them by the name of the superclass, Barker.

I then decided to convert the array into a Kennel class. I confess that I mainly did it because I thought it was cute to have a Kennel full of Barkers.[4] Although that new class was premature, it was probably justified after I decided to make the different Barkers bark simultaneously, rather than one after the other. That required some tricky code, and it's right to isolate it in its own class. That way, someone who doesn't have to care about it doesn't have to look at it.

And that's how I ended up with the classes I did.

23.2   What Happens Where?

One of the challenges of scripting with objects, especially once you start making superclasses and subclasses, is that no method ever seems to *do* anything—it just asks some other method to do something. It can be frustrating to figure out what's going on, even in code you wrote. There are ways to ease the frustration.

Don't go wild with new classes, especially superclasses and subclasses. Don't write code your experience hasn't prepared you to read.

Pick good names, ones that are *memorable* and *specific*. If they're memorable, you'll be able to keep more of them in your head at once as you try to figure out the purpose of the whole collection. My early use of send was far inferior to my final bark. First, I was overriding a method that's available to all objects. (Recall that "foo".send(:upcase) is the same as "foo".upcase.) Second, it's vague—there might be lots of objects in a script that send something to something else. But in a program named watchdog, bark must be the method that finally communicates with the outside world.

I am lousy at naming, so I'm resigned to picking bad names and having to change them later. Even if you're great at picking names, the purposes of your classes and methods will shift over time. You need to change their names to match. A completely obscure name is probably better than one that clearly suggests what the class no longer does.

Difficulty finding a good name may be a sign you're coding down the wrong path. Once when I was extracting a superclass, the best name I could think of was PageThing. That turned out to be a sign that the

---

4.   I toyed with the idea of giving all Barkers a class method named whelp to be used instead of new but stopped myself in time.

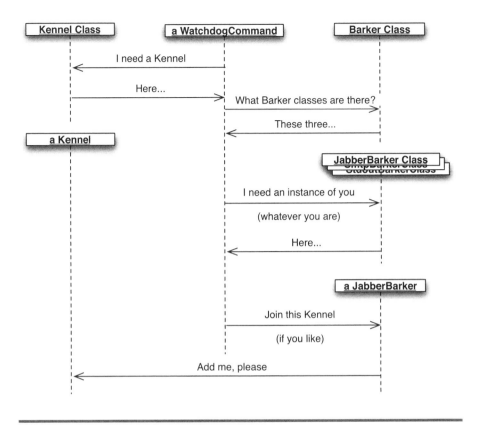

Figure 23.2: A SEQUENCE DIAGRAM

duplicate code really belonged in only one of the classes. Eventually, I realized that, so I gradually made the superclass go away. Whenever a change to add a new feature brought me in contact with the clumsy code, I took a little time to make it better.

An Example

sequence diagram

Figure 23.2 is a *sequence diagram* showing the communication among some of watchdog's classes. It should make it easier to understand the code explained in this section. Time increases from top to bottom. The arrows describe messages flowing between objects and (if helpful) the return values.

Let's look at the different steps in this calculation.

```
code/watchdog/lib/watchdog/choices.rb
```
❶ @kennel = Kennel.new
❷ Barker::Subclasses.each do | barker_class |
❸   barker = barker_class.new(@user_choices)
❹   errors += barker.errors
❺   barker.invite_into(@kennel)
   end

❻ raise errors.join("\n") unless errors.empty?

watchdog/lib/watchdog/choices.rb

Figure 23.3: STOCKING A KENNEL

"I Need a Kennel"

As its last action, the WatchdogCommand's postprocess_user_choices method asks for a new Kennel instance. That's done in the usual way, by sending new to the appropriate class. See line ❶ in Figure 23.3.

"What Barker Classes Are There?"

Barker contains a constant, Subclasses. At any given moment, that constant names an array of all Barker subclasses. That array lets the WatchdogCommand stock the Kennel without ever having to care specifically which classes it's using.

It's interesting how that array is filled. By using a nice Ruby feature, no human ever has to maintain a list of subclasses. When any subclass is defined, its superclass is sent the inherited message. Its single argument is the new child class. The default implementation of inherited does nothing, but Barker responds to that message like this:

```
code/watchdog/lib/watchdog/barkers.rb
```
Subclasses = []

def self.inherited(new_child_class)
  Subclasses << new_child_class
end

"I Need an Instance of You (Whatever You Are)"

Line ❸ shows that a class can be named by any old variable, not just a capitalized class name. So new can be sent to it without ever knowing what class will receive the message.

The Barker subclass is given the UserChoices object that has already been filled. During initialize, the Barker subclass checked the suitability of the choices and stashed any errors found in an instance variable. The errors method (used at ❹) will fetch a list of error messages to be printed to the screen. All the messages are gathered for all the Barkers before any are printed.

"Join This Kennel (If You Like)"

At ❺, the new Barker is invited into the Kennel. No object except the Barker itself needs to know or care whether it accepts the invitation. The Kennel just operates on the Barkers it has, oblivious to whether there are other kinds out there.

Every Barker decides whether to accept the invitation the same way:

```
code/watchdog/lib/watchdog/barkers.rb
def invite_into(kennel)
  return unless errors.empty?
  return unless wanted?
  kennel.add(self)
end
```

(**return** is a handy way of returning from a method before the end. This method shows a common idiom: if there are unusual or error cases, they're handled at the top of the method. After the **returns**, the main part of the method worries only about the common case, not the oddities. Separating these two concerns makes the code easier to read.)

That code is defined in the Barker, not in the specific subclasses. It uses a helper method, wanted?, that's also defined in the superclass:

```
code/watchdog/lib/watchdog/barkers.rb
def wanted?
  @user_choices[self.symbol]
end
```

All that a particular Barker subclass needs to define is symbol, the @user_choices key used to discover whether the user wants that Barker. So, for example, the JabberBarker needs to define only this:

```
code/watchdog/lib/watchdog/barkers.rb
def symbol; :jabber; end
```

Once it has done that, all the rest of initialization comes for free.

"Add Me, Please"

Suppose the Barker decides to accept the invitation. It could do that in one of two ways:

- It could ask the Kennel for the array it uses to hold Barkers. Then it could add itself to that array:

  kennel.barkers << self

- Or it could ask the Kennel to do the work:

  code/watchdog/lib/watchdog/barkers.rb

  kennel.add(self)

The second is usually better. By analogy, suppose you want someone to take a pill. The first approach is like reaching down their throat, pulling out their stomach, and putting the pill in it. The second is like giving them the pill and asking them to take it. Which is more appealing?[5]

The first is usually the worst because it requires you to know something about Kennel's innards. Once again, there's duplication: both Kennel and Barker know how a Kennel holds onto Barkers. If that knowledge changes in one, it has to change in the other.

The first is not *always* the wrong choice. Kennel's add method is one line long—easy to write:

code/watchdog/lib/watchdog/kennel.rb

```
def add(*barkers)
  @barkers += barkers
end
```

If getting rid of duplication required me to make a whole new class, I probably wouldn't do it.[6]

Sometimes you won't be able to decide which of two choices to make. Just pick one. Agonizing over it won't produce a better decision. If you take care to keep your script clean, you can easily change your mind later.

"Oops! Changed My Mind!"

After all the Barkers have added themselves, the code checks whether any errors were found. If so, it raises an exception (❻). That will travel

---

5. I adapted this analogy from one I heard from Joseph Bergin.
6. Although the Barkers add themselves one at a time, this method can add several at once. I use that in the Kennel tests.

all the way to with_pleasant_exceptions, where it will be printed. All that work of adding will have been done for nothing. Big deal: it's work that a computer does in a vanishingly small fraction of a second. Don't worry about wasted effort unless you *know*—by measurement—that the waste is noticeable and important. Always favor the clean code you need over the fast code you *might* need.

23.3 Modules Instead of Superclasses

From the point of view of a subclass, what does this do?

```
class Subclass < Superclass
end
```

It makes the methods of Superclass available to the Subclass. And what does this do?

```
class AnyClass
  include SomeModule
end
```

It makes the methods of SomeModule available to AnyClass.

Superclasses and modules are closely related. Just as *superclass* methods can send messages whose receiving methods are expected to be defined in all *subclasses*, *module* methods can send messages whose receiving methods are expected to be defined in *all classes that include the module.*

Whew! That's hard for me to follow, and I wrote it. Maybe this will help:

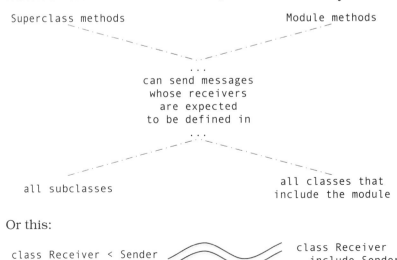

Or this:

```
class Receiver < Sender                  class Receiver
                                           include Sender
```

A module that makes heavy use of such an expectation is Enumerable. It defines all the collection methods you're used to—collect, find, include?, etc.—in terms of each. If your class defines each, you need only includeEnumerable to get all those methods for free. Like this:

`code/inheritance/module-inclusion.rb`

```
class Threeer
  include Enumerable

  def each
    yield(1)
    yield(2)
    yield(3)
  end
end
```

Having done that:

```
irb(main):002:0> Threeer.new.collect { | e | e * 2 }
=> [2, 4, 6]
irb(main):003:0> Threeer.new.include?(3)
=> true
```

When Do You Use Which?

The only important difference between modules and classes is that a class can have only one superclass, but it can include many modules. So you'll often be faced with a choice between extracting methods into a superclass or into a module. I decide by trying to pick a good name for the code I'm extracting. Class names are almost always nouns, like Kennel or Barker. Module names are typically adjectives that modify nouns, like Enumerable, Comparable, or Observable. Including a module adds, or *mixes in*, a new kind of property to objects, but it'd be a stretch to say a module defines any kind of thing. For that reason, you can't create new instances from a module—they don't respond to new.

mixes in

## Chapter 24

Final Thoughts

Right now, you have the tools to become a truly accomplished scripter. What you need is experience. The way to get experience is to write scripts. But there's an old question among readers of resumes: "Does this person have ten years of experience or one year of experience repeated ten times?" Unless each script you write teaches you something, you will not become accomplished.

Many scripters fail because they *always* write a straightforward script that's mostly one big method, add lots of duplication when they change it, get bogged down, and throw the script away.

Throwing scripts away is, in itself, not a problem. Your job is not to write scripts; it's to solve problems. Once you've solved the problem, it's fine to discard the script. Even if you face a similar problem next year, it may be easier to write a new script than to adapt an old one.

But you should throw scripts away because you *choose to*, not because you *have to*. If you spend all your time making throwaway scripts, you won't build up your toolbox, and you'll stop getting better too soon.

Economics being what it is, we're all under enormous pressure to do a barely acceptable job as fast as possible. If you want to get good, you'll have to resist that pressure. You'll have to do at least a little bit better than barely good enough.

As I've mentioned, the way I do that is to spend twenty or so minutes at the end of a task improving something that needs improving (either me or the code). Something that I wish I did more often is to explore other people's packages to see how they do things and what tricks they use. When you find a bug in someone's package, consider fixing the bug, not just reporting it. That will give you a much more concrete understanding of how that author approaches scripting.

What I tell people on my consulting trips is that every week you spend at your job should make you worth at least a little more money. Make a habit of asking yourself whether that has been true of the past week.

Some fraction of scripters fall into the opposite trap: they get so enthralled with scripting that they build elaborate, gorgeous (to them, at least) frameworks far in excess of what their job demands. The trick in scripting is to push yourself beyond the minimum while still regularly producing results that justify your salary. To do that, you have to grow your scripts bit by bit, satisfying one real and immediate need after another, while still keeping the code clean. This book won't surgically implant that skill in your skull, but it's given you some of the tools you need:

- Test-driven scripting with Test::Unit

- A wary attitude toward duplication

- Places to extract duplicate code into: methods, classes, and modules

- An emphasis on picking good names, a realization that the right name for a method or class will likely change over time, and a willingness to change the name until you get it right

- Scripting by assumption: the habit of assuming that Ruby provides exactly the methods and classes you need, using those methods, and creating them when they turn out not to exist

I hope this book helps you remove a little of the tedium and frustration from your job. Thanks for reading it.

Champaign, Illinois; March 17, 2005–September 30, 2006

Part V

The Back of the Book

Glossary

abstract superclass

> An incomplete *class*, one whose *instances* would be useless. Only instances of *subclasses* should be created. An abstract class is a template or *framework* for its subclasses.

accessor

> A *method* that's either a *reader* or a *writer*.

anchor

> In a *regexp*, a character that requires the match to either begin at the beginning of the string or end at the end of the string.

argument

> One of the *objects* passed, along with a *message*, to a *method*. The name of the argument appears in the method's argument list and is treated as a *local variable*.

array

> An array is a *composite object* that is *indexed* by a number, starting with 0.

assignment

> Assignment causes some human-readable name to refer to a particular *object*. The usual jargon is "foo is assigned 5."

base class

> A *class* that another class *inherits* from. Also: *superclass* or *parent class*.

block

> A chunk of Ruby code that acts much like a *method* without a name. Like a method, it takes *arguments* and *returns* some *object*.

body

> In a conditional statement like **if** or **unless**, the Ruby code that's sometimes executed, sometimes not.

boolean-valued

> Having a value that's either true or false.

bootstrapping test

> Instead of manufacturing test *objects* directly, a bootstrapping test uses already-tested *methods* to make them. Contrast with *direct test*.

case sensitive

> Ruby is case sensitive because words with different capitalization are different *variables*.

character class

> In a *regexp*, a backslashed character that stands in for a whole set of characters.

class

> A class is an *object* that specializes in creating other objects, typically called *instances* of that class.

class method

> A *method* that is reached by sending a *message* to a *class* rather than to one of its instances. new is the most common class method.

class variable

> A *variable* visible to all *instances* of a *class* and its *subclasses*, as well as to *class methods* of the classes themselves.

client

> A client of an *object* sends it *messages*.

command-line argument

> On the command line, all the space-separated words after the name of the script are its command-line arguments. They're given to the script in *array* named ARGV.

composite object

> A composite object is one *object* that names a whole set of objects. A composite object can typically be *indexed* to pick one object out of the set. *Arrays* and *hashes* are composite objects.

continuation prompt
> A *prompt* that tells you an *interpreter* (the command-line inter-
> preter or irb) needs more information before it can respond to a
> command.

core (Ruby)
> Those *classes* a Ruby script can use without having to require
> them.

coupling
> Two *classes* are coupled when one can't work without the other.

current working folder
> If a file is in your current working folder, it can be used as a
> *command-line argument* without having to specify what folder it's
> in.

data type
> A synonym for *class*.

descend from
> To make a *class* a *subclass* of some *superclass*. Also: to inherit
> from, to subclass, to extend.

direct test
> A test that itself manufactures *objects* given as *arguments* (or other
> kind of input) to a *method* under test. Contrast to *bootstrapping
> test*.

dynamic (decisions)
> Decisions made (by Ruby) at the time a script is run. Consider this
> code:
>
> ```
> obj.update
> ```
>
> There might be many *classes* that define an update *method*. Ruby
> chooses which method to run at the moment the *message* is sent.
>
> Contrast to *static*.

dynamic language
> A language that favors *dynamic* decisions over static.

elaborative test
> A test that confirms something you already suspected. Contrast
> to *generative test*.

element
> One of the *objects* a *composite object* names.

environment variable
> A named value that's accessible to any program (not just Ruby programs). For example, the environment variable HOME usually names a user's home folder.

escape character
> In a *regexp* or *string*, the escape character \ removes any special meaning from the following character.

exception
> An *object raised* by Ruby code to indicate that something unusual has happened. Often used in error handling.

extend
> To make a *class* a *subclass* of some *superclass*. Also: to inherit from, to subclass, to descend from.

extract (a superclass)
> Suppose you have two *classes* that don't have *superclasses* (other than Object, which all classes *inherit* from). Suppose also they both have a copy of a particular *method*. You can then extract a superclass by creating a new class, putting the common method there, deleting it from the two classes, and declaring that they *inherit* from the superclass.

floating-point number
> A number with a decimal point, like 5.3.

framework
> A collection of interrelated *classes*. You use a framework by *extending* some of those classes through *inheritance*.

fully qualified (name)
> A name prefixed by all the nested *modules* that include it, as in Test::Unit::TestCase.

generative test
> A test that the current version of a *method* fails. A generative test causes you to write new code. Contrast to *elaborative test*.

global namespace
> The collection of names that's visible to a Ruby script before any *modules* are *included*. It contains names like ARGV, $:, File, and

puts. The names in the global namespace can be used *unqualified* both inside any module or *class* or outside all modules and classes.

global variables

Global variables are visible everywhere.

greedy (regexp)

A greedy *regexp* finds the largest possible match.

group (regexp)

In a *regexp*, a group is formed by surrounding some regexp text with *unescaped* parentheses. Groups allow you to select pieces of matches.

hash

A *composite object* that looks much like an *array*, except that it can be *indexed* by any object, not just integers.

include (a module)

When a *class* or *module* includes a module, all the names in the module can be used in their *unqualified* form.

index (noun)

Most commonly, an integer used to select one *element* of an *array*. *Hashes* are indexed, too, but their index is usually called a *key*.

index (verb)

You *index* a *composite object* to pick out one of its *elements*.

inherit

A *class* inherits from another class if it is a *subclass* of that class. The connotation is that the subclass has everything the *superclass* does, except for certain specified differences. Also: to subclass, to extend, to descend from.

inheritance

Creating a *class* by pointing at another one and saying, "this new class is just like that old one, except...." The exceptions are expressed as *method* definitions.

instance

An instance is an *object* created by sending a *class* the new message.

instance method

A *method* that's reached via an *instance* of a *class*, not via the *class* itself. The word "method," unqualified, usually refers to an instance method.

instance variable

An *instance* variable is a *variable* that can be seen only by the *methods* of a particular *object*.

integer

A number without a decimal point, like 5. A counting number.

interpreter

An interpreter is a program that responds to commands typed by a person.

iterator

A *method* that takes a *block* and potentially applies it to every *element* of a *compound object*.

key

An *object* used to pick an *element* out of a *hash*.

keyword

All those words in Ruby that aren't the names of *methods*, *classes*, *variables*, etc. **if**, **def**, and **return** are all keywords.

keyword argument

A named *message argument*, like this:

```
center(:spread => 2, :padding => '-')
```

library

A collection of files for scripts to require. In practice, *library*, *package*, and *project* are used pretty much interchangeably. I'll often use library when I want to emphasize that none of the files are scripts to be run from the command line.

literal

Strings, *hashes*, *arrays*, and *symbols* can be created as literal expressions. Rather than constructing the *object* with new, it's constructed by typing to Ruby what you'd expect irb to print for that object. So, for example, a hash is made with h = {'key' => 'value'} rather than h = Hash.new; h['key'] = 'value'.

load path

A list of folders in which Ruby looks for files named in a require or load command.

local variable
> A *variable* that's visible only within a single *method*. A method's *argument* names are treated as local variables.

message
> Messages are sent to objects to cause them to do something (by executing a *method*) and then return *results*.

method
> A method is snippet of Ruby code that an *object* runs in response to a *message*.

mix in (verb)
> To *include* a *module* with the specific intent of making *mixin methods* available to the *class* doing the including.

mixin method
> A *method* inside a *module* that can be used only by a *class* or module that *includes* it. The methods collect, reject, and find_all are mixin methods of module Enumerable.

module
> A Ruby *object* that restricts the visibility of a set of names to code that *fully qualifies* them or that *includes* the module.

module method
> A *method* inside a *module* that can be used only by (1) sending the *message* with the same name to the module (File.open) or (2) *qualifying* the message name with the module (File::open).

namespace
> A collection of names; a *module*.

natural order
> For numbers, increasing value. For strings, increasing alphabetical order.

object
> An object is a bundle of *instance variables* and *methods* that operate on the objects the *variables* name.

operator
> A way of making Ruby look more appealing. Strictly, adding two numbers ought to look like this: 5.plus(3). That's ugly, so Ruby converts 5+3, which looks like ordinary addition, into the usual *message*-sending form. The plus sign, minus sign, asterisk for

multiplication, brackets for *array indexing*: all of those are operators that don't look like messages, but they really are.

optional argument

An *argument* that, if not provided by the *message* sender, is assigned some default *object*. The default is declared when the *method* is written.

override

When a *subclass* and a *superclass* both have a *method* with the same name, the subclass version overrides the superclass version. When the *message* of the same name is sent to an *instance* of the subclass, the overriding version is the one that's run.

package

A collection of Ruby files. Strictly, a package can contain scripts while a *library* cannot. In practice, package, library, and project are used interchangeably.

parent class

A *class* that another class *inherits* from. Also: *superclass* or *base class*.

polymorphic message

If more than one *class* of *object responds to* a *message*, that message is called "polymorphic."

precedence

Precedence is used to remove ambiguity from expressions. Expressions are normally evaluated left to right, but a||b&&c is evaluated like a||(b&&c) (that is, right to left) because **&&** has a higher precedence than ||.

project

A common synonym for *package*.

protocol

The rules governing communication between two computer programs, especially over a network.

qualified (name)

A name that's prefixed with the *module* that controls its visibility.

question-mark operator

The conditional expression boolean ? truecase : falsecase. A shorthand version of **if**.

raise (an exception)

> Execution of the current *method* does not proceed to the next Ruby *method* statement. Instead, it begins inside the first available *handler* for the *exception*.

reader (method)

> A *method* is a reader if it returns the *object* named by an *instance variable*.

receiver

> An *object* that's sent a *message* by another object. When it receives the message, it activates the corresponding *method* and then returns a *result*.

redirect (output)

> To send output that would otherwise show on the screen to a file.

refactoring

> Changing a script in a way that doesn't change its behavior. It's often done to clean up the code after making a test pass.

regexp

> Slang for "regular expression." Regular expressions are ways of describing a large number of matching strings.

rescue (an exception)

```
begin
  ...
  raise Exception.new
  ...
rescue Exception
  ...
end
```

> An *exception raised* during execution of the **rescue** statement's **begin**. . . **end** block is handled by the **rescue** statement's body if the exception's *class* matches the class named in the **rescue** statement.

responds to

> An *object* responds to a *message* if it has a *method* with the same name.

rest argument

> An *argument* assigned all unused *objects* in a *message*'s *argument list*. Declared like this:

```
def all_args(required, *rest)
```

result
> A Ruby *method* returns a *object* as its result.

sender
> An *object* that sends a *message* to another object and then awaits the *result*.

separation of concerns
> The design guideline that a *class* or *method* should do one thing and do it well.

sequence diagram
> A diagram that shows how *messages* flow among a set of *objects*. See Figure 23.2 on page 236.

short-circuiting evaluation
> In an expression like a and b, b doesn't need to be evaluated if a is false. Ruby already knows the whole expression will be false. The evaluation of b is "short-circuited."

slice
> A subarray of an *array*. For example, you might pick out the slice of a twelve-element array that extends from element 3 through 8. Some ways of picking out a slice remove it from the original array; others don't.

spaceship operator
> <=>, the generalized comparison *operator*. It returns -1, 0, or 1, depending on whether its left side is less than, equal to, or larger than the right, in the *class*'s *natural order*.

stack trace
> A list of *methods* that have begun execution and have not yet returned.

standard library (Ruby)
> *Classes* delivered with Ruby that have to be required before they can be used.

static (decisions)
> Decisions made (by a person) at the time a script is written. Consider this code:

```
obj.update
```

There might be many *classes* that define an update *method*. In a *static language*, a human would have to declare (in script code) which class of *object*obj is allowed to name.

Contrast to *dynamic*.

static language
:   A language that favors *static* decisions over dynamic.

stderr
:   The place a program normally sends error output. May be *redirected*. Short for "standard error."

stdout
:   The place a program normally sends nonerror output. May be *redirected*. Short for "standard output."

string
:   A Ruby *object* of *class* String. It is essentially a sequence of characters.

subclass (noun)
:   A *class* that *inherits* from another class.

subclass (verb)
:   To make a *class* a *subclass* of some *superclass*. Also: to inherit from, to extend, to descend from.

superclass
:   A *class* that another class *inherits* from. Also: *base class* or *parent class*.

symbol
:   A symbol is a simplified *string*. Most places you can use a string, you can also use a symbol. Using the symbol tells the reader that you're using it as a pure name or marker, not because you will ever want to send it *messages*. So, for example, symbols are often used as *hashkeys*. *Literal* symbols are written with a leading colon: :my_symbol.

ternary operator
:   The conditional expression boolean ? truecase : falsecase. A shorthand version of **if**.

test-driven programming
:   The same thing as *test-first* programming.

test expression

In a conditional statement like **if** or **unless**, the Ruby code that determines whether a *body* is executed. A test expression is either false or true.

test-first programming

Write code by writing a test, watching the program fail it, writing the minimal amount of code that passes the test, and then writing the next test. Along the way, clean up code whenever it starts to get messy. Also called test-driven programming or test-driven design.

unqualified (name)

A name not prefixed by the nested *modules* that include it. TestCase is the unqualified version of the *fully qualified* Test::Unit::TestCase.

variable

A variable gives a name to an *object*. More than one variable may name the same object. Variables are caused to name objects via *assignment*.

writer (method)

A *method* is a writer if it changes which *object* an *instance variable* names.

Appendix B

Solutions to Exercises

You can find all solutions in your downloaded code folder. In the sub-folder exercise-solutions, there's one folder for each chapter with exercises. Each exercise solution is named after the exercise. For example, exercise-1.rb.

B.1 Solutions for Chapter 3

The solution files are in exercise-solutions/inventory.

Exercise 1

The value of x is 4, because new_inventory - old_inventory is the list of files in the first but not in the second—that is, the number of new files. There are four of those: new-inventory.txt, recycler, recycler/inst-39.tmp, and temp/inst-39.

So a better name than x would be new_file_count or new_count or even number_of_new_files.

Exercise 2

I exited from irb before doing this exercise. I was too lazy to read in the files again, so I just made up some values for new_inventory and old_inventory and then typed the new line. Here's what happened:

```
irb(main):001:0> new_inventory = ['a', 'b', 'c']
=> ["a", "b", "c"]
irb(main):002:0> old_inventory = ['old']
=> ["old"]
irb(main):003:0> new_inventory - old_inventory.length
TypeError: cannot convert Fixnum into Array
    from (irb):4:in '-'
    from (irb):4
```

The length message is sent to old_inventory's object first. It returns some number. Then the subtraction is done. That means Ruby is now trying to subtract a number from an array—which doesn't make sense.

Exercise 3

Here is the number of new and deleted messages:

```
new_count = (new_inventory - old_inventory).length
deleted_count = (old_inventory - new_inventory).length
```

The number of messages in common is a little trickier to calculate. Consider the size of the new inventory. That's the number of elements in common *plus* the number of new elements. So we can get the number of elements in common like this:

```
common_count = new_inventory.length - new_count
```

There's actually an easier way, but it depends on a fact you don't know about arrays. Just as - gives the difference between two arrays, & gives the elements they have in common:

```
irb(main):007:0> ['1', '2', '3'] & ['2', '3', '4']
=> ["2", "3"]
```

So a better way to find common_count is this:

```
common_count = (new_inventory & old_inventory).length
```

I say that's better because it's more obviously right. And it would probably have taken me less time to say, "there must be a Ruby method that does this" and find it than it did to convince myself that the other way was correct.

Having calculated the values, we can print them. I'd like a tidy, compact printout, something like this:

```
13 new files; 2 deleted files; 5 files in common.
```

But I'm going to defer teaching you how to format output until Chapter 7, *The Churn Project: Writing Scripts without Fuss*, on page 59. So for now let's print the strings and values on separate lines:

```
code/exercise-solutions/inventory/exercise-1.rb
```

```
old_inventory = File.open('old-inventory.txt').readlines
new_inventory = File.open('new-inventory.txt').readlines

puts "The following files have been added:"
puts new_inventory - old_inventory

puts ""
```

```
puts "The following files have been deleted:"
puts old_inventory - new_inventory
new_count = (new_inventory - old_inventory).length
deleted_count = (old_inventory - new_inventory).length
common_count = new_inventory.length - new_count

puts ""
puts "New files added:"
puts new_count
puts "Old files deleted:"
puts deleted_count
puts "Files in common:"
puts common_count
```

Exercise 4

Array subtraction doesn't depend on order. This example shows that:

```
irb(main):002:0> ['a', 'b', 'c', 'd'] - ['b', 'c']
=> ["a", "d"]
irb(main):003:0> ['d', 'b', 'c', 'a'] - ['c', 'b']
=> ["d", "a"]
```

B.2   Solutions for Chapter 5

The solution files are in exercise-solutions/more-inventory.

Exercise 1

When differences-version-8.rb is loaded, this happens:

```
prompt> irb
irb(main):001:0> load 'snapshots/differences-version-8.rb'
Usage: differences.rb old-inventory new-inventory
prompt>
```

This happens because everything in the file is executed as it's loaded. Here are the first lines loaded:

```
unless ARGV.length == 2
  puts "Usage: differences.rb old-inventory new-inventory"
  exit
end
```

As soon as that construct is read, Ruby checks the length of ARGV. What's ARGV? It's the list of command-line arguments given to the original script. In this case, the original script is irb (which is, remember, itself a Ruby script). Since I gave irb no arguments, ARGV is the empty array, whose length is 0.

Therefore, the body of the unless is executed. First a message is printed to the screen, and then the script—irb—exits (just as if you'd typed exit at the irb prompt).

Exercise 2

Here's the original version of boring?:

```
def boring?(line)
  line.split('/').include?('temp') or
    line.split('/').include?('recycler')
end
```

Here's the version with chomp added:

```
code/exercise-solutions/more-inventory/exercise-2.rb
```

```
def boring?(line)
  line.chomp.split('/').include?('temp') or
    line.chomp.split('/').include?('recycler')
end
```

Exercise 3

Here's the result of splitting boring? into two methods:

```
code/exercise-solutions/more-inventory/exercise-3.rb
```

```
def boring?(line)
  contains?(line, 'temp') or contains?(line, 'recycler')
end
```

```
def contains?(line, a_boring_word)
  line.chomp.split('/').include?(a_boring_word)
end
```

Question: as long as we're trying to make the code clearer, what about that variable line? Is what we're working with any old line? What would be a better name?

Exercise 4

```
code/exercise-solutions/more-inventory/exercise-4.rb
```

```
def boring?(line, boring_words)
  boring_words.any? do | a_boring_word |
    contains?(line, a_boring_word)
  end
end
```

Checking it:

```
irb(main):004:0> load 'differences.rb'
=> true
```

```
irb(main):005:0> boring?("temp", ["temp", "recycler"])
=> true
irb(main):006:0> boring?("/foo/bar", ["food", "bart", "quux"])
=> false
```

Exercise 5

The script fails like this:

```
prompt> ruby differences.rb before.txt after.txt
```
❶ differences.rb:32:in 'boring?': wrong number of arguments (1 for 2)
(ArgumentError)
```
        from differences.rb:30:in 'inventory_from'
        from differences.rb:29:in 'reject'
        from differences.rb:29:in 'inventory_from'
        from differences.rb:35:in 'compare_inventory_files'
        from differences.rb:48
```

Line ❶ of the error message tells you what line of the script failed. That's
the one also marked ❶ here:

```
def inventory_from(filename)
  inventory = File.open(filename)
  downcased = inventory.collect do | line |
    line.downcase
  end
  downcased.reject do | line |
```
❶
```
    boring?(line)
  end
end
```

Now that boring? takes two arguments, it has to be called with two
arguments. I could change line ❶ to this:

code/exercise-solutions/more-inventory/exercise-5.rb

```
boring?(line, ['temp', 'recycler'])
```

Call this the *first solution*. A question is whether I should go to a further
solution where inventory_from takes a boring_words argument as well and
passes that array onto boring?. Here's what that would look like, with
the further changes marked at ❶ and ❷:

code/exercise-solutions/more-inventory/exercise-5-rejected.rb

❶
```
def inventory_from(filename, boring_words)
  inventory = File.open(filename)
  downcased = inventory.collect do | line |
    line.downcase
  end
  downcased.reject do | line |
```
❷
```
    boring?(line, boring_words)
  end
end
```

Whereas the first solution gives responsibility of deciding what's boring to inventory_from, the proposed solution moves it to inventory_from's client, compare_inventory_files—or perhaps even to *its* client.

But I think I want the responsibility left with inventory_from. Suppose the script were to be used on some Unix derivative. It would have to be changed in two ways. First, the list of boring files would be different. For example, Unix derivatives use tmp where Windows uses temp. Second, case matters, in that Manifest.txt names a different file than does manifest.txt. (In fact, a folder could have files with both names at the same time.) So the code that downcases all the lines would need to be removed.

Both those changes would be made in compare_inventory_files in the first solution. That's good: it increases the chance they'll both actually *be* made. In the second solution, a switch to a new operating system affects more than one place in the code, making it more likely that one will be overlooked. For that reason, I reject the second solution.[1]

B.3 Solutions for Chapter 7

The solution files are in exercise-solutions/churn.

Exercise 1

Here's one possible solution:

```
def header(an_svn_date)
  "Changes between #{an_svn_date} and #{svn_date(Time.now)}:"
end
```

That would require no changes to the rest of the script, but it would be impractically hard to test (since the expected results would depend on the time the test was run). For the benefit of testing, I'll pass in the date to use. I can pass it as either a Time object or a date string. Since header's first argument is a date string, and it seems safest to be consistent, I'll choose to pass a date string. Here's the new test:

```
code/exercise-solutions/churn/exercise-1-tests.rb
```

```
def test_header_format
  assert_equal("Changes between 2005-08-05 and 2006-12-30:",
        header(svn_date(month_before(Time.local(2005, 9, 2))),
            svn_date(Time.local(2006, 12, 30))))
end
```

---

1. That's not to say that this script is as good as it could be—it certainly doesn't draw attention to where such OS dependencies live—but it's good enough for now.

Here's the code that passes that test:

code/exercise-solutions/churn/exercise-1.rb

```
def header(starting_svn_date, ending_svn_date)
  "Changes between #{starting_svn_date} and #{ending_svn_date}:"
end
```

And here's how it's used:

```
start_date = svn_date(month_before(Time.now))

puts header(start_date, svn_date(Time.now))
```

Exercise 2

Here is the complete set of tests for asterisks_for. Notice the long names. I name tests as sentences in the hope that someone can skim down the list of names and get a pretty good idea of what the method does. More detail means reading the body of the test, and the ultimate detail comes from reading the method definition.

code/exercise-solutions/churn/exercise-2-tests.rb

```
def test_asterisks_for_divides_by_five
  assert_equal('****', asterisks_for(20))
end

def test_asterisks_for_rounds_up_and_down
  assert_equal('****', asterisks_for(18))
  assert_equal('***', asterisks_for(17))
end

def test_asterisks_for_zero_is_a_dash
  assert_equal('-', asterisks_for(0))
end

def test_asterisks_for_rounds_up_small_numbers
  assert_equal('*', asterisks_for(1))
  assert_equal('*', asterisks_for(2))
  # Just in case, check nearby boundaries.
  assert_equal('*', asterisks_for(5))
  assert_equal('*', asterisks_for(7))
  assert_equal('**', asterisks_for(8))
end
```

Note the last 3 assertions in test_asterisks_for_rounds_up_small_numbers. I was pretty sure that an implementation that passed the first two asserts would pass the last three. The logic should be the same divide-by-five-and-round as before. But it's easy to check, so I decided to make sure.

elaborative tests

Bill Wake calls those *elaborative tests* because they elaborate on what the code does without the expectation that they'll make you write new code. The kind that *does* make you write new code is called a *generative test*. The implementation is a simple if construct:

generative test

`code/exercise-solutions/churn/exercise-2.rb`

```
def asterisks_for(an_integer)
  if an_integer == 0
    '_'
  elsif an_integer < 3
    '*'
  else
    '*' * (an_integer / 5.0).round
  end
end
```

Exercise 3

I wrote two tests for the change:

```
def test_normal_subsystem_line_format
  assert_equal('audit          (45 changes)    *********',
          subsystem_line("audit", 45))
end
def test_subsystem_line_has_special_format_for_zero_changes
  assert_equal('data           -              -',
          subsystem_line("data", 0))
end
```

I could have put both assertions into one test, but I adhere to my practice of having the test method name be a second description of what the test is about.

Even though I wrote both tests in advance, I ignored the second one until I'd made the first pass, with this code:

```
def subsystem_line(subsystem_name, change_count)
  name = subsystem_name.ljust(14)
  change_description = "(#{change_count} changes)".ljust(14)
  asterisks = asterisks_for(change_count)
  "#{name} #{change_description} #{asterisks}"
end
```

Making the second test pass would force the code to check whether the change count is zero. It seemed appropriate to farm that work out to another change-count-creation method, just as the calculation of the asterisks was. I had some trouble naming that method, but then I hit on the idea that a subsystem line really has two descriptions of the change: the row of asterisks is really an image to be seen as a whole, whereas the other is text to be read. That gave me two words to use in variable names: text and image. Here's what I wrote:

```
code/exercise-solutions/churn/exercise-3.rb
def subsystem_line(subsystem_name, change_count)
  image = image_for(change_count)
  text = text_for(change_count)

  "#{subsystem_name.ljust(14)} #{text.ljust(14)} #{image}"
end
```

Notice that I've also decided to separate two concerns: getting a descriptive string and justifying it within a blank-padded field.

The next step was to implement text_for and change asterisks_for's name to image_for.

I was tempted not to write tests for text_for. After all, both cases it has to handle are tested, indirectly, by the tests for subsystem_line. But I decided to err on the side of being explicit. I probably wouldn't have done that if it hadn't been blindingly easy and if I hadn't already had tests for asterisks_for (now image_for). I mention this because I don't want you to think you *must* have direct tests for every method. That belief can dissuade you from making little methods when you really should, which is worse than having indirect tests.

Here are the tests:

```
code/exercise-solutions/churn/exercise-3-tests.rb
def test_normal_text_for_format
  assert_equal('(45 changes)', text_for(45))
end

def test_special_text_for_no_changes
  assert_equal('-', text_for(0))
end
```

And here's the code that passes them:

```
code/exercise-solutions/churn/exercise-3.rb
def text_for(an_integer)
  if an_integer == 0
    '-'
  else
    "(#{an_integer} changes)"
  end
end
```

Given the smaller tests for text_for and image_for, all that the previous subsystem_line tests speak to is how the pieces are put together. They both say the same thing: "the subsystem name is left-justified in a fourteen-space field, then there's a space, then the change-count text is left-justified. . . ."

So I decided to delete this one (once I'd seen it pass):

`code/exercise-solutions/churn/exercise-3-tests.rb`

```
def test_subsystem_line_has_special_format_for_zero_changes
  assert_equal('data          -          -',
          subsystem_line("data", 0))
end
```

Why delete it? After all, maybe it accidentally tests something that none of the other tests does. It might be the only test that finds a bug.

True, but it will also fail when other tests do. If I change the script again in four months and both tests fail, I'll have to spend time wondering why they both exist. What does the second one tell me that the first doesn't? It's annoying to spend time asking that question when the answer is "nothing."

Worse, I'm likely to think that I must have had *some* reason for writing the test, even if I can't remember it, so I'll keep it around just in case. Now I've bought myself the obligation to keep changing and changing and changing a test that does nothing for me.

I think most people are too skittish about throwing tests away once they've outlived their usefulness, and I include myself among "most people." So I'll sometimes give a test one more chance: if I think it's useless, but it's not failing right now, I'll leave it around until it does. If that failure tells me nothing new, the test is history.

B.4 Solutions for Chapter 9

The solution files are in exercise-solutions/churn-regexp.

Exercise 1

I'll make a method, interesting, that filters out the uninteresting lines in an array. Here it is in use (at ❶), here is the test I wrote, and here is the resulting implementation:

```
code/exercise-solutions/churn-regexp/exercise-1.rb
```

```
if $0 == __FILE__
  subsystem_names = ['audit', 'fulfillment', 'persistence',
                'ui', 'util', 'inventory']
  start_date = svn_date(month_before(Time.now))

  puts header(start_date)
  lines = subsystem_names.collect do | name |
    subsystem_line(name, change_count_for(name, start_date))
  end
❶ puts order_by_descending_change_count(interesting(lines))
end
```

```
code/exercise-solutions/churn-regexp/exercise-1-tests.rb
```

```
def test_interesting_lines_contain_at_least_one_asterisk
  boring_line =       "     inventory  (0)"
  interesting_line = "         ui * (3)"
  big_line =          "        util ************ (61)"

  original = [interesting_line, boring_line, big_line]
  expected = [interesting_line, big_line]

  assert_equal(expected, interesting(original))
end
```

```
code/exercise-solutions/churn-regexp/exercise-1.rb
```

```
def interesting(array)
  array.find_all do | line |
    /\*/ =~ line
  end
end
```

Exercise 2

Even if the subsystem name contains an asterisk, the format of the line is still *subsystem-name asterisks (count)*. Asterisks that indicate changes are surrounded by spaces, but asterisks in names are not. I'm going to build my solution around this observation.

That's a more fragile observation than the one in the previous exercise, which was just that interesting lines contain asterisks. It would be easier for subsystem_line to change in a way that breaks it.

That's a worry because the test in the previous example gave explicit strings to interesting. Those strings match today's subsystem_line, but they might not match tomorrow's.

It would be better to test interesting by getting its input from subsystem_line, like this:

```
code/exercise-solutions/churn-regexp/exercise-2-tests.rb
```
```
def test_interesting_lines_contain_at_least_one_asterisk
  boring_line = subsystem_line("inventory", 0)
  interesting_line = subsystem_line("ui", 3)
  big_line = subsystem_line('util', 61)

  original = [interesting_line, boring_line, big_line]
  expected = [interesting_line, big_line]

  assert_equal(expected, interesting(original))
end
```

Having done that, I'm inspired to document explicitly—in tests—the behavior of subsystem_line that I'm depending on:

```
code/exercise-solutions/churn-regexp/exercise-2-tests.rb
```
```
def test_subsystem_line_surrounds_asterisks_with_spaces
  assert_match(/ \* \(3\)/, subsystem_line("ui", 3))
  assert_match(/ \*\* \(10\)/, subsystem_line("ui", 10))
end

def test_subsystem_line_surrounds_even_no_asterisks_with_spaces
  # ... so interesting can depend on this, if it needs to.
  assert_match(/  \(0\)/, subsystem_line("ui", 0))
end
```

If I ever do break something, that'll make it easier to figure out what I've done. It also gives me a little more confidence that the observation I'm working from is indeed correct.

Having done all that—and seen that the tests pass—I'm ready (at last!) for the new test:

```
code/exercise-solutions/churn-regexp/exercise-2-tests.rb
```
```
def test_interesting_lines_subsystem_can_have_asterisk_at_end
  boring_line = subsystem_line('inventory*', 0)
  interesting_line = subsystem_line('ui*', 3)

  original = [interesting_line, boring_line]
  expected = [interesting_line]

  assert_equal(expected, interesting(original))
end
```

And the code to pass that is remarkably simple. Simply look for one or more asterisks with spaces on either side:

code/exercise-solutions/churn-regexp/exercise-2.rb

```ruby
def interesting(array)
  array.find_all do | line |
    / \*+ / =~ line
  end
end
```

I debated whether I should check that the asterisks are followed by a count in parentheses. That would work correctly with a subsystem name ending in a space and an asterisk (fast ui two *). I decided not to.

Exercise 3

code/exercise-solutions/churn-regexp/exercise-3.rb

```ruby
def rearrange(string)
❶    match = /(\w+), (\w+) (\w+)/.match(string)
    last_name = match[1]
    first_name = match[2]
    middle_name = match[3]
❷    "#{first_name} #{middle_name[0,1]}. #{last_name}"
end
```

We want the three groups of word characters to be plucked out of the string. Those groups are defined at line ❶ and plucked out in the three following lines.

Notice the string operation on line ❷ that extracts a single-character string from the middle_name. A mistake I often make is to write such an expression like this: middle_name[0]. That extracts a single *character*, not a one-character *string*. That's particularly confusing because individual characters are actually represented by integers. Here's the difference:

```
irb(main):001:0> "Elaine"[0]
=> 69
irb(main):002:0> "Elaine"[0,1]
=> "E"
```

It may help to think of a string as an array of characters. You want to extract a *slice* of an array—a one-element subarray—rather than a single element. Compare the previous to this:

```
irb(main):003:0> [69, 108, 97, 105, 110, 101][0]
=> 69
irb(main):004:0> [69, 108, 97, 105, 110, 101][0,1]
=> [69]
```

Exercise 4

`code/exercise-solutions/churn-regexp/exercise-4.rb`

```
def rearrange(string)
❶  has_middle_name = /(\w+), (\w+) (\w+)/.match(string)
❷  no_middle_name =  /(\w+), (\w+)/.match(string)

❸  if has_middle_name
     last_name = has_middle_name[1]
     first_name = has_middle_name[2]
     middle_name = has_middle_name[3]
     "#{first_name} #{middle_name[0,1]}. #{last_name}"
   elsif no_middle_name
     last_name = no_middle_name[1]
     first_name = no_middle_name[2]
     "#{first_name} #{last_name}"
   end
end
```

The two kinds of name can be represented by two patterns, matched separately (❶ and ❷). In one of the lines, the match will return a Match-Data object; in the other, it will return nil. In an **if** statement, a Match-Data counts as true, and nil counts as false, so rearrange can use match's return value to tell which kind of name it was given. (See ❸.)

There's a lot of duplication in that method, isn't there? You'll remove it in the next chapter's exercises.

B.5 Solutions for Chapter 10

The solution files are in exercise-solutions/regexp.

Exercise 1

The necessary insight here is that no matter *what* the subsystem name looks like, the end of the line has to be a space followed by a parenthesized number. If there's an asterisk just before that, the line is interesting. If there's a space just before that, that means the line must look something like *"subsystem (0)"*, which is uninteresting.

Here's the code:

`code/exercise-solutions/regexp/exercise-1.rb`

```
def interesting(array)
  array.find_all do | line |
    /\* \(\d+\)$/ =~ line
  end
end
```

Exercise 2

`code/exercise-solutions/regexp/exercise-2.rb`

```
def rearrange(name)
❶   match = /(\w+), (\w+)( \w+)?/.match(name)

    last_name = match[1]
    first_name = match[2]
    if match[3]
❷     separator = "#{match[3][0,2]}. "
    else
❸     separator = ' '
    end

❹   "#{first_name}#{separator}#{last_name}"
  end
```

The difference between *"Marick, Dawn Elaine"* and *"Marick, Paul"* is that the former ends in a space and a name. At first, I thought I wanted only the name, but then I realized I could use the space to construct the return value, so I wrapped both in a group that could occur zero or one times (line ❶).

When constructing the final string, I flailed around trying to get the right number of spaces in the right places. Then I realized I was confusing myself by thinking about three chunks of name separated by spaces. Instead, I should think about a first and last name separated by a separator (❹). If there's a middle name, the separator is a space and the middle initial (❷). (The space is the first character in the group; that's why the slice extracts two characters.) Otherwise, it's just a space (❸). As it so often is when you look at the problem right, the right code became easy.

B.6 Solutions for Chapter 11

The solution files are in *exercise-solutions/churn-classes.*

Exercise 1

I would add all the methods except month_before. Those are header, subsystem_line, asterisks_for, order_by_descending_change_count, and churn_line_to_int. I wouldn't add month_before because it has nothing in particular to do with formatting.

Suppose I used a script to plan my vacations, and there was some company rule about not taking two vacations in one month. I might very well borrow month_before for that other script, but I wouldn't want all the rest. That's a sign that month_before has a distinct responsibility and should not be lumped in with them.

Exercise 2

See Figure B.1, on the facing page, for the Formatter tests. There are three things to note:

❶ If the methods are grouped into a class, it makes sense to group the test methods as well.

❷ It's likely that you had something like this at the beginning of your tests:

```
formatter = Formatter.new
```

That way, each test method works with its own independent Formatter. The repetition is a little boring, and I got rid of it with a Test::Unit feature I haven't told you about: if the test class has a setup method defined, it's run before each test method.

In this particular case, I had setup make a Formatter and name it with an instance variable. That way, all the tests can use it. Since setup runs before each test method, it's still a new instance per test.

There's also a message teardown that's sent to the object after the test method is finished, but I had no use for it.

❸ The only change to the actual tests is to use @formatter to refer to the Formatter object.

Exercise 3

Figure B.2, on page 276, shows the Formatter class. Notice that there's no initialize method. If there's nothing to initialize, there's no need for the method.

Exercise 4

When the Formatter class is finished, there will be two kinds of methods in it. Three of them—the three we're testing in this exercise—are for public consumption. The rest will be used by those public methods. I decided to test the new ones in a new test class, FormatterNormalUseTests.

When thinking about the test, I realized that there's only one sensible way to use the methods: create a Formatter, give it a date, add data for

code/exercise-solutions/churn-classes/exercise-2.rb

❶   class FormatterTests < Test::Unit::TestCase

❷   def setup
      @formatter = Formatter.new
    end

    def test_header_format
      assert_equal("Changes since 2005-08-05:",
❸   @formatter.header('2005-08-05'))
    end

    def test_normal_subsystem_line_format
      assert_equal('   audit ********* (45)',
             @formatter.subsystem_line("audit", 45))
    end

    def test_asterisks_for_divides_by_five
      assert_equal('****', @formatter.asterisks_for(20))
    end

    def test_asterisks_for_rounds_up_and_down
      assert_equal('****', @formatter.asterisks_for(18))
      assert_equal('***', @formatter.asterisks_for(17))
    end

    def test_churn_line_to_int_extracts_parenthesized_change_count
      assert_equal(19, @formatter.churn_line_to_int("   churn2 **** (19)"))
      assert_equal(9, @formatter.churn_line_to_int("   churn ** (9)"))
    end

    def test_order_by_descending_change_count
      original = ["all that really matters is the number in parens - (1)",
             "   inventory (0)",
             "   churn ** (12)"]

      expected = ["   churn ** (12)",
             "all that really matters is the number in parens - (1)",
             "   inventory (0)"]

      actual = @formatter.order_by_descending_change_count(original)

      assert_equal(expected, actual)
    end
  end

exercise-solutions/churn-classes/exercise-2.rb

Figure B.1: FORMATTER TESTS

code/exercise-solutions/churn-classes/exercise-3.rb

```
class Formatter
  def header(a_date)
    "Changes since #{a_date}:"
  end

  def subsystem_line(subsystem_name, change_count)
    asterisks = asterisks_for(change_count)
    "#{subsystem_name.rjust(14)} #{asterisks} (#{change_count})"
  end

  def asterisks_for(an_integer)
    '*' * (an_integer / 5.0).round
  end

  def order_by_descending_change_count(lines)
    lines.sort do | first, second |
      first_count = churn_line_to_int(first)
      second_count = churn_line_to_int(second)
      - (first_count <=> second_count)
    end
  end

  def churn_line_to_int(line)
    /\((\d+)\)/.match(line)[1].to_i
  end
end
```

exercise-solutions/churn-classes/exercise-3.rb

Figure B.2: CODE THAT PASSES THE FORMATTER TESTS

some subsystems, and get the output. That done, some things ought to be true about the output:

- The header comes before the subsystem lines.
- Any data given appears in descending order of change count.
- The header and the lines are all that's printed.

I could also make claims about how many asterisks there are or what the lines look like exactly, but I've already made those claims in other tests (the tests for the other methods). These claims are what's special and new about the new code.

Tests become helpful as documentation when their names are sentences like the previous claims. So I made a test for each of them, as you can see in Figure B.3, on the facing page (at ❷, ❸, and ❹). Each

`code/exercise-solutions/churn-classes/exercise-4.rb`

```
class FormatterNormalUseTests < Test::Unit::TestCase

  def setup
    formatter = Formatter.new
    formatter.use_date('1960-02-19')
    formatter.add_subsystem_change_count('sub1', 30)
    formatter.add_subsystem_change_count('sub2', 39)
❶   @output_lines = formatter.output.split("\n")
  end

❷ def test_header_comes_before_subsystem_lines
    assert_match(/Changes since 1960-02-19/, @output_lines[0])
  end

❸ def test_both_lines_are_present_in_descending_change_count_order
    assert_match(/sub2.*39/, @output_lines[1])
    assert_match(/sub1.*30/, @output_lines[2])
  end

❹ def test_nothing_else_is_present
    assert_equal(3, @output_lines.size)
  end
end
```

exercise-solutions/churn-classes/exercise-4.rb

Figure B.3: NEW FORMATTER TESTS

of the tests needs some output to work with. Instead of putting code to create the output in each test, I put it in the setup method.

Did I choose for output to return an array or a single string? I picked a single string. You can tell that from ❶, where I split the string apart into separate lines. I don't have a strong argument for that choice, only that using a string implies that, yes, this is it; this is all the output there is. It's so easy to push data onto arrays that returning one might imply that a client should feel free to tack on more lines. Returning a string makes it (slightly) clearer that all the responsibility for producing output strings belongs to Formatter.

If I later change my mind, not much has to be changed in these tests. I just have to remove the split.

Exercise 5

use_date takes a date string as its argument. That string at some point has to be given to header to construct a header. That header will be returned by output. Here's one solution:

code/exercise-solutions/churn-classes/exercise-5.rb

```
def use_date(date_string)
  @date_string = date_string
end
```

It stores the date string for later use in output. output will use header to make the header string:

```
def output
  ... header(@date_string) ...
end
```

Alternately, I could have use_date immediately use header to construct the line to be printed. That line could be stashed in an instance variable and used by output. That would look like this:

```
def use_date(date_string)
  @date_line = header(date_string)
end

def output
  ... @date_line ...
end
```

I chose the first way because I don't like to limit my options. By storing the date string, I reserve the option to use it in methods other than header.

Exercise 6

Again, I have the choice: do I stash away the raw data, or do I construct the output line and stash that away? In this case, there are two bits of data: the subsystem name and its change count. It's more convenient to stash away a single datum—like an output line—so that's what I do. I stash the line away by pushing it onto an array:

code/exercise-solutions/churn-classes/exercise-6.rb

```
def use_subsystem_with_change_count(name, count)
  @lines.push(subsystem_line(name, count))
end
```

@lines has to start out as an empty array. I'll set that up in initialize:

```
def initialize
  @lines = []
end
```

Why do I store lines in an array instead of appending them together into one big string as I construct them? It's because I don't know how to order the lines yet. I have to sort them once I've got them all.

Note: the convenience advantage of storing a line goes away if I know about Ruby's *hashes* (see Chapter 16, *Ruby Facts: Hashes*). With a hash, add_subsystem_change_count could be written like this:

```
def add_subsystem_change_count(name, count)
  @changes.push( { :name => name, :change_count => count } )
end
```

Instead of storing a single datum, the line, I store a single datum that contains what's used to construct the line.

Exercise 7

code/exercise-solutions/churn-classes/exercise-7.rb
```
def output
❶  ordered_lines = order_by_descending_change_count(@lines)
❷  output_array = [header(@date_string)] + ordered_lines
   output_array.join("\n")
end
```

The line at ❷ is a bit confusing. First, a single-element array is created. It contains the header. Then that array and the array of ordered lines are concatenated to form the output_array.

Someone else might instead change ordered_lines to put the header in front. That looks like this:

```
def output
  ordered_lines = order_by_descending_change_count(@lines)
  ordered_lines[0,0] = header(@date_string)
  ordered_lines.join("\n")
end
```

```ruby
class Formatter
  # Public interface

  def initialize
    @lines = []
  end

  def use_date(date_string)
    @date_string = date_string
  end

  def use_subsystem_with_change_count(name, count)
    @lines.push(subsystem_line(name, count))
  end
  def output
    ordered_lines = order_by_descending_change_count(@lines)
    output_array = [header(@date_string)] + ordered_lines
    output_array.join("\n")
  end

  # Helpers
  def header(a_date)
    "Changes since #{a_date}:"
  end

  def subsystem_line(subsystem_name, change_count)
    asterisks = asterisks_for(change_count)
    "#{subsystem_name.rjust(14)} #{asterisks} (#{change_count})"
  end

  def asterisks_for(an_integer)
    '*' * (an_integer / 5.0).round
  end

  def order_by_descending_change_count(lines)
    lines.sort do | first, second |
      first_count = churn_line_to_int(first)
      second_count = churn_line_to_int(second)
      - (first_count <=> second_count)
    end
  end

  def churn_line_to_int(line)
    /\((\d+)\)/.match(line)[1].to_i
  end
end
```

Figure B.4: THE COMPLETED FORMATTER (OR IS IT?)

Figure B.4, on the preceding page, shows the completed Formatter.[2] You can test the code like this:

```
prompt> ruby exercise-4.rb
Loaded suite exercise-4
Started
.............
Finished in 0.089908 seconds.

13 tests, 16 assertions, 0 failures, 0 errors
```

In the first two lines of output, notice that header and order_by_ descending_change_count take instance variables as arguments. That bugs me.

If they're private methods intended to work on an instance variable, they ought to refer to it directly, like this:

```
code/exercise-solutions/churn-classes/exercise-7b.rb
```

```ruby
def header
  "Changes since #{@date_string}:"
end

def lines_ordered_by_descending_change_count
  @lines.sort do | first, second |

def output
  ([header] + lines_ordered_by_descending_change_count).join("\n")
end
```

That makes their purpose clearer. (I had to change the tests, too.)

Exercise 8

I decided to make the header look like this:

Changes between November 23, 2005, and December 21, 2005:

---

2. Notice that I've divided the class into two parts, marked as the public interface and helper methods. It can be argued that code outside Formatter has no business using the helper methods and should therefore be *unable* to use them. That can be accomplished by putting the word private between the public and helper methods (just before header). The problem with that is that the *tests* are "code outside Formatter," so they couldn't check those methods. There are ways around that, though not with the tools you know about yet. I tend not to use private, especially on small scripts—its theoretical benefits don't exceed the annoyance.

That required a change to header's test:

```
code/exercise-solutions/churn-classes/exercise-8-tests.rb
```

```ruby
def test_header_format
  @formatter.report_range(Time.local(2001, 3, 3),
                  Time.local(2002, 2, 2))
  assert_equal("Changes between March 3, 2001, and February 2, 2002:",
          @formatter.header)
end
```

I also had to change the way the regular use tests were set up:

```ruby
def setup
  formatter = Formatter.new
  formatter.report_range(Time.local(2005, 1, 1),
                  Time.local(2005, 2, 1))
  formatter.use_subsystem_with_change_count('sub1', 30)
  formatter.use_subsystem_with_change_count('sub2', 39)
  @output_lines = formatter.output.split("\n")
end
```

The older version of test_header_comes_before_subsystem_lines depended on the header format, since it looked for /Changes since 1960-02-19/. I changed it to match the new format (but to be a little less dependent on the details of date formatting):

```ruby
def test_header_comes_before_subsystem_lines
  assert_match(/Changes between/, @output_lines[0])
end
```

Then I had to change the code to match the tests. First I stashed away the date range:

```
code/exercise-solutions/churn-classes/exercise-8.rb
```

```ruby
def report_range(from, to)
  @from = from
  @to = to
end
```

Then I put it to use:

```
code/exercise-solutions/churn-classes/exercise-8.rb
```

```ruby
def date(time)
  date_format = "%B %d, %Y"
  time.strftime(date_format).sub(' 0', ' ')
end

def header
  "Changes between #{date(@from)}, and #{date(@to)}:"
end
```

I made a little utility method so that I didn't have to repeat the formatting of the different dates inside header. strftime prints a leading zero on days earlier than the 10th, probably so that columns line up neatly when you print many lines of dates. The sub method changes a zero after a space into just a space, giving me the format I want.

None of the SubversionRepository tests had to change. The code changed a little:

`code/exercise-solutions/churn-classes/exercise-8.rb`

```
def change_count_for(name, a_time)
  extract_change_count_from(log(name, date(a_time)))
end
```

change_count_for no longer gets a string already converted into Subversion format, so it has to do it itself.

Notice that there are two methods named date: one in SubversionRepository, one in Formatter. Each converts a Ruby Time object into a string format appropriate to its class. There's no chance of confusing Ruby because the message date is always sent to one class of object or the other.

Exercise 9

I broke churn.rb into three files: churn.rb, subversion-repository.rb, and formatter.rb. churn.rbrequires the other two files:

`code/exercise-solutions/churn-classes/exercise-9/churn.rb`

```
require "subversion-repository"
require "formatter"

def month_before(a_time)
  a_time - 28 * 24 * 60 * 60
end
```

month_before is the only method defined in churn.rb.

The tests are more interesting. If churn is divided into three files, it makes sense for the tests to be divided as well. But how do you run all three tests? The following does *not* work:

```
prompt> ruby churn-tests.rb formatter-tests.rb subversion-repository-tests.rb
Loaded suite churn-tests
Started
.
Finished in 0.003016 seconds.

1 tests, 1 assertions, 0 failures, 0 errors
```

Only the first file is used, so only one test—for month_before—is run. One way to run all the tests is to require them in a single master test file, like this:

<code>code/exercise-solutions/churn-classes/exercise-9/annoying-test-all.rb</code>

```
require 'churn-tests.rb'
require 'formatter-tests.rb'
require 'subversion-repository-tests.rb'

prompt> ruby annoying-test-all.rb
Loaded suite annoying-test-all
Started
.............
Finished in 0.085509 seconds.

13 tests, 18 assertions, 0 failures, 0 errors
```

I called that file annoying-test-all.rb because I have to remember to add new test files to it. I'm lousy at that kind of thing, so I prefer this version, called test-all.rb:

<code>code/exercise-solutions/churn-classes/exercise-9/test-all.rb</code>

```
Dir.glob("*tests.rb").each do | testfile |
  puts testfile
  require testfile
end
```

Dir is an object that knows about handling directories (folders). glob is ancient Unix slang for the way wildcard characters are used in filenames. *tests.rb refers to all files in the current folder that end in "tests.rb". Dir returns those as an array of string filenames.

statically

dynamically

dynamic languages

Each of those is then required. Instead of building the list of files to require *statically*, at the time the Ruby script is written, it's built *dynamically*, at the time the script is run. Languages like Ruby are sometimes called *dynamic languages* because they prefer (and encourage you to prefer) putting decisions off until runtime.

So as long as I follow the naming convention of ending all test files (and no others) with *test.rb*, I won't have to worry that test-all.rb won't run all the tests.

B.7 Solutions for Chapter 12

The solution files are in exercise-solutions/classes.

Exercise 1

Here's my test:

code/exercise-solutions/classes/exercise-1-tests.rb

```
require 'test/unit'
require 'exercise-1.v5'

class CounterTests < Test::Unit::TestCase
  def test_Counter_counts
    assert_equal(0, Counter.count)
    Counter.counted_new
    assert_equal(1, Counter.count)
    Counter.counted_new
    assert_equal(2, Counter.count)
  end
end
```

It immediately finds a bug:

```
 1) Failure:
test_Counter_counts(CounterTests) [exercise-1-tests.rb:6]:
<0> expected but was
<nil>.
```

The failure here is caused by Counter.count being called before Counter.counted_new. But only Counter.counted_new sets the nil instance variable to zero.

My first solution looked like this:

code/exercise-solutions/classes/exercise-1.v2.rb

```
class Counter
  def self.counted_new
    @count = 0 if @count.nil?
    @count += 1
    new
  end

  def self.count
❶    @count = 0 if @count.nil?
    @count
  end
end
```

At ❶, Counter.count initializes the count just as Counter.counted_new does. The problem here is duplication. I toyed around with pulling all the duplication into another method, defined at ❶ below and used at ❷ and ❸ in the code below.

code/exercise-solutions/classes/exercise-1.v3.rb

```
class Counter
❶    def self.maybe_initialize
       @count = 0 if @count.nil?
     end

❷    def self.counted_new
       maybe_initialize
       @count += 1
       new
     end

❸    def self.count
       maybe_initialize
       @count
     end
   end
```

That's no help, really. Previously, there was a twenty-five-character line duplicated between two methods. Now there's a sixteen-character line duplicated—and it's not clear to me that maybe_initialize is all that much clearer than the **if** statement.

Moreover, the next time I add a method that uses the count, I might forget to maybe_initialize the count. I don't want to risk that.

There's a simple solution—not perfectly foolproof, but better. Suppose every method that needs the count gets it through Counter.value. Then that method is the only one that needs to worry about whether initialization is needed. Here's an example of how the two methods would look:

code/exercise-solutions/classes/exercise-1.v4.rb

```
class Counter
     def self.counted_new
❶      @count = self.count + 1
       new
     end

     def self.count
       @count = 0 if @count.nil?
       @count
     end
   end
```

It's pretty creepy, though, to use an instance variable in the first part of line ❶ and a reader method in the latter half. It'd be better to write the code on the next page.

```
def self.counted_new
  self.count = self.count + 1
  new
end
```

If you'll remember, x+=1 is shorthand for x=x+1. That works even when x is a reader, provided the corresponding writer exists. So the final version of Counter can look like this:

```
class Counter
  def self.counted_new
    self.count += 1
    new
  end

  def self.count
    @count = 0 if @count.nil?
    @count
  end

  def self.count=(value)
    @count = value
  end
end
```

Exercise 2

One solution is to put each test method in a file of its own and run it with a separate Ruby command. That's the only way to get an absolutely unused version of Counter. That's more than a little annoying, though:

```
prompt> ruby Counter-test-1.rb
prompt> ruby Counter-test-2.rb
prompt> ruby Counter-test-3.rb
prompt> ruby Counter-test-4.rb
...
```

Instead, I'll simulate an unused Counter by putting everything back as it started. ("Everything" in this case means @count.) A test script can do that by sending a Counter.reset message:

```
def self.reset
  self.count = nil
end
```

The Counter.reset method can be sent before every test by putting it in the test class's setup method:[3]

code/exercise-solutions/classes/exercise-2-tests.rb

```
def setup
  Counter.reset
end
```

There's a risk that I've misunderstood the right way to reset a Counter. If I have, the tests will pass, but the class will be buggy. I'm sure of myself (in this case), so I'm ready to move on.

Exercise 3

Add this line anywhere within the class definition:

code/exercise-solutions/classes/exercise-3.rb

```
attr_accessor :birth_order
```

Exercise 4

Here's the test:

code/exercise-solutions/classes/exercise-4-tests.rb

```
def test_birth_order
  assert_equal(1, Counter.counted_new.birth_order)
  # Test another one, just for luck.
  assert_equal(2, Counter.counted_new.birth_order)
end
```

(Some might argue that the birth order of the first Counter should be 0, not 1. They might be right. The test shows what I intended; it has nothing to say about whether that intention was mistaken. That's a matter of human judgment and debate.)

In the previous exercise, I added both a read and a write accessor for @birth_order. I knew I would need the writer to make this test pass. Even though Counter is intimately related to its instances, it still has no access to their instance variables.

Just like any other object, the only way it has of changing them is to ask the instance by sending a writer message:

---

3. setup was described on page 274.

code/exercise-solutions/classes/exercise-4.rb

```
def self.counted_new
  self.count += 1
  new_counter = new
  new_counter.birth_order = self.count
  new_counter
end
```

B.8 Solutions for Chapter 21

The solution files are in exercise-solutions/error-handling.

Exercise 1

code/exercise-solutions/error-handling/exercise-1.rb

```
def check_args(args)
  raise "Exactly one argument is required." unless args.length == 1
  only_arg = args[0]
  raise "'#{only_arg}' is not an integer."  unless /^\d+$/ =~ only_arg
end

if $0 == __FILE__
  begin
    check_args(ARGV)
    puts ARGV[0].to_i
  rescue Exception => ex
    puts ex.message
  end
end
```

Exercise 2

code/exercise-solutions/error-handling/exercise-2.rb

```
class Array
  def my_each
    index = 0
    while index < self.length
      yield self[index]
      index += 1
    end
    self
  end
end
```

Exercise 3

`code/exercise-solutions/error-handling/exercise-3.rb`

```ruby
class Reserver
  def reserve(machine_name)
    machine = Machine.new(machine_name)
    yield machine
    puts "Reserved #{machine.name}."
    machine
  rescue Exception => ex
    puts "Test failure: #{ex.message}"
  ensure
    release(machine) if machine
  end

  def release(machine)
    puts "Released #{machine.name}."
  end
end
```

Appendix C

Bibliography

[ASS84]   Harold Abelson, Gerald Sussman, and Julie Sussman. *Structure and Interpretation of Computer Programs*. MIT Press, 1984.

[Bec00]   Kent Beck. *Extreme Programming Explained: Embrace Change*. Addison-Wesley, Reading, MA, 2000.

[Fri97]   Jeffrey E. F. Friedl. *Mastering Regular Expressions*. O'Reilly & Associates, Inc, Sebastopol, CA, 1997.

[TFH05]   David Thomas, Chad Fowler, and Andrew Hunt. *Programming Ruby: The Pragmatic Programmers' Guide*. The Pragmatic Programmers, LLC, Raleigh, NC, and Dallas, TX, second edition, 2005.

[TH01]   David Thomas and Andrew Hunt. *Programming Ruby: The Pragmatic Programmer's Guide*. Addison-Wesley, Reading, MA, 2001.

Index

Symbols

%r{}, 137
* character, 100, 102, 167
\+ character, 92, 100, 102
\d, 92, 93
\d, 100f
\n, 15, 22, 44, 72
==, 53, 92
=~ operator, 92, 94, 138
@ character, 111
@@, 129
\# character, 61
#{} marker, 71, 72, 78
$ character, 99, 129
$: variable, 178
% character, 69
ˆ character, 99, 101
| character, 101
<<, 155

A

Abstract superclasses, 233
Accessors, 119–122
  defined, 120
Affinity list, 142
Affinity trip, 133–134
  for a book, 134f
  and comma-separated values, 153,
    155–156
  defined, 133
Agile Web Development with Rails
  (Thomas et al), 142
Akira, Tanaka, 135
Amazon, *see* Scraping script; Affinity
  trip
args, 166
Arguments, 165–168
  command-line, 33–36
  defined, 21

keyword, 167–168
optional, 142, 165–166
rest, 166–167
ARGV, 33, 34
Arrays, 29–32
  ARGV, 33
  of Barkers, 234
  and block, 37
  change an element of, 30
  combining and expanding, 167
  comparing, 23–24
  and CSV files, 154
  defined, 22
  deleting elements, 30
  empty, 29, 34
  exclusive range and, 30
  and flatten, 140
  inclusive range and, 30
  index for, 29
  and iterators, 37
  last element, selecting, 30
  and length, 27, 29
  literal, 29
  naming, 22
  negative indices and, 30
  and numbers, 31
  popping elements off, 31
  printed, 22
  and puts, 25, 52
  putting arrays in, 31
  putting objects in, 31
  reordering, 95–97
  and ri, 32
  and scan, 139
  shifting, 31
  slices and, 31
  and unshift, 31
assert-equal, 64
Associative arrays, *see* Hashes

asterisks, 70, 73, 77, 79
Attributes, defining multiple, 122

B

Backslash, 72, 76, 93, 100
Backticks, 78, 228
Barker, 232–235
Bergin, Joseph, 239n
bin, 184, 188
Black-box testing, 77
Blank-filling methods, 225–227
Block, 37
Blocks
    defined, 45
    delimiting, 40
    for cleanup, 154–155
    and hashes, 162
    and sort, 96
    yielding control to, 206–208
Body, 35, 52
Boolean-valued, 53
Booleans, 87–90
    object selection and, 89–90
    operators, 87
    precedence and, 87–89
    precedence rules for, 88
    values, 87
Bootstrapping test, 68, 69
Brackets, 100
Bugs
    and error handling, 201
    avoiding, 63
    fixing, 43–45
    and test-driven programming, 82
Bundling data,exercises for, 112–118

C

center, 165, 167
change_count_for, 75, 78
change_count, 71
Character classes, 100, 100f
chomp, 44
churn
    see also Version control script
churn.rb, 66, 93
churn
    and error handling, 82
    methods for Subversion, 107
    and scripting by assumption, 61
clash-check.rb, 179
class, 106, 124

Class variables, 129
Classes, 119–130
    adding onto, 107
    augmenting a superclass, 220
    for Barker code, 232–235
    bundling methods into, 109f
    defined, 106, 119
    defining accessors, 119–122
    defining attributes, 122
    defining methods, 106–108
    documentation for, 111
    exercises for, 112–118, 129–130
    for Subversion, 105
    and instance variables, 221, 222f
    vs. instances, 107
    methods, 126–128
    as modules, 197–198
    modules vs. classes, 241
    names, 179–181
    overriding, 219
    and self, 122–126
    structure of, 232f
    and subclasses, 218
    see also Frameworks
collect, 37, 91, 140, 163
Comma-separated values, 153–160
    <<, 155
    and affinity-trip.rb, 155–156
    and blocks, 154–155
    documentation on, 156, 158f
    library for, 154
    output, 153
    replacing code with data, 158–160
Command, 223, 227, 228, 232
Command-line arguments, 33–36
Command-line interpreter
    backticks and, 78
    defined, 8
    in Mac or Unix, 9–10
    in Windows, 8–9
Comment character #, 61
Composite objects, 140
Continuation prompt, 15, 16
CSV, see Comma-separated values
Current working folder, 8, 10

D

Data types
    see also Arrays
Dictionaries, see Hashes
Direct test, 68, 69

Double-quoted strings, 72
downcase, 35
Downloads, 171–176
   locating packages, 171
   RubyGems, 172–175
   setup.rb, 172–173
   understanding, 175–176
Driving a browser, 150

E

each, 37, 38, 91, 163
Editors, 11, 26
else statement, 52
elsif statement, 52, 53
End-of-line character, 15, 22, 44
End-of-line comments, 61
Ensuring actions, 206
Environment variables, 174–175
Errors *vs.* failures, 67
Exceptions, 200
   ensuring actions, 206
   handled, 202f
   handling, 202
   handling options, 202–206
   raised, 200, 201f
   raising, 204
   reraising, 205, 205f
   rescuing, 203
Exclusive range, 30
execute, 228
Exercises
   for bundling data and methods,
      112–118
   for classes, 129–130
   for directory customization, 48–50
   for error handling, 208–209
   for version control script, 83–84
   for inventory scripts, 27
   for regular expressions, 97, 103
   for scraping web info, 143–144
   for scripts, polishing, 190–191
exit, 208
External programs, 75–82

F

Failures, 135
fetch, 162
File, 21
Filenames, 178–179
find_all, 77
flatten, 140

Floating-point numbers, 74, 155
Folder structure, 183f
Formatting time, 68–70
Frameworks, 213–228
   add_choices, 226
   add_sources, 225
   advice about, 231
   blank-filling method, 225–227
   challenges with, 213
   configuring watchdog script,
      214–217
   defined, 213
   and inheritance, 217–221
   postprocess_user_choices, 226–227
   pp, 227
   subclass responsibility, 223
   user choices, 224f, 223–228
   UserChoices, 217, 225
   Watchdog's code, 229f
   see also Superclasses

G

gedit, 11
GET request, 151
Global namespaces, 193, 195, 197
Global variables, 129, 178
Groups, 94

H

Hash keys, 141, 161
Hash value, 141
Hashes, 140–141, 161–163
   default value, 161
   defined, 161
   empty, 161, 162
   key/value pairs, 161, 162
header, 62, 69
hello, 107
HTML, book information in, 136f
HTTP GET request, 151
HTTP POST request, 151

I

if statement, 51–54
"In the Beginning Was the Command
    Line" (Stephenson), 8
include, 42, 180, 196
Including modules, 180, 195–197
Inclusive range, 30
index, 138

Indices
- negative, 30
- out of bounds, 30, 34
- for strings, 93
- zero-based, 29

Inheritance, 217, 221
- instance variables, 221
- and superclasses, 222f

initialize, 109, 110, 200
inspect, 25
install, 174
Instance methods, 126
Instance variables, 221
- and class methods, 128
- defined, 110
- super- and subclasses and, 222f
- uninitialized, 121

Instances, 105–107, 109, 126
Integers *vs.* floating-point numbers, 74
Inventory scripts, 19–27
- no arguments in, 34
- comparing arrays, 23–24, 42
- for comparison, 25–26
- exercises for, 27
- filtering files, 41
- fixing bugs, 43–45
- new file, create, 20
- printing to screen, 24–25
- problems with, 33
- testing uses for, 20

IO.read, 149
irb, 12
- File, 21
- command-line arguments and, 34
- exiting from, 13
- load, 65
- and loadable scripts, 47f
- mistakes in, 14–16
- prompts for, 12
- return values and, 25
- and strings, 22
- syntax errors in, 14

ISBN, 134
Iterations, 37
Iterators, 37
- collect, 37
- each, 37, 38
- polymorphic, 38

J
Jabber, 214, 215, 233

K
Keyword arguments, 167–168

L
length, 27
line_format, 75
Literal array, 29
load, 65, 178
Load path, 178
Loadable scripts, 46, 47f
Local variables, 110, 114, 121, 125
Location-independent tests, 188–190
log, 109, 110

M
Mastering Regular Expressions (Friedl), 103
Match strings, 92–93, 101
MatchData, 101
McMahon, Chris, 20n
Messages, 20, 39
- *see also* puts
Methods, 39–40
- accessor, 119
- and blocks, 206–208
- and classes, 106–108, 109f, 126–128
- creating synonyms, 126, 127
- documentation for, 111
- exercises for, 112–118
- instance, 126
- and local variables, 114
- *vs. messages*, 39
- and objects, 112
- overriding, 219

Modules, 193–198
- classes as, 197–198
- content availability, 181, 182f
- including into classes, 180, 195–197
- namespaces and, 193
- naming, 196, 198
- nested, 194–195
- nesting, 189f, 194, 195f
- qualified names, 193
- S4TUtils, 188
- *vs.* superclasses, 240
- uses for, 194f
- visibility of objects, 195

N
Name rules (Ruby), 23
Names, 20

convention for, 241
and files, 178–179
and methods, 40
and modules, 179–181, 196, 198
qualified *vs.* unqualified, 180
Namespaces, 193, 195
Negative indices, 30
Nested modules, 194–195
new, 106, 109, 110, 126, 197
nil
and hashes, 161
and indices, 30
and instance variables, 121, 122
and open-uri library, 135
and Ruby messages, 25

O

Objects, 20
File as, 21
attributes of, 120
challenges with, 235
and data, 109–112
equality in, 53
and instance variables, 111
and methods, 112
naming, 22–23
putting in arrays, 31
sending messages, 122–126
sending/receiving messages, 20–22
truth value of, 89
and variables, 112
see also Classes, *see also* Exceptions
open, 21, 35, 37, 135
open-uri library, 135, 147, 150–152
Optional arguments, 142, 165–166
Overriding methods, 219

P

Parentheses, 24, 36, 93–95, 101, 125
Parsers, 148
pico, 11
Polymorphic messages, 38
POST request, 151
Practice files
downloading, 7–8
overview of, 3
where to save, 13
Prettyprint, 227
Programming, *see* Scripting
Programming Ruby (Thomas, et. al.), 5,
69, 103, 134, 156

Prompts, 8, 9
command line *vs.* irb, 12
continuation, 15, 16
working with, 13
push, 31
puts
and arguments, 166
and arrays, 25
as message, 24
nil and, 25
and printing, 24
and quotes, 25

Q

Question-mark operator, 54–55

R

RAA, *see* Ruby Application Archive
Rails, 2
Raising exceptions, 204
rake, 173, 175
rakefile, 184–189
rake commit, 187
rake fast, 187
rake increment-version, 187
rake install-into, 187
rake install, 187
rake move-on, 188
rake rdoc, 188
rake test, 186
rake update-peers, 188
Rdoc, 157f
Refactoring, 63
Regular expressions, 91–103
%r{}, 137
and case sensitivity, 99
challenges in, 147
character classes, 100f
dissecting strings with, 94–95
exercises for, 97, 103
groups, 94, 101
if, 99
match strings, 92–93, 101
nil, 99
options, 102–103
reordering arrays, 95–97
and scan, 139
for searching strings, 137
spaces in, 136
special characters, 99–101
and substrings, 136

taking strings apart, 101–102
testing, 95
and variables, 102
and whitespace, 137
see also Scraping script
reject, 42
require, 65, 135, 178, 180
Reraising exceptions, 205, 205f
Rescued exceptions, 203
respond_to, 106
Rest arguments, 166–167
Returning values, 21
REXML, 148
ri, 32, 69, 111, 157
rjust, 70
Rounding, 74, 77
Ruby
    arguments, 165–168
    arrays in, 29–32
    benefits of, 2, 46
    boolean values, 87–90
    and case sensitivity, 21, 23, 35
    classes, 105
    classes in standard library, 156–158
    CSV library, 154
    delimiting blocks, 40
    else statement, 52
    elsif statement, 52, 53
    end, 35, 36
    environment variable in, 174–175
    equal signs in, 35n
    Extensions, 186
    Facets, 186
    fixing bugs, 43–45
    folder separator character, 41n
    format characters, 69
    helper scripts and applications for,
        171–176
    if statement, 51–54
    installation of, 10
        in Mac OS X, 11
        in Unix, 172, 173
        in Windows, 10, 173
    installation root, 173
    iterators in, 37
    library documentation, making own,
        158f
    load path for, 178
    mailing list for, 176
    messages in, 20
    methods, 39–40

    modules, 193–198
    name rules for, 23
    names in, 20
    namespaces in, 193
    negations in, 54
    nil and, 25
    objects in, 20
    parentheses in, 24
    polymorphic messages and, 38
    question mark operator, 54–55
    receivers in, 24
    regular expressions in, 99–103
    REXML, 148
    setup.rb, 172
    and short-circuiting evaluation, 89
    string multiplication, 74
    strings in, 15
    Test::Unit, 64, 64f
    truth value of objects, 89
    unless, 35, 54
    variables in, 22
    XML, support for, 148
    and YAML, 216n
ruby -S, 177, 178
Ruby Application Archive (RAA), 171
RubyForge, 171–172
RubyGems, 189
    installing, 172
    and rake, 173
    using, 173–175
Russell, Sean, 148n

S

scan, 136, 139
SciTE, 11, 26, 174
Scraping script, 133–145
    and affinity trip, 133–134
    and Amazon, 133
    author and title info, 136–140
    challenges of, 136, 138, 147
    and comma-separated values,
        153–160
    driving a browser, 150
    exercises, 143–144
    failures in, 135
    first draft of, 141–143
    and hashes, 140–141
    HTML book info, 136f
    m, 139
    testing, 144
    web pages as files, 134–136

whitespace in, 137
and XHTML, 147–149
Screen scraping, *see* Scraping script
Script files
  and require, 65
  syntax errors in, 15
  test files for, 64
Scripting
  adding variables, 63
  advice on, 243–244
  by assumption, 61
  benefits of using Ruby, 2
  challenges of, 235–240
  and complexity, 2
  and computer speed, 2
  defined, 1, 45
  duplicate code in, 39
  and frameworks, 213–228
  if, use of, 52
  improvement in, 243–244
  number of tests, 79
  process of, 59
  test-driven, 63, 82, 144
Scripts, 177–191
  class names and, 179–181
  executing, 177
  exercises for, 190–191
  filenames and, 178–179
  for folder and module structure,
    183f, 181–185
  frameworks for, 213–228
  handling errrors in, 199–209
  load path, 178
  location-independent test, 188–190
  rakefile, 185–189
  skeleton files and, 184
  see also Scraping script; Version
    control script; Watchdog script
Selenium, 150
self, 122–126
  and class methods, 126
  defined, 123
  uses for, 123–125
Sender, 21, 39
Separation of concerns, 62
setup.rb, 172–173, 177
Short-circuiting evaluation, 89
Single-quote strings, 72
Skeleton files, 184
Slices, 30–32, 102
SMTP, 232

sort, 95–97
Spaceship operator, 95–97
Special characters, 99–101
split, 42
Stack trace, 200, 201f, 202
stderr, 208
stdout, 208
Stephenson, Neal, 8
Strings
  and \n, 44
  backslash in, 16
  in CSV files, 155
  defined, 15, 22
  dissecting, 41–43, 94–95
  downcase, 35
  equality in, 53
  formatting, 70–75
  indexing, 93
  and IO.read, 149
  match, 92–93, 99
  multiplication, 74
  printed, 22
  searching through, 137
  single-quoted *vs.* double-quoted, 72
  substitution, 71
  and symbols, 120, 121
  taking apart, 101–102
  see also Arrays
*Structure and Interpretation of Computer
  Programs* (Abelson and Sussman),
  61n
Subclasses
  Barker classes for, 237
subsystem_line, 62, 70, 71, 77, 79
Subtraction, 23
Subversion
  changes to a subsystem, 60f
  as external program, 75
  formatting for, 78
  methods for, 107
  repository class, 105, 113f
  website for, 60
super, 220
Superclasses, 218, 220, 222f, 231–241
  abstract, 233
  and Barker, 232–235
  challenges with, 235–240
  vs. classes, 240
  creating, 231
  extracting, 231
  instances and, 237

watchdog sequence diagram, 236f
Supplements, 149
svn_log, 75, 77, 78
Symbols, 120, 121
Synonyms, 126, 127
Syntax errors, 14
   in script files, 15
   source of problem, 36

T

Ternary operator, 54–55
Test expressions, 52
Test::Unit, 217–221
   assertions, 115f
   failure, 67
   name option, 73
   overriding, 219
   testing with, 64f
   uses for, 64
Testing
   snapshots in Unix, 66
   and rakefile, 184
   automation of, 4
   bootstrapping, 68, 69
   directly, 68, 69
   failures, 65n, 66, 67, 135
   and inventory scripts, 20
   location independently, 188–190
   number of, 79
   in Ruby, 2
   scraping script, 144
   selecting, 77
   snapshots in Windows, 65
   speed of, 144
   suites, 64
   with Test::Unit, 64f
   time format, 68–70
   and version control, 60
TextMate, 11, 26
third-party, 184, 185
Thomas, Dave, 5
times, 142
to_i, 94
trip, 142
Troubleshooting, 199–209
   with blocks, 206–208
   ensuring actions, 206
   exception raised, 201f
   exception-handling options, 202–206
   exercises for, 208–209
   strategy for handling errors, 201

U

uninstall, 174
unless, 35, 54
unshift, 31
User choices, gathering, 224f, 223–228
UserChoices framework, 217, 225, 232
Utilities library, 186

V

Variables, 22–23
   and accessors, 119
   adding to a script, 63
   class, 129
   composite objects and, 140
   environment, 174–175
   global, 129, 178
   instance, 110, 111, 121, 128, 221, 222f
   local, 110, 114, 121
   and objects, 112
   and regular expressions, 102
Version control script, 59–84
   churn code, 81f
   corrections to, 78–83
   direct *vs.* indirect approach, 62
   exercises for, 83–84
   and external programs, 75–82
   formatting time, 68–70
   ordering the lines, 91–98
   refactoring time, 67
   requirements for, 61
   and rounding, 74
   separation of concerns and, 62
   time and test-driving, 62–68

W

Watchdog script
   accepting invitation to join, 239
   add_choices, 226
   add_source, 225
   and Barker, 232–235
   challenges with, 235–240
   configuring, 214–217
   exceptions, 240
   and --help, 215
   and inheritance, 217–221
   instances, 237
   instant message, 214f
   join this kennel, 238
   and kennel, 237

mail message, 215f
postprocess_user_choices, 226–227
pp, 227
sequence diagram, 236f
stocking a kennel, 237f
subclassing a class, 223
user choices and, 224f, 223–228
and UserChoices framework, 217, 225
watching code, 229f
Watir, 2, 150
Web pages
    driving a browser, 150
    and JavaScript, 147, 150
    treating like files, 134, 136f,
        136–140
    XHTML *vs.* HTML, 147–149
Websites
    for Agile Alliance, 85
    for Amazon script, 134
    for Extensions, 186
    for Facets, 186
    for failure help, 135
    for this book, 5
    for gems installed, 176
    for practice files, 7
    for Rails, 2
    for Ruby Application Archive, 171
    for Ruby installation, 10, 11
    for Ruby library classes, 156

for Ruby mailing list, 176
for RubyForge, 171, 189
for RubyGems, 173, 189
for Selenium, 150
for Subversion, 60
for TextMate, 11
for this book, 173
for W3C, 148
for Watir, 2, 150
for Wildfire, 214n
for WinZip, 7
Weirich, Jim, 185
Whitespace, 137
with_pleasant_exceptions, 199–201, 207

X

XML
    and REXML, 148
    supplement for, 149
    and W3C, 149
    and watchdog configuration file,
        216n
XPath
    supplement for, 149
    and XML documents, 149

Z

Zero-based indexing, 29

A Pragmatic Career

Welcome to the Pragmatic Community. We hope you've enjoyed this title.

Interested in improving your career? Want to make yourself more valuable to your organization, and avoid being outsourced? Then read *My Job Went to India*, and find out great ways to keep yours. If you're interested in moving your career more towards a team lead or mangement position, then read what happens *Behind Closed Doors*.

My Job Went to India

The job market is shifting. Your current job may be outsourced, perhaps to India or eastern Europe. But you can save your job and improve your career by following these practical and timely tips. See how to: • treat your career as a business • build your own brand as a software developer • develop a structured plan for keeping your skills up to date • market yourself to your company and rest of the industry • keep your job!

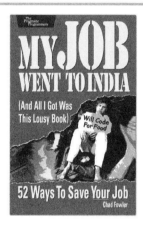

My Job Went to India: 52 Ways to Save Your Job
Chad Fowler
(185 pages) ISBN: 0-9766940-1-8. $19.95
http://pragmaticprogrammer.com/titles/mjwti

Behind Closed Doors

You can learn to be a better manager—even a great manager—with this guide. You'll find powerful tips covering:

• Delegating effectively • Using feedback and goal-setting • Developing influence • Handling one-on-one meetings • Coaching and mentoring • Deciding what work to do-and what not to do • . . . and more!

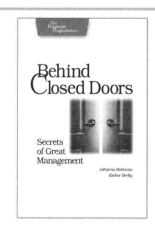

Behind Closed Doors Secrets of Great Management
Johanna Rothman and Esther Derby
(192 pages) ISBN: 0-9766940-2-6. $24.95
http://pragmaticprogrammer.com/titles/rdbcd

Pragmatic Methodology

Need to get software out the door? Then you want to see how to *Ship It!* with less fuss and more features. And every developer can benefit from the *Practices of an Agile Developer*.

Ship It!

Page after page of solid advice, all tried and tested in the real world. This book offers a collection of tips that show you what tools a successful team has to use, and how to use them well. You'll get quick, easy-to-follow advice on modern techniques and when they should be applied. **You need this book if:** • You're frustrated at lack of progress on your project. • You want to make yourself and your team more valuable. • You've looked at methodologies such as Extreme Programming (XP) and felt they were too, well, extreme. • You've looked at the Rational Unified Process (RUP) or CMM/I methods and cringed at the learning curve and costs. • **You need to get software out the door without excuses**

Ship It! A Practical Guide to Successful Software Projects
Jared Richardson and Will Gwaltney
(200 pages) ISBN: 0-9745140-4-7. $29.95
http://pragmaticprogrammer.com/titles/prj

Practices of an Agile Developer

Agility is all about using feedback to respond to change. Learn how to apply the principles of agility throughout the software development process • Establish and maintain an agile working environment • Deliver what users really want • Use personal agile techniques for better coding and debugging • Use effective collaborative techniques for better teamwork • Move to an agile approach

Practices of an Agile Developer: Working in the Real World
Venkat Subramaniam and Andy Hunt
(189 pages) ISBN: 0-9745140-8-X. $29.95
http://pragmaticprogrammer.com/titles/pad

Facets of Ruby Series

Sharpen your Ruby programming skills with James Edward Gray's *Best of Ruby Quiz*, or see how to integrate Ruby with all varieties of today's technology in *Enterprise Integration with Ruby*.

Best of Ruby Quiz

Sharpen your Ruby programming skills with twenty-five challenging problems from Ruby Quiz. Read the problems, work out a solution, and compare your solution with answers from others.

• Learn using the most effective method available: *practice* • Learn great Ruby idioms • Understand sticky problems and the insights that lead you past them • Gain familiarity with Ruby's standard library • Translate traditional algorithms to Ruby

Best of Ruby Quiz
James Edward Gray II
(304 pages) ISBN: 0-9766940-7-7. $29.95
http://pragmaticprogrammer.com/titles/fr_quiz

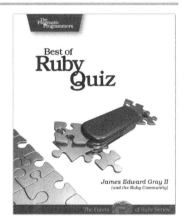

Enterprise Integration with Ruby

See how to use the power of Ruby to integrate all the applications in your environment. Lean how to
• use relational databases directly, and via mapping layers such as ActiveRecord • Harness the power of directory services • Create, validate, and read XML documents for easy information interchange • Use both high- and low-level protocols to knit applications together

Enterprise Integration with Ruby
Maik Schmidt
(360 pages) ISBN: 0-9766940-6-9. $32.95
http://pragmaticprogrammer.com/titles/fr_eir

Facets of Ruby Series

If you're serious about Ruby, you need the definitive reference to the language. The Pickaxe: *Programming Ruby: The Pragmatic Programmer's Guide, Second Edition*. This is *the* definitive guide for all Ruby programmers. And you'll need a good text editor, too. On the Mac, we recommend TextMate.

Programming Ruby (The Pickaxe)

The Pickaxe book, named for the tool on the cover, is the definitive reference to this highly-regarded language. • Up-to-date and expanded for Ruby version 1.8 • Complete documentation of all the built-in classes, modules, and methods • Complete descriptions of all ninety-eight standard libraries • 200+ pages of new content in this edition • Learn more about Ruby's web tools, unit testing, and programming philosophy

Programming Ruby: The Pragmatic Programmer's Guide, 2nd Edition
Dave Thomas with Chad Fowler and Andy Hunt
(864 pages) ISBN: 0-9745140-5-5. $44.95
http://pragmaticprogrammer.com/titles/ruby

TextMate

If you're coding Ruby or Rails on a Mac, then you owe it to yourself to get the TextMate editor. And, once you're using TextMate, you owe it to yourself to pick up this book. It's packed with information which will help you automate all your editing tasks, saving you time to concentrate on the important stuff. Use snippets to insert boilerplate code and refactorings to move stuff around. Learn how to write your own extensions to customize it to the way you work.

TextMate: Power Editing for the Mac
James Edward Gray II
(200 pages) ISBN: 0-9787392-3-X. $29.95
http://pragmaticprogrammer.com/titles/textmate

The Pragmatic Bookshelf

The Pragmatic Bookshelf features books written by developers for developers. The titles continue the well-known Pragmatic Programmer style, and continue to garner awards and rave reviews. As development gets more and more difficult, the Pragmatic Programmers will be there with more titles and products to help you stay on top of your game.

Visit Us Online

Everyday Scripting's Home Page
http://pragmaticprogrammer.com/titles/bmsft
Source code from this book, errata, and other resources. Come give us feedback, too!

Register for Updates
http://pragmaticprogrammer.com/updates
Be notified when updates and new books become available.

Join the Community
http://pragmaticprogrammer.com/community
Read our weblogs, join our online discussions, participate in our mailing list, interact with our wiki, and benefit from the experience of other Pragmatic Programmers.

New and Noteworthy
http://pragmaticprogrammer.com/news
Check out the latest pragmatic developments in the news.

Save on the PDF

Save PDF version of this book. Owning the paper version of this book entitles you to purchase the PDF version at a terrific discount. The PDF is great for carrying around on your laptop. It's hyperlinked, has color, and is fully searchable.

Buy it now at pragmaticprogrammer.com/coupon.

Contact Us

Phone Orders:	1-800-699-PROG (+1 919 847 3884)
Online Orders:	www.pragmaticprogrammer.com/catalog
Customer Service:	orders@pragmaticprogrammer.com
Non-English Versions:	translations@pragmaticprogrammer.com
Pragmatic Teaching:	academic@pragmaticprogrammer.com
Author Proposals:	proposals@pragmaticprogrammer.com